Preventing Sexual Harm

Preventing Sexual Harm provides an overview of current criminal justice strategies for tackling sexual violence, and highlights existing positive criminological approaches that could help prevent sexual abuse and harm.

Sexual violence is a complex, multi-faceted crime. Its causes and consequences are both multiple and enduring and our understanding of sexual violence is embedded within our social, cultural, and political constructs. As such, a response to sexual violence ought to be equally complex and multi-faceted. Alternative approaches might therefore be needed, such as positive criminology. This book explores positive criminology as a mechanism to reduce the risk of recidivism, eradicate harm, prevent reoffending as well as to help reintegrate those with histories of sexual abuse back into the community. In light of recent historic cases of sexual abuse and poor institutional response to these allegations, it opens with an overview of the current landscape of sexual offending. The book then reviews the current positive criminological approaches already in existence in the effort to prevent sexual abuse by outlining the approach of positive criminology and by demonstrating the many gaps in practice that might benefit from this new way of working to prevent sexual abuse.

By highlighting that an alternative response to sexual violence is needed, and by presenting the idea that a positive criminological paradigm is worthy of further examination, this book will be of great interest to scholars of criminology, criminal justice, and forensic psychology.

Stephanie Kewley is Senior Lecturer in Forensic Psychology at Liverpool John Moores University. Stephanie supports, advocates, and promotes the safe and healthy functioning of marginalised and highly stigmatised populations involved in criminal justice systems.

Sarah Pemberton is Associate Professor in Criminology at Birmingham City University. Sarah's current research interests include discourse and identity management of those with convictions for sexual offences; teaching sensitive subjects and vicarious trauma; making sense of coercive control; and media representation of intimate partner homicide.

Mohammed Rahman is Senior Lecturer in Criminology at Birmingham City University. His academic work concerns serious violence – namely organised crime. Mohammed has used his teaching and research experiences to inform the public and international press about crime, harm, and crime control.

Routledge Studies in Crime and Society

Crime, Harm and Consumer Culture
Edited by Steve Hall, Tereza Kuldova and Mark Horsley

Legalizing Cannabis
Experiences, Lessons and Scenarios
Edited by Tom Decorte, Simon Lenton and Chris Wilkins

Risk and Harm in Youth Sexting
Young People's Perspectives
Emily Setty

Gendered Responses to Male Offending in Barbados
Patriarchal Perceptions and Their Effect on Offender Treatment
Corin Bailey

Crime and Fear in Public Places
Towards Safe, Inclusive and Sustainable Cities
Edited by Mahesh K Nalla and Vania Ceccato

Preventing Sexual Harm
Positive Criminology and Sexual Abuse
Stephanie Kewley, Sarah Pemberton and Mohammed Rahman

Female Capital Punishment
From the Gallows to Unofficial Abolition in Connecticut
Lawrence Goodheart

Redefining Murder, Transforming Emotion
An Exploration of Forgiveness after Loss due to Homicide
Kristen Hourigan

For more information about this series, please visit: www.routledge.com/Routledge-Studies-in-Crime-and-Society/book-series/RSCS

The only subject that evokes a more extreme reaction than sex in modern society is violence, so it is little wonder that the subject of sexual violence is fraught with hyperbole, myth and misunderstanding. The authors' 'positive criminology' approach is therefore both badly needed and quietly ground-breaking, broadening the lens from one of 'risk' and psychological deficits, to a focus on resilience, reparation and protective factors – a very important new direction for the field.

– **Shadd Maruna**, author of *Making Good: How Ex-Convicts Reform and Rebuild Their Lives*

While the authors do not make the claim for this text to be one that is all-singing and all-dancing, in fact they could have justifiably made such a claim. The chapters cover a broad array of relevant areas, including important standard ones (definitions and prevalence, sentencing, management and risk assessment, prevention strategies) together with more forward-thinking chapters. The positive criminology approach is a welcome guest to the table, and this volume certainly contributes 'new ways of thinking' around sexual abuse, whilst covering the old favourites and standard fare one would expect.

– **Belinda Winder**, Research Director of the Sexual Offences, Crime and Misconduct Research Unit at Nottingham Trent University

The major goal of positive criminology is to equip individuals who have committed crimes with the resources to living more meaningful and less harmful lives. It has its roots in the understanding that all human beings have intrinsic value and that therefore punishment should always be delivered in ways that demonstrate respect, and seek community healing. In this exciting new book, Stephanie Kewley, Sarah Pemberton, and Mohammed Rahman apply the key ideas of positive criminology to the area of sexual abuse. In the process they demonstrate admirable scholarship, an appreciation of the complexity of crime prevention and treatment, and an excellent introduction to positive criminology for practitioners and researchers.

– **Tony Ward**, developer of the Good Lives Model, Victoria University of Wellington

Preventing Sexual Harm

Positive Criminology and Sexual Abuse

Stephanie Kewley, Sarah Pemberton and Mohammed Rahman

Routledge
Taylor & Francis Group
LONDON AND NEW YORK

First published 2021
by Routledge
2 Park Square, Milton Park, Abingdon, Oxon OX14 4RN

and by Routledge
605 Third Avenue, New York, NY 10017

First issued in paperback 2022

Routledge is an imprint of the Taylor & Francis Group, an informa business

Publisher's Note
The publisher has gone to great lengths to ensure the quality of this reprint but points out that some imperfections in the original copies may be apparent.

British Library Cataloguing-in-Publication Data
A catalogue record for this book is available from the British Library

Library of Congress Cataloging-in-Publication Data
A catalog record for this book has been requested

ISBN: 978-0-367-62409-5 (pbk)
ISBN: 978-0-815-35366-9 (hbk)
ISBN: 978-1-351-13579-5 (ebk)

DOI: 10.4324/9781351135795

Typeset in Times New Roman
by Apex CoVantage, LLC

I dedicate this work to my Mum who continues to shower me in unconditional love and endless support, and to the memory of my Dad; without him, life is a little less colourful.

Stephanie Kewley

Contents

Foreword x
NATTI RONEL

Introduction 1

1 Definition, causes, and prevalence of sexual abuse 5

2 Current approaches to sentencing and management 26

3 Current approaches to the assessment of sexual offending 39

4 Current approaches to the treatment of sexual offending 57

5 Prevention strategies of sexual harm 68

6 Positive criminology as an alternative 86

7 Current positive criminology applications in terms of assessment 103

8 Current positive criminology applications in terms of treatment and management 114

9 Religion, spirituality, and positive criminology 128

Conclusion 142

Index 147

Foreword

Imagine a place, within the ancient city of Acre, not far from the harsh and vibrant oriental market, inside the big stone walls of which there is an enduring silence unbroken by what is happening outside. Even with ongoing construction work, the knocking of hammers and the sounds of machines, the silence is not disturbed. The workers keep quiet throughout the hard day's work, as they do not want to disturb the sacred serenity of the place. They work with appreciation, with dignity, with inner intention. However, they all are ex-prisoners, accustomed to loud, aggressive, and violent behaviour, and to criminal behaviour. Most of them regularly abuse – and are addicted to – drugs and alcohol, although some have quit altogether. How did they become serious workers who confront their ordinary frustration with such quietness? How are they able to retain the change?

The secret was revealed in an insightful positive criminology study of a unique Sufi-Islamic way of rehabilitation (Hawa-Kamel, 2018), that is, a way of 'non-doing' or 'Wu-Wei' (Koptseva & Kirko, 2015; Loy, 1985), a non-doing of even intentional rehabilitation. Ideally, the Sufis provide the ex-prisoners with their own human presence and a physical, social, psychological, and spiritual surrounding different from any other that the ex-prisoners have met hitherto. It is peace-making, positive, sacred; based on unconditional acceptance, faith, authentic modelling, and loving care. Is it enough for a self-transformation? For some ex-prisoners the change was gradual but solid. Others initially experienced some change but then relapsed. But even the latter remember the Sufi place with awe and sorrow for themselves, knowing they were unable to achieve a transformation (Amitay, Hawa-Kamel, & Ronel, n.d.).

The positive perspective of criminology confronts us with an unexpected challenge – instead of doing more and harder at the same time, it gently but firmly indicates a possibility for an alternative direction. Particularly in law enforcement, where we are consumed with calls for harsher social and personal responses, notwithstanding evidence proving that such responses to reduce criminality are failing, positive criminology suggests a novel approach. This perspective aspires for constructing a solid rehabilitation that is based on self-change rather than on fear from an external response (Ronel, 2015). In the chosen sub-field of sexual violence, where the public calls for even more excessive punishment based on the consequences victims experience at any level of victimisation, understandable fears, combined with the known risks and inevitable myths, the unexpected challenge raised by positive criminology is even more profound. Accordingly, one may genuinely appreciate the professional courage of Stephanie Kewley, Sarah Pemberton, and Mohammed Rahman, the authors of this remarkable book, who very systematically connect up-to-date knowledge and practice to prevent and end sexual offending within the existing perspective defined as positive criminology (Ronel & Elisha, 2020).

Throughout time, victims of sexual violence and abuse have been unable to discuss or report their experiences as the dominant perspective in society deemed it a private matter. Fortunately, today there is some change with recognition of the prevalence of sexual violence (e.g. the 'Me-Too' movement), increasing awareness of the consequences to individuals, families, and society, and a greater understanding of the responses needed, including its prevention. This book is highly aware of the existing social climate and the professional tools for evaluating the problem and eliminating its risks. However, by interweaving positive criminology strategies into present knowledge of the response to sexual abusers, this book goes beyond the known towards the positively envisioned, and clearly presents how this vision can become a reality. Based on their deep comprehension of the fundamentals of a positive criminology perspective, Stephanie, Sarah, and Mohammad succeeded in providing a first-of-its-kind handbook on the application of this perspective, which can be easily adapted to other topics of criminology.

Interestingly, and in coincidence with the current book, the first study that stemmed out of the perspective of positive criminology focussed on sexual offenders who were in prison (Elisha, Idisis, & Ronel, 2013). That study presented the rehabilitative power of social acceptance for the prisoners, especially by significant others. Following it, other studies explored the possibilities and meaning of positive criminology. For example, Ben Zvi–Uzan (2016) and Ben Zvi and Haimoff-Ayali (2015) carefully explored the complex interplay of being exposed to genuine goodness and the self-centredness of youth-at-risk. Ronel, Frid, and Timor (2013) deeply explored the potential impact on addicted prisoners of meaningfully participating in an intensive *vipassana* course while in prison. Ronel, Chen, and Elisha (2015) focussed on the recovery experience of clients of a therapeutic community through the lens of positive criminology. This distinct community – named Retorno – is the only Orthodox Jewish one (open to any willing individual regardless of their religious background) and it combines Jewish values with the spiritual 12-step programme and the more formal therapeutic community methods. Following principles of positive criminology, it also demonstrates another development of this innovative approach, that is, spiritual criminology. Spiritual criminology stems from the essential fact that different ages, spiritual schools, methods, and communities attempted to address criminality by applying various spiritual paths, providing a variety of spiritual responses to the issues of criminality (Baier & Wright, 2001; Ronel & Ben Yair, 2017). Spiritual criminology appreciates the spiritual worldview and refrains from providing a secular explanation for it. As specific examples of spiritual criminology, Ben Yair (2018) conducted an intensive study of Jewish spiritual criminology, including its peculiar attitude towards punishment and rehabilitation, and Hawa-Kamel (2018) thoroughly studied the rehabilitation of ex-prisoners in a Sufi-Islamic *zawia* (meeting place), as described earlier. Another research-based development of positive criminology is that of positive victimology (Shechory & Ronel, 2015; Toren, 2015a, 2015b), which holds a parallel perspective and guiding principles and adapts it to the complex field of victimology. Lastly, spiritual victimology faithfully represents an essential development and its academic study is currently ongoing, including spiritual victimology and recovery from past sexual victimisation, to close the circle.

The described developments of positive criminology – spiritual criminology, positive victimology, and spiritual victimology – already have an echo in this book since it also has in mind victimological issues as well as a reference to spirituality. That naturally makes it a prominent model for a comprehensive analysis of positive criminology and a promising, timely contribution to the field of criminology.

Natti Ronel

References

Amitay, G., Hawa-Kamel, D., & Ronel, N. (n.d.). *Wu-Wei criminology: An Islamic Sufi non-doing offender rehabilitation – positive and peacemaking criminology in practice*. Paper in preparation.

Baier, C. J., & Wright, B. R. E. (2001). If you love me, keep my commandments: A meta-analysis of the effect of religion on crime. *Journal of Research in Crime and Delinquency*, *38*(1), 3–21.

Ben Yair, Y. (2018). *Jewish criminology – the establishment of theory and practice based on Jewish resources* (Unpublished PhD dissertation), Bar-Ilan University (in Hebrew, English abstract, Ramat Gan, Israel).

Ben Zvi, T. (2016). *Between generosity and self- centeredness in the reality of youth at risk* (Unpublished PhD dissertation), Bar-Ilan University (in Hebrew, English abstract, Ramat Gan, Israel).

Ben Zvi, T., & Haimoff-Ayali, R. (2015). The effect of "the good" and the self-centeredness barrier – positive criminology in the lived reality of youth at risk. In N. Ronel & D. Segev (Eds.), *Positive criminology* (pp. 32–51). New York and London: Routledge.

Elisha, E., Idisis, Y., & Ronel, N. (2013). Positive criminology and imprisoned sex offenders: Demonstration of a way out from a criminal spin through acceptance relationships. *Journal of Sexual Aggression*, *19*(1), 66–80.

Hawa-Kamel, D. (2018). *Spiritual criminology of Sufi Islam: Theory and practice of positive peacemaking criminology* (Unpublished PhD dissertation), Bar-Ilan University (in Hebrew, English abstract, Ramat Gan, Israel).

Koptseva, N. P., & Kirko, V. I. (2015). Aspects of political wisdom in the treatise Lao Tzu "Tao Te Ching." *Mediterranean Journal of Social Sciences*, *6*(5), 119–126. https://doi.org/10.5901/mjss.2015.v6n5s2p119

Loy, D. (1985). Wei-wu-wei: Nondual action. *Philosophy East and West*, *35*(1), 73–87. Retrieved from http://ccbs.ntu.edu.tw/FULLTEXT/JR-PHIL/loy3.htm

Ronel, N. (2015). How can criminology become positive? In N. Ronel & D. Segev (Eds.), *Positive criminology* (pp. 13–31). New York and London: Routledge.

Ronel, N., & Ben Yair, Y. (2017). Spiritual criminology: The case of Jewish criminology. *International Journal of Offender Therapy and Comparative Criminology, 62*(7), 2081–2102.

Ronel, N., Chen, G., & Elisha, E. (2015). Application of positive criminology in Retorno – a Jewish therapeutic community for people with addictions. *Journal of Offender Rehabilitation, 54*(2), 122–141.

Ronel, N., & Elisha, E. (2020). Positive criminology: Theory, research, and practice. In *Oxford Research Encyclopedia of Criminology and Criminal Justice*. http://dx.doi.org/10.1093/acrefore/9780190264079.013.554

Ronel, N., Frid, N., & Timor, U. (2013). The practice of positive criminology: A Vipassana course in prison. *International Journal of Offender Therapy and Comparative Criminology, 57*(2), 133–153.

Shechory, M., & Ronel, N. (2015). Posttraumatic growth and positive victimology: The case of ultra-orthodox Jewish women who resided in a shelter. In N. Ronel & D. Segev (Eds.), *Positive criminology* (pp. 250–260). New York and London: Routledge.

Toren, T. Y. (2015a). *The effect of social relationship between offender and victim of sexual assault, on the rehabilitation strategy and healing process of the victim* (Unpublished PhD dissertation), Bar-Ilan University (in Hebrew, English abstract, Ramat Gan, Israel).

Toren, T. Y. (2015b). Theoretical and practical aspects of positive victimology. In N. Ronel & D. Segev (Eds.), *Positive criminology* (pp. 237–249). New York and London: Routledge.

Introduction

Experiencing sexual abuse is a traumatic and often life changing event. Survivors will often experience its consequences throughout their life span and across numerous domains within their lives. Preventing abuse from occurring in the first place must, therefore, be a priority for all in society; yet in the absence of an effective global prevention solution, we continue to respond to victims and perpetrators of sexual violence only after the abuse has occurred. General public responses to incidents of sexual abuse and violence and to those who sexually abuse others is, understandably, one of outrage and vilification (Burke, 2015). Instinctive in this response is the need to protect those at risk of harm and/or those victims who are already harmed, using resources available, whilst harshly punishing and sanctioning those responsible for perpetrating harm. Indeed, much Western legislation and policy has been implemented in direct response to such public and media outcries, with at times little empirical evidence to support its effectiveness (McCartan & Kemshall, 2015). In reality, 'community protection' approaches focus on an identified perpetrator alongside increased penalties such as civil commitment, chemical castration, registration, and residency restrictions, which often result in a barrage of unintended and harmful consequences for perpetrators and their families and friends (Tabachnick, McCartan, & Panaro, 2016). However, as our understanding of sexual abuse and how to respond to it develops, there is increasing pressure to move away from a 'justice only' solution, and towards a more integrated, positive, and public health approach (McCartan & Brown, 2019).

Positive criminology is a relatively new conceptual perspective in the criminological field. Although not a theory per se, it incorporates several models and theories under one unified umbrella. Ronel and Elisha first introduced the concept in 2011. In their paper, they outlined how dominant criminological traditions have tended to focus on an examination of causal explanations to criminal behaviour. Yet up until recently, examination of factors or processes needed to help prevent crime or support a person to move away from crime has been lacking in the field. Indeed, a disproportionate degree of attention has historically focussed on individual deviance and pathology, each of which are of course important areas that have helped improve our understanding of crime and deviant behaviour, but this single focus of interest provides only a partial picture. Instead of focussing solely on the negative aspects within a person's life, positive criminology requires researchers, practitioners, and policy makers to consider a broader range of factors related to crime and the desistance of crime. Human behaviour is complex and positive criminology highlights how incomplete our understanding of crime and our responses to it presently are.

Thus, in response to the current and arguably limited criminological examination of crime and prevention of crime, Ronel and Elisha (2011) presented the notion of positive criminology. It is important to note here that positive criminology does not claim any new knowledge or insight; instead it provides a unification of already existing knowledge and theories. Indeed, Ronel and Segev (2015) demonstrate this with a comprehensive collection of existing work. Positive criminology brings together models and theories of criminology in which a positive focus is central to their philosophy. Several existing positive criminological concepts are embedded into our criminal justice systems. These already share the essence of positive criminology, in that they feature positive characteristics, processes, and influences on people's lives that help them move away from, avoid, or desist from committing crime. These include, for example, the notions of protective factors and resilience, post-traumatic growth, exposure to goodness, social acceptance, desistance, peace-making criminology, restorative justice, and reintegrative shaming. It is the unification of these approaches that is important, and as in the early stages of the development of the field of positive criminology, there needs to be, at the very minimum, a common language with which researchers and practitioners can engage and explore within the context of mainstream/traditional criminology. Positive criminology is therefore best defined as:

> a focus on the encounter with significant force and effects that are experienced positively and that distance the individual from deviance and crime, whether by means of formal and informal therapy programs and interventions (such as self-help organisations), through emphasis on positive social elements (such as reintegrative shaming, human kindness, or social acceptance), or based on positive personal factors (such as factors of protection and resilience, positive emotions and subjective attitudes, coherence, faith, and morality).
>
> (Ronel & Elisha, 2011, p. 307)

The text is organised into two parts. The first aims to outline current practice and policy in terms of assessment, treatment, and management of people convicted of sexual offending. Chapter 1 presents some definitions of sexual abuse from both legal and organisational perspectives, followed by some insight into prevalence and incidence rates and the impact of these rates on our understanding of the scale and nature of sexual violence. Types of abuse, perpetrators, and victims are outlined, along with a summary of some theoretical explanations of sexual abuse. Chapter 2 presents the current sentencing and management responses to those convicted of sexual offences in England and Wales. It outlines the range of current options and sanctions available to sentencers and details the statutory management requirements of people with sexual conditions through the English and Welsh system known as Multi-Agency Public Protection Arrangements

(MAPPA). Chapter 3 introduces readers to the field of risk assessment. It summarises the variety of standard tools and assessment methods used in the industry, such as case formulation, psychometrics, phallometry and polygraph. Chapter 4 provides a brief history of the treatment of sexual offending behaviours, as well as contemporary approaches to treatment. Focus in this chapter includes a summary of different approaches and their effectiveness in treating the factors known to contribute to sexual offending behaviour. The final chapter in this first part of the text includes an ecological overview of a public health approach to preventing sexual violence including primary, secondary, and tertiary approaches.

The second part of the text, beginning with Chapter 6, introduces the notion of positive criminology. It outlines a suggested criterion for models, describes interventions or approaches classified as positive criminological, and includes some examples that fall under this umbrella. In keeping with the format of the first part of the book, Chapter 7 considers current assessment tools and assessment approaches that include and consider strength or protective factors as part of their assessment for those with convictions for sexual offending. Following this, Chapter 8 considers the degree to which current interventions or treatment supports a positive criminological approach. A review of nine studies that meet these criteria is considered. Finally, Chapter 9 considers the notion of religion, spirituality, and crime, an area robustly examined in non-offending populations, but far less for offending populations, and even lesser for those with a history of sexual offending.

The purpose of this text is to provide a new perspective in which policymakers, practitioners, and academics might begin to engage with the notion of preventing sexual harm and abuse, not only through the current community protection measures, but also through positive and strengths-based approaches. Using positive criminology as a framework, this text explores how prevention of sexual harm and abuse, and growth from trauma and perpetration of abuse, might be applied in the current criminal justice context. The arguments presented in this text aim to supplement and incorporate our current understanding of the prevention of sexual harm and abuse by presenting an alternative positive criminological perspective. Our text does not claim to have all the answers or solutions to this global and complex issue; instead, we simply provide a worthy complementary perspective that requires legitimate consideration. We encourage fellow scholars and policy makers to explore, investigate, and test the possibilities of a criminal justice system that incorporates strength-based and positive criminological solutions to sexual violence.

References

Burke, L. (2015). Sexual offending: Past injustice and present risks. *Probation Journal*, *62*(4), 315–319.

McCartan, K., & Brown, J. (2019). The prevention of sexual abuse: Issues, challenges and resolutions. *Journal of Sexual Aggression*, *25*(1), 1–3.

McCartan, K., & Kemshall, H. (2015). Sex offender (re) integration into the community: Realities and challenges. *Journal of Sexual Aggression*, *21*(1), 1–3.

Ronel, N., & Elisha, E. (2011). A different perspective: Introducing positive criminology. *International Journal of Offender Therapy and Comparative Criminology*, *55*(2), 305–325.

Ronel, N., & Segev, D. (2015). *Positive criminology*. Oxon: Routledge.

Tabachnick, J., McCartan, K., & Panaro, R. (2016). Changing course: From a victim/offender duality to a public health perspective. In D. R. Laws & W. O'Donohue (Eds.), *Treatment of sex offenders: Strengths and weaknesses in assessment and intervention* (pp. 323–342). Switzerland: Springer.

1 Definition, causes, and prevalence of sexual abuse

Definition

The concept of crime, including crimes that are sexual in nature, is socially constructed. They are crimes "not fixed but vary(ing) across time, culture and even from one situation to the next" (Burke, 2014, p. 194). As such, defining sexual abuse is dependent upon temporal and cultural contexts. To demonstrate recent definitional shifts, it is worth noting for example that in England and Wales, prior to 1991, it was not a criminal offence for a man to rape his wife (McGregor, 2011) and in many countries across the world, homosexuality is still deemed illegal (Beyrer, 2014). Definitions, therefore, reflect changing political, legal, cultural, and contextual perspectives and without a clear or stable definition, it becomes a challenge for policymakers, legislators, researchers, as well as well as clinicians and practitioners to work in a consistent manner to prevent abuse.

For sexual harm and abuse to be prevented, a greater understanding and clarity of the definition of what sexual abuse is, is needed. The World Health Organisation (WHO) defines sexual violence as:

> Any sexual act, attempt to obtain a sexual act, unwanted sexual comments or advances, or acts to traffic or otherwise directed against a person's sexuality using coercion, by any person regardless of their relationship to the victim, in any setting, including but not limited to home and work.
>
> (Garcia-Moreno, Guedes, & Knerr, 2012, p. 2)

The current legal framework in which most of England and Wales operate when responding to sexual and violent abuse includes legislation under the Protection of Children Act, 1978, Criminal Justice and Immigration Act, 2008, the recently drafted Domestic Abuse Bill, 2019, and the most relevant, the Sexual Offences Act, 2003. The Sexual Offences Act, 2003 does not define sexual abuse or sexual harm in one succinct definition, as the World Health Organisation does; instead, it provides specific details of individual behaviours and the conditions under which these acts are illegal. These include the acts of:

> Rape; Assault; Causing sexual activity without consent; Rape and other offences against children under 13; Child sex offences; Abuse of position

> of trust; Familial child sex offences; Offences against persons with a mental disorder impeding choice; Inducements etc. to persons with a mental disorder; Care workers for persons with a mental disorder; Indecent photographs of children; Abuse of children through prostitution and pornography; Prostitution; Trafficking; Preparatory offences; Sex with an adult relative; Other offences (exposure, voyeurism, intercourse with an animal etc.); and Offences outside the United Kingdom.
>
> (Sexual Offences Act, 2003)

Whilst in a legal context, this type of definition provides greater clarity, in areas such as health, education, or social care, further elaboration of what constitutes abuse is still required. Without clarity of definition, people are vulnerable, as was highlighted in the publication of an independent inquiry commissioned by Rotherham Metropolitan Borough Council (Jay, 2014), whereby approximately 1,400 children were sexually exploited over a 16-year period in the town of Rotherham alone. The inquiry into this case identified a significant failure to act in several child abuse situations by different statutory authorities. This was because of a lack of understanding concerning what constituted child sexual exploitation (CSE).

While many factors account for the scale of this case, one factor is the authorities' lack of definitional agreement or understanding. A definition of what constitutes sexual abuse or CSE is therefore important for all stakeholders, but key for practitioners and professionals who might encounter victims or perpetrators of this crime.

While definitions of sexual crime remain complex, so too do the descriptions of the actors involved in a sexual crime. The labels society place and construct around these actors can serve to both help – and at times hinder – the justice system. For decades, people behaving outside of social norms are often perceived to be threatening the fabric of society, and as such are labelled and stigmatised. Cohen's work on "folk devils" and "moral panics" provides great insight into this phenomenon (Cohen, 1972) and people with criminal convictions are a good example of this labelling process. The label associated with 'criminal' is problematic in that it tends to be permanent and pathological. Likewise, the label 'sex offender' produces perhaps a greater threat to social stability, and it is thus emotionally charged and laden with fearful and frightening connotations. Labels of those convicted of sexual offences include, for example, predator, paedophile, pervert, very high risk, mentally disturbed, monster; indeed, media narratives often present family members and people working with this group as gullible do-gooders (Hanvey, Wilson, & Philpot, 2011). From the perspective of prevention, this type of language raises two key issues. First, such social constructions are often ill-informed and driven by the popular media following the detection, sentencing, or the release of a high-profile case. While motivations to publish such stories are claimed to be in public interest, and perhaps serve as a warning of the risks children potentially face, stories are very rarely produced as an educational or informative notice of sexual abuse. Instead, one of the common consequences is moral panic. A good example of this was the tabloid *News of the World*'s "naming and shaming" campaign in response to the abduction and murder of Sarah Payne in 2000 in West Sussex. Sarah was eight years old when in July 2000 she was abducted while playing outside her grandparents' house. Her body was found several days later. Roy Whiting was convicted of her abduction and murder. During the investigation, it emerged that he was already on the sex offender register, having previously abducted and indecently assaulted another young girl (Lipscombe, 2012). In response to this, the *News of the World* printed names, addresses, and photographs of alleged sex offenders, claiming that this was an effort to protect the public. However, vigilante groups emerged, and many people's homes and lives were ruined after these groups wrongly targeted innocent people in what became a modern-day witch hunt (Cross, 2005). Arguably, such media discourse defeats the objective of raising public awareness in the first place, as the general public fixates on inaccurate information. Second, governments and policymakers tend to respond to such labels with the greatest of force in order to satisfy public demands, resulting in criminal justice systems being dominated by controlling and punitive policy and practice (Harrison, 2011). While it is important, therefore, when developing definitions of sexual crime, use of labels that define perpetrators of such crimes is equally important. Accurate and factual labels are far more helpful to tackle and prevent sexual violence. Demonising and 'othering' people who commit an offence provides distance from lawful citizens (Spencer, 2009). Thus, the problem becomes external to society, and the solution is to displace people from the society. This approach is problematic for two reasons. First, society is encouraged to reject and fear those who are labelled, creating isolated 'others'; second, people given such labels carry the stigma of said labels, accepting social rejection, or perhaps worse, internalising labels, thus jeopardising opportunities to desist from future crime (Maruna, Lebel, Mitchell, & Naples, 2004).

Having a shared definition of the behaviour and the person perpetrating the harm further helps us understand and define the nature of sexual abuse as well as the scale and scope of the problem. This is because understanding the nature and prevalence of abuse enables policy makers to develop strategies and policies that incorporate all stakeholders exposed to the issue. Indeed, applying varying and inconsistent definitions makes evaluation and identification of the problem extremely complex. Furthermore, without it, designing, implementing, and evaluating strategies to prevent sexual abuse from occurring in the first place becomes meaningless and perhaps impossible.

Causes of sexual abuse

To understand how to prevent sexual abuse, an understanding of the causes of abuse is first needed. While it is not our aim to give a comprehensive review of the literature explaining the aetiology of sexual offending, as this is of course beyond the scope of this chapter and indeed this text, a brief overview is needed. Readers interested in exploring the theory of sexual violence are directed to the numerous excellent texts dedicated to just this purpose, for example, Beech, Craig, and Browne (2009a), Craig, Browne, and Beech (2008), Harrison (2011), Laws and

Ward (2011), Marshall, Marshall, Serran, and O'Brien (2011), Ward, Polaschek, and Beech (2006), Wilcox, Garrett, and Harkins (2015).

As we do not intend on providing an in-depth review of existing theory, we turn to one of the most current and comprehensive edited collections of theory to date to support this chapter. Ward, Beech and colleagues (2017) discuss a broad range of theoretical explanations of sexual offending. They include theories that are multi-factorial; single factor; process models; theory for special populations; and practice theories. Rather than discuss each in turn, they are briefly summarised in Table 1.1.

Nature of sexual abuse

Consequences

The nature of sexual abuse is diverse and broad. Abuse is perpetrated by men, women, and children; likewise, victims of abuse include men, women, and children. Abuse can be carried out by one perpetrator; however, it can also be organised and facilitated by pairs or groups of people. Abuse occurs in people's homes, places of work, educational institutions, public areas, and in many of our institutions such as health care or prison environments. Abuse takes place in the virtual world through the World Wide Web where many victims are likely to be unaware of the reach abusive images may have. Some may be unaware that illegal images of them have even been published and shared through the Internet. Images of sexual abuse can be produced and distributed throughout the Internet with ease. Indeed, sexual abuse and the distribution of images can take place via social applications such as chat rooms and networking platforms; images of abuse can be (re) produced and (re)distributed through websites, emails, messaging apps, as well as the more recent phenomena of live streaming abuse via the Internet. Thus, the nature of abuse is diverse and broad in its scope.

The impact that sexual abuse has on individuals and on society is equally vast. In their 1986 review of the literature, Browne and Finkelhor found the short- and long-term consequences of being a victim of sexual abuse to include impaired emotional, physical, sexual, and social functioning. They reported initial effects of abuse to include feelings of fear, anger, guilt, and shame, with physical effects such as disruption to sleep and eating habits, as well as unwanted pregnancy. Their review also found young victims to be acting out sexually or engaging in excessive masturbation, dropping out of school, running away from home, or presenting with delinquent behaviours. The longer-term effects of abuse were reported as depression, anxiety, low self-esteem, and for many, self-harm and/or suicide. Browne and Finkelhor reported that victims faced interpersonal difficulties such as relating with parents or being a parent and not trusting partners; indeed, younger female victims, likely vulnerable as a result of early sexual abuse, were further revictimised through non-consensual sexual experiences as adults. Victims report struggling with sexual intimacy, engaging in promiscuous behaviours, prostitution, or substance abuse. The findings of Browne and Finkelhor (1986) have been

Table 1.1 Summary of existing theories on the aetiology, assessment, and treatment of people convicted of sexual offending[1]

Theory/model	*Key theorist(s)*[2]	*Summary of theory or model*
1 Attachment-Based Theory	Marshall and Marshall	Theory relates only to male affiliated child abusers. It aims to explain the onset of offending across the life span. It argues that attachment issues are central to problems across the life span and can occur at any stage, not just develop in childhood. The theory states that two factors are required for a man to commit a sexual offence: a) disposition to offend and b) the opportunity to offend. 'Disposition,' it is argued, is rooted in the attachment experiences and stays current to the man. Attachment is changeable.
2 The Four Preconditions Model	Finkelhor and Araji	Best described as a conceptual framework rather than a falsifiable theory. Argues that for a sexual offence to take place, the following four conditions are needed: a) The offender must be predisposed to sexually abusing a child. This element is further broken down to include the need for the offender to have an emotional congruence with children, be able to be sexually aroused by children, and have blockages in his life preventing him from securing healthy adult sexual relationships; b) The offender must be able to overcome internal disinhibitors to carrying out such an act; c) The offender must overcome external barriers or a lack of access to children; and finally, d) The offender must overcome the resistance of the child. The framework is supported by empirical evidence examining emotional congruence, emotional loneliness, poor attachments, sexual arousal developed through own abuse, learned behaviour, biological factors, cognitive distortions, empathy deficits, decreased inhibitions, situational factors, environmental factors, targeting or grooming behaviours.
3 The Confluence Mediational Model of Sexual Aggression	Malamuth	The first multifactorial model in which sexual aggression is correlated with behavioural, developmental, and personality factors. The model was narrowed down to two constellations: a) Hostile masculinity (HM) and b) Impersonal sex (IS). The HM pathway is a personality construct made up of narcissistic, insecure, defensive, hypersensitive, hostile, and distrustful orientation, particularly towards women, and sexual gratification from controlling or dominating women. The IS pathway is developmental and is representative of a person who has grown up in a violent, abusive, or antisocial environment, with they themselves becoming promiscuous or detached from sexual relationships. Both constellations are strongly predictive of sexual aggression in non-criminal justice men as well as those in the system and when low empathy traits are included, prediction is increased.

(*Continued*)

Table 1.1 (Continued)

Theory/model	*Key theorist(s)*[2]	*Summary of theory or model*
4 A Theoretical Integration of Aetiological and Typological Models of Rape	Knight and Sims-Knight	Initially developed from the Malamuth model, the authors test for both aetiological and typological models for rape and found both converge to support the three core traits of antisociality, callous/unemotional, and sexualisation. These traits are therefore predictive of rape, but are also supported in the literature to predict general recidivism and sexual recidivism.
5 Multimodal Self-Regulation Theory of Sexual Offending	Stinson, Sales and Becker	This theory explains sexual offending by drawing on the extant literature on self-regulation. It states that by poor coping and maladaptive self-regulation, sexual offending behaviours become reinforced over time. The model details the biological, developmental, behavioural, personality-based, and perceived environmental factors. There have been two studies testing this theory to date, with work ongoing.
6 The Integrated Theory of Sexual Offending – Revised	Ward and Beech	This theory integrates a diverse range of factors that are comprehensive and descriptive. It is multi-field and offers an interlevel theoretical framework. It argues that human behaviour needs to be understood on four levels: a) Aetiological (genetic/environmental); b) Brain mechanisms (developmental and subsequent functioning); c) Neuropsychological (brain based psychological systems); d) Symptom of phenomenological level. Four sets of facts converge to cause sexual offending behaviour: biological, ecological, neuropsychological, and agency level factors. The theory posits that offending occurs when distal and proximal variables dynamically interact.
7 Incentive Theory of Sexual Motivation	Bindra, Both, Singer and Toates	The theory argues that sexual excitement and desire are an emotional response to a stimulus. That is, the stimulus is an important trigger for initiating the response of sexual desire, which is then influenced by hormones and neurotransmitters that push forward the behaviour – it is the attraction to a stimuli that triggers sexual motivation rather than a deficit in the hypothalamus. Once excited by stimulus, desire is activated, and behaviour will be dictated by previous sexual experiences/rewards, etc. In addition, other factors influence the process, such as internal or external (dis)inhibitors such as the use of chemical substances (alcohol, drugs), impulsivity, or antisocial orientation.

8	Theories of Deviant Sexual Fantasy	McGuire, Carlisle and Young; Laws and Marshall; Beech, Harkins and Bartols	A number of theories include accounts of Deviant Sexual Fantasy. During a single initial sexual experience, deviant fantasies are learned. This fantasy is then usually used for later masturbation and by repeatedly using the fantasy, the sexual excitement of it increases. Theorists also argue that the development of deviant fantasy occurs through classical conditioning, by regularly masturbating to a stimulus and ejaculating, which will eventually result in sexual stimulation to said fantasy. Further, argument has been made for secondary conditioning whereby, for example, after a child has been sexually abused they may experience high levels of arousal and aggression. Thus, over time, when the individual experiences anger, they may experience sexual arousal. The Dual Process Model of Sexual Thinking (DPM-ST) draws on existing theories and aims to explain the cognitive process associated with sexual thoughts/fantasy. It is argued that associative processes are responsible for intrusive sexual thoughts whereas controlled processes are responsible for deliberate fantasy.
9	Intimacy Deficits/ Attachment Problems in Sexual Offenders	Bowlby, Marshall, Ward and Beech	The desire for intimacy is a basic human need. The quality of the bond between an individual and their initial care giver influences future adult relationships and the ability to determine. Thus this model determines that regardless of the positive or negative experience, it is the expectations of the individual in terms of how they then see themselves within the world and with others that matters. Secure attachment, for example, helps develop individuals who are supportive, nurturing, and safe, whereas insecure attachments produce individuals who are callous, fearful, reject relationships or exert power over others. While much of this development is learned, there are also neurobiological explanations, for example those with paedophilic attraction, or those with social phobias. Likewise, there are neurochemical explanations, such as the actions of oxytocin and vasopressin, which are argued to cause intimacy deficits.
10	Cognitive Distortions of Child Sexual Abusers	Abel, Becker, Cunningham-Rathner and Ward; Keenhan and Gannon	Cognitive distortions (CDs) are historically known as dysfunctional thinking styles, beliefs, justifications, defensiveness, denials, minimisations, rationalisations, etc., generally associated with psychological problems. In the context of sexual offending, this is best described as beliefs/thoughts that violate accepted sexual norms and influence the onset/maintenance of sexually abusive behaviour.

(Continued)

Table 1.1 (Continued)

Theory/model	*Key theorist(s)*[2]	*Summary of theory or model*
11 Theories of Empathy Deficits	Mann, Marshall, Miller and Eisenburg; Pithers	There are a number of different ways in which empathy deficits contribute to sexual offending. These include offenders having a) General empathy deficits; b) Specific deficits to groups; or c) Failure to engage in the process of empathy in certain situations. It is generally agreed that empathy involves both a cognitive and affective process. One theory argues that the process in empathy linked to sexual offending takes place in five parts: a) Limitations in ability to take perspective of others in given situation; b) Viewing others in a hostile and aggressive way in particular situations; c) Restricted ability to experience emotion; d) Inability to manage emotion; and e) Failure of a–d as a result of substances, stress, sexual arousal, etc.
12 Theories of Emotion Regulation	Gilespie and Beech, Ekman, Gross	Authors note that the literature suggests that people convicted of sexual offending tend to have problems with emotional regulation. This arguably derives from poor attachments and maladaptive responses to early experience. Neurobiological explanations also support explanations for poor emotional regulation. Techniques to support self-regulation include mindfulness and controlled breathing techniques.
13 Situational Theories	Smallbone and Cale; Wortley, Cornish, and Clarke; Eck	Situational theories exist within the debate regarding the causes of crime being of individual disposition and/or situational factors. Scholars accept that both are important in the commission of a crime; however, research policy and practice has tended to focus on the individual. Situational crime prevention draws on rational choice theory, routine activities theory, and the dynamic properties of criminal situations. These include the four ways in which a situation may support and promote the motivation of the perpetrator. Situation can prompt criminal activity, exert social pressure, give permission to a criminal response, and induce arousal and thus provoke criminality. Wortley and Smallbone (2006) proposed a typology based on offender dispositions and varying situation type. They classify the predatory offender as an opportunistic vendor and a situational offender; for all offender types, the situation is precipitating, in that the offender either reacts to or exploits the situation. Should a situation be tempting, a situational offender is unlikely to respond, whereas the opportunistic and predatory type will exploit this situation, and only in challenging situation types will predatory offenders manipulate the situation.

14 Theories of the Offence and Relapse Process	Polaschek; Pithers, Marques and Marlatt; Ward and Hudson	Process theories aim to help explain and describe the steps or stages offenders take that take them closer to offending or lapsing/relapsing into harmful behaviours. Offence models (OM) include models to explain rape, child abuse, and self-regulation. They break down the various stages in an offence chain including the time before, during, and after the offence. The Relapse Model (RM) follows closely models designed to explain relapse in alcoholics. The RM assumes that the person has been through treatment and is thus aware of areas of concern or high-risk situations. The RM enables strategies to be developed to help avoid – or deal with – these situations in the future. The process is therefore a learned behaviour and is skills based.
15 Models of Modus Operandi in Sexual Offending: A Criminological Perspective	Beauregard and Proulx	Models of Modus Operandi (MO) link closely to typologies of sexual offenders (e.g. sadistic, anger, opportunity, and compensatory) in that the pattern of action and behaviour prior to, during, and after a crime is determined. MOs are, however, not fixed, and can change from crime to crime. Arguably, MOs tend to focus only on the offender, when understanding the whole event can help explain MO. Thus, exploring the offender's crime script regarding all aspects of the crime – including the victim, the offenders themselves, and the crime context – provides understanding of the development of an MO in relation to internal and external constraints.
16 Integrated Model of Change for the Treatment of Sexual Offending	Carter and Mann	This model provides an overall framework to support and enable treatment programmes so that change can be more readily achieved. The framework includes details of the model of change and six organising principles required to help facilitate change. The framework aligns closely to the Risk, Need, and Responsivity Principles. This model of change requires treatment programmes to address biological, psychological, and social factors empirically related to sexual offending. Sexual risk factors can be described in several ways. Carter and Mann draw on the earlier works of Mann and frame four domains, namely a) Sexual interests; b) Offence supportive attitudes; c) Social and emotional functioning; and d) Self-management. Each of these domains can be divided into psychological, biological, and social components. Six organising principles help arrange the model of change. Principle 1 states that treatment should be designed and delivered in a way that is proportionate to the risk of each participant. Principle 2 states that treatment will be delivered in a way that makes it accessible and appealing to participants whatever the biological, psychological, and social circumstances. Principle 3 mentions that in addressing criminogenic needs, treatment will strengthen biological resources such as neurocognitive functioning. Principle 4 states that in addressing criminogenic needs, treatment will strengthen psychological resources, such as cognitive and emotional flexibility and empathetic relating. Principle 5 says that treatment t will strengthen social resources such as social capital. Principle 6 states that treatment will strengthen the intention to desist from offending. All treatment activities/sessions must connect to biological, psychological, and social risk and need factors, as well as the organising principles.

(Continued)

Table 1.1 (Continued)

Theory/model	*Key theorist(s)*[2]	*Summary of theory or model*
17 Strengths-Based Theories and Sexual Offending	Willis, Yates, Stewart, Ward, Marshall, and Maruna	Drawing on the positive psychology movement, strengths-based theories for sexual offending aim to draw on personal strengths helping people to make alternative healthy choices in life that help steer them away from harmful behaviours. The Good Lives Model (GLM) is one example that has been embraced (although less empirically tested than Risk-Need-Responsivity models) in the treatment of sexual offending. The central assumption of the GLM is that all humans are intrinsically driven to seek out opportunities that result in feelings of satisfaction and well-being. As such, humans strive to achieve goals or primary goods. Primary goods are states of affairs, states of mind, personal characteristics, activities, or experiences that are sought for their own sake and are likely to increase psychological well-being if achieved (Ward & Brown, 2004). Drawing on a range of disciplines like psychology, anthropology, and biology, at least ten primary goods are identified: "Life (including healthy living and functioning), knowledge, excellence in work and play (including mastery experiences), excellence in agency (i.e., autonomy and self-directedness), inner peace (i.e., freedom from emotional turmoil and stress), friendship (including intimate, romantic, and family relationships), community, spirituality (in the broad sense of finding meaning and purpose in life), happiness, and creativity. Instrumental or secondary goods provide concrete ways (or the means) of securing these goods, for example, certain types of work (i.e., good of mastery), relationships (i.e., good of intimacy), or leisure activities (i.e. good of play)" (Ward & Brown, 2004, p. 247). To achieve primary goods, secondary goals or instrumental goods take the form of activities or means by which these goods might be achieved. For example, the primary good of friendship could be achieved by the secondary goal of spending time with friends or meeting new people. However, people who sexually offend engage in maladaptive secondary goals to achieve the primary goods. GLM argues that it is a result of inappropriate choices/means to obtain primary goods, a lack of scope, a conflict in goals set, and a lack of internal or external capabilities that lead to offending behaviour.

18	The Risk–Need–Responsivity Model	Andrew and Bonta	The Risk-Need-Responsivity Model (RNR) has three main principles: a) The risk principle – the level of intervention or service must match the offender's level of actuarial risk of recidivism. As such, treatment designed for high risk offenders should be more intensive than for lower risk offenders; b) The need principle – criminogenic needs of the offender must be assessed and targeted by appropriate interventions. Treatment should only target factors known to be related to recidivism. While non-criminogenic factors are important (such as mental health), they are not related to reducing recidivism and are therefore less important in this context; c) The responsivity principle – most effective interventions tend to include theories based on cognitive, behavioural, and social learning theories which ensure that treatment is responsive to the needs of clients by delivering interventions by therapists displaying warmth, respect, prosocial modelling, and collaboration with the client. Responsivity also ensures that barriers to treatment are reduced, so that issues of diversity, learning needs, and gender are responded to.
19	Theories of Desistance from Sexual Offending	Harris, Laws, Ward, Maruna, Willis, Levenson	Debate regarding the need for a separate desistance theory for those convicted of sexual offending exists in the literature. The answer to this question, however, is currently unknown. As such, general theories of desistance are applied, tested, and considered for this population, although far greater examination of this is needed. In terms of general desistance, there is no single working definition, rather, an agreement that desistance is a process and not a specific point in time where criminal behaviour is terminated. It is perhaps more helpfully understood as the maintenance of abstinence from crime in an ongoing process that interacts between internal and external factors, influenced by the structural, situational, and cultural contexts. Thus, the desistance process for all 'offender types' is complex and challenging. The process of desistance is perhaps best viewed in two phases – a primary and a secondary phase. In the primary phase, a behavioural change occurs, the offender ceases offending, and a crime free period is experienced. The secondary phase, perhaps the most important, sees not only a crime-free offender but one who reinvents and redefines their identity and self through new narratives and roles. Given that there is no single overarching theory to explain desistance, the concept is best viewed as a paradigm that consists of several models, theories, and approaches, each of which draw on different explanations at varying ecological levels. Desistance, even for sexual offending populations, can therefore only be understood by considering criminal behaviour and the desistance of such behaviour through a multifaceted and interdisciplinary lens. Thus, theories of desistance are conceptually divided into at least four domains: Individual and agentic; Social and structural; Interactionist; and Situational theories.

1 Theories drawn from Boer (2017)
2 List is not exhaustive/exclusive, nor presented in any priority

replicated in more recent reviews of the literature including those that suggest that experiences between men and women are relatively equal (Dube et al., 2005) and others reporting differences, for example, that women tend to internalise their suffering and men externalise it (Sigurdardottir, Halldorsdottir, & Bender, 2014). Either way, both genders experience trauma of some sort with increasing reports that victims of sexual abuse present symptoms of post-traumatic stress disorder (Hébert, Langevin, & Daigneault, 2016; Hébert, Lavoie, & Blais, 2014).

While people as individuals are inevitably impacted by abuse, a socioeconomic cost to society is incurred as well. Fergusson, McLeod, and Horwood (2013), who compared the outcomes of over 900 people in New Zealand at the ages of 18, 21, and 30 years, found that those who were victims of sexual abuse visited their medical practitioners and health centres at a far greater rate than others and had a greater dependency on welfare. Fang et al. (2015), when using the 2010 World Health Organisation's global burden of disease estimates, found the economic cost of sexual abuse in China in 2010 to be 0.39% of the gross domestic profit (GDP). In South Africa, the cost of violence against children to the economy was estimated at nearly 5% of the country's GDP (Hsiao et al., 2018). Furthermore, using data from the United Nations, Fearon and Hoeffler (2014) report the overall cost of recorded sexual abuse for children worldwide at US $36.8 billion; and for lifetime economic burden for interpersonal violence (in the US alone), US $1.3 trillion is the estimated cost to the government (Peterson et al., 2018). These costs are also likely to be underestimated, as figures only account for certain types of violence against certain victims and in many cases where offences have been officially recorded. Thus, individual and socioeconomic costs are massive following an incident of sexual abuse. However, it is important to note that the impact and harm of experiencing sexual abuse and recovering from it is a unique experience to each individual, and therefore likely to incur further problems and costs that are not officially mentioned.

Classification

Although perpetrators and victims of sexual abuse are a heterogeneous population (Beech et al., 2009a), both legal and academic literature frequently classifies them into distinct groups. For example, perpetrators are often classified by gender (male/female), age (adult or juvenile), number of perpetrators (lone, co-offender, group, or gang), relational (stranger, inter-familial, extra-familial), and contact or non-contact offender. Victims are classified in a similar fashion, along with recognition of both primary and secondary victims (e.g. family/friends of the victim).

Similarly, offences are typically categorised by type (Lockmuller, Fisher, & Beech, 2008). For example, 'child abuse' is an offence type used to describe a range of sexual assaults against a child or children that vary from non-contact offences (e.g. grooming) to contact offences (e.g. penetrative and sadistic rape). 'Rape' is an offence type in which a male perpetrator sexually assaults the victim through vaginal/anal/oral penetration with his penis. The victim can be either an adult or a child. Perpetrators of rape are often classified further to include the motivation for the offence, such as a sexual, anger, or sadistic rapist. 'Internet offending' is a type of offence that is also sub-divided and can include perpetrators who produce, supply/distribute, or download illicit images of (usually) children being sexually abused. Victims can be adults, children, or animals but the greatest demand appears to be for images of child abuse. 'Exhibitionists' are types of perpetrators who engage in non-contact sexually abusive behaviours, which primarily involves the exposure of the genitals, usually while masturbating, and victims include both adults and children. Finally, 'sexual murder' involves the murder of a victim (adult or child) as the result of a sexual assault. The murder often occurs as a result of the perpetrator needing to prevent disclosure or as part of the sexual gratification process.

Prevalence, incidence, and prosecution rates

Sexual abuse is an under-reported crime. Therefore, reported incidents of sexual assault cannot be assumed to represent the actual prevalence of the abuse (Brown & Walklate, 2012). Indeed, as noted by the difficulties in defining sexual abuse, understanding, researching, and recording this type of crime is complex and challenging. The very nature of sexual abuse requires the perpetrator to exert power and control over the victim, making the reporting of sexual abuse less likely for several reasons. Victims are often young children, unable or unaware of ways of reporting such crimes; teenage children may be groomed to the extent of being fearful of reprisals and further attacks, or even blame themselves (Smallbone, Marshall, & Wortley, 2013). While sexual perpetrators are a heterogeneous group (Beech, Craig, & Browne, 2009b), sexual abuse is most frequently carried out by family members or people known to the family (Browne, 2009). Victims, therefore, fear they will not be believed if they report the abuse (Finkelhor, 1984). The criminal justice system can also be a hostile environment for victims of sexual abuse. Many expect that they will not be listened to or believed, particularly, for example, if they had been drinking alcohol prior to the assault (Fisher, Daigle, Cullen, & Turner, 2003). Likewise, they may be afraid of the potential trauma of having to engage with the judicial system (Smith & Freyd, 2014) and testify publicly before their assailant.

While determining actual and accurate rates of sexual abuse is a challenge, three sources are useful to explore when considering this figure: official police recorded crime; victim and victim family reports; and perpetrator self-reports. According to the Office of National Statistics in the UK (2018), police recorded crime for sexual offences has steadily risen over the last decade. Table 1.2 details this trend.

This is also reflected in the international picture, as demonstrated in Figure 1.1. The data in this figure was collected using statistics provided by the United Nations Office on Drugs and Crime (2017). However, as with all large data sets, caution is required when interpreting the figures. While Figure 1.1 shows an apparent increase in trends, with Europe having the most police recorded incidents of violence, this of course does not mean that Europe has the greatest prevalence rates.

Table 1.2 Annual police recorded sexual offences 2002–2017 (UK)

Recorded year	*Total recorded sexual offences*
Apr '02 to Mar '03	56,652
Apr '03 to Mar '04	60,412
Apr '04 to Mar '05	60,924
Apr '05 to Mar '06	60,287
Apr '06 to Mar '07	56,042
Apr '07 to Mar '08	52,166
Apr '08 to Mar '09	50,185
Apr '09 to Mar '10	53,006
Apr '10 to Mar '11	53,940
Apr '11 to Mar '12	52,760
Apr '12 to Mar '13	53,599
Apr '13 to Mar '14	64,232
Apr '14 to Mar '15	88,402
Apr '15 to Mar '16	106,111
Apr '16 to Mar '17	121,187

For example, each region within each continent has different definitions of sexual abuse and varying laws. Therefore, what constitutes a sexual offence in one country in Europe may be different from a country in Africa. Indeed, even within each continent, very large variants in practice and legislation are found.

Findings from studies that explore the prevalence rates of sexual abuse from the perspectives of the victim, that is, through self-reports of sexual abuse, are also mixed. For example, Finkelhor, Ormrod, Turner, and Hamby (2005) examined a 12-month period to determine the rate of sexual abuse and found that in their sample of 2,030 US children aged 2 to 17 years, 1 in 12 children had been abused in the prior year. Indeed, of those children, up to 97% were victimised in other ways such as physical assaults or witnessing abuse. In a follow up study, Finkelhor, Ormrod, and Turner (2007) discovered that in the children's second year following the initial sexual assault, as many as 39% were revictimised. Victimisation is rarely, therefore, a one-off incident. Instead, it occurs within a climate of ongoing physical and sexual abuse and harm.

In the analysis of the Crime Survey for England and Wales in 2017 (Office for National Statistics, 2018), it was estimated that 12.1% of adults (aged between 16 and 59) had experienced attempted and actual sexual assaults since the age of 16, which is equivalent to 4 million victims. Also, 11.5% experienced indecent exposure (equivalent to 3.8 million) and an estimated 3.6% of adults experienced domestic sexual assault. These figures do not include assaults against children and so are, yet again, an underestimation of actual prevalence.

Examination of abuse over a lifetime, rather than a one-off incident of abuse, arguably gives a more complete picture. In one systematic review of the prevalence of sexual abuse in children worldwide, researchers reviewed 55 studies with sample sizes ranging from 106 to 127,097 and showed child sexual abuse (CSA)

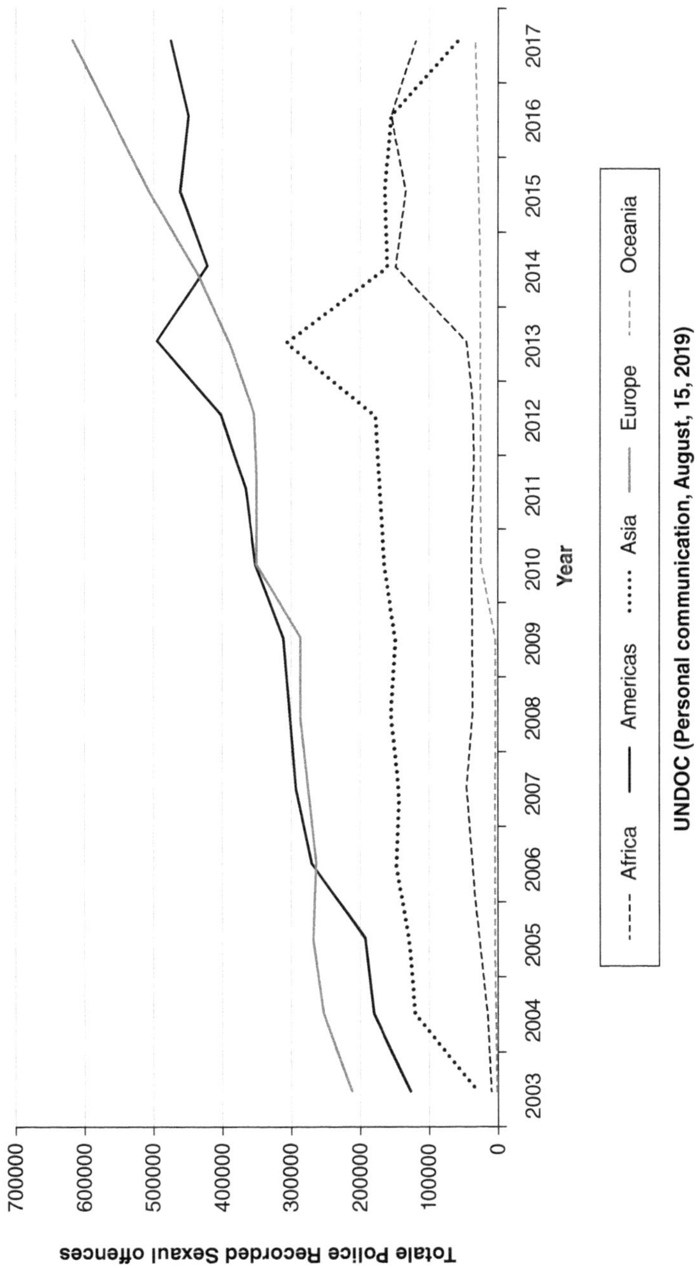

Figure 1.1 Global police recorded data of sexual offences by region between 2003 and 2017

to be highly prevalent worldwide (Barth, Bermetz, Heim, Trelle, & Tonia, 2013). They found that globally, 9% of women and 3% of men have experienced forced intercourse, and 15% of women and 8% of men experienced 'mixed sexual abuse' (varying abusive behaviours were reported but the type of abuse was not specified). In another meta-analysis, Stoltenborgh, Bakermans-Kranenburg, Alink, and IJzendoorn (2015) considered 244 global studies, of which 217 studies examined the prevalence of sexual abuse. They found higher prevalence rates with a 22% rate of abuse in girls and 18% among boys. Of course, meta-analyses have a number of methodological shortcomings and both studies reported inconsistencies, for example, in measures used to gather data in the studies examined, the shortage of studies in non-Western countries, and the lack of consistent definition across studies due to differing legal status within each country, potentially undermining actual prevalence rates.

A final method for gathering data is through self-reports. While this type of design is relatively rare, due to the ethical and legal difficulty in generating a disclosure, it provides a useful perspective. When considering Internet-based offences, Seto et al. (2015) found in their male sample of 1,978 non-offender Swedish 17–20 year olds that 4.2% disclosed viewing illicit images of children online. Seigfried, Lovely, and Rogers (2008) reported greater disclosure rates, with 16% of males and 5% of females reporting the use of pornography that included viewing images of child sexual abuse. When considering contact offences, one study by Ybarra and Mitchell (2013) found that of their 1,058 young people, aged between 14 and 21 years of age, 9% reported engaging in some form of sexual perpetration, with 4% of this group reporting an attempted or actual rape.

Prosecution rates

While many victims do not appear to disclose abuse, for those that do, most cases never reach the criminal justice system, with data suggesting that arrest and prosecution is unlikely (Spohn, Tellis, & O'Neal, 2013). Offences of rape are the least likely to result in a charge, and many assault cases do not make it to court due to evidential challenges. For those that do, cases can take on average over a year to conclude (Elkin, 2018). Within this process, significant attrition occurs at each stage in the criminal justice system. While all cases reported to criminal justice authorities are investigated by gathering physical evidence (where possible), gathering witness statements, and interviewing alleged perpetrators, in the UK, a decision by the Crown Prosecution Service (CPS) is made on a case-by-case basis as to whether to charge and prosecute. While the CPS has a duty to consider each case and make appropriate decisions on whether to proceed, they are only able to do so by considering the available evidence. Prosecutors' primary purpose is to serve justice, and as such, they are obligated to consider the chances of obtaining a successful prosecution. Thus, when deciding to prosecute or not, the CPS considers all aspects of the case presented, including legal factors such as physical evidence or a guilty plea, as well as extra-legal factors, such as the background and cooperation of the victim, how the perpetrator or victim might present in court, the relationship between the two, and so on (O'Neal, Tellis, & Spohn, 2015). If a perceived legal weakness is detected, the decision and strategy to proceed with the case is influenced. Discretion and subjectivity are perhaps rightly ubiquitous, but this is often at the victims' cost.

In their study of 47 interpersonal perpetrator sexual assault cases referred to the Los Angeles Attorney's Office, O'Neal et al. (2015) found that only 14% culminated in charges against the perpetrator. While there is a case to make that only 14% of the cases were prosecutable, the authors found that in many of the remaining cases, decisions not to charge were influenced by unhelpful beliefs by prosecutors. These included, for example, beliefs about the victims' intimate relationship with the perpetrator (assuming consent); the private location of the assault (assuming a false allegation); and the use of alcohol or substances by the victim (victim blame and therefore reduced credibility).

Police practitioners/investigators are subject to similar bias when making decisions regarding whether to charge the accused or not. Both legal (such as physical evidence or independent witnesses) and extra-legal factors (such as the characteristics of the victim, the use of alcohol, the relationship between victim and perpetrator) are found to strongly influence the likelihood of arrest. When a greater number of extra-legal factors are present, a piling up effect occurs (Morabito, Pattavina, & Williams, 2016). For example, if an investigative officer believes the victim to be mentally unwell, or that the victim was intoxicated at the time of the offence, they are less likely to proceed with a criminal charge, as they question the victim's credibility. Similar prejudice was found in a study analysing the closing arguments of attorneys (Stolzenberg & Lyon, 2014). Researchers found that in cases where the relationship between the alleged victim and perpetrator continued after the assault, or when the victim and or witnesses' character was brought into question, the case was acquitted.

Even if a case makes it to the court room, for children, the process of being cross examined is questionable, although the process has somewhat improved in recent years. This issue is examined in some detail by Lyon, Stolzenberg, and McWilliams (2017) who highlight problems when obtaining information from child witnesses about abuse. They highlight the nature of the questioning of children. When children are asked mainly closed questions their testimony becomes less credible. Likewise, where time has lapsed between the alleged assault, the disclosure, and the court case, defence barristers will argue that the child's testimony is flawed and cannot be relied upon. This tactic is also known to be used when asking children to recall the number of assaults that have taken place, when clearly knowing that this is a complex task for any child. Although Lyon et al (2017) conclude that not all acquittals are wrongful, they argue that a number of them will be. Indeed, false reports of sexual abuse are made. It is the responsibility of investigators and professionals in the criminal and legal system to determine these on society's behalf.

While we cannot be certain of the exact prevalence rates of sexual abuse, we can be certain that the current figures are an underestimation of the true figure. Thus, when considering strategies based on prevalence rates or when developing policy to help prevent future harm, or more preferably, prevent harm from occurring in the first place, it is important to be aware of the limitations of existing data on child sexual abuse and its investigation. Policy makers must look beyond only official statistics to explore this issue.

Conclusion

The landscape in which criminal justice and legal practitioners operate when attempting to tackle sexual crime is complex and embedded within social and political structures. With inconsistent definitions and unclear prevalence and incidence rates, the starting point for policymakers to develop strategies and policy to target sexual crime and prevent abuse from occurring in the first place is problematical. Instead, current solutions to sexual abuse tend to be reactive and limited by subjective, biased ideas of what constitutes a victim, a sexual crime, and a perpetrator. As such, options available for courts to respond to those convicted of sexual crime appear, in the main, to be punitive and controlling. While there are some options for the courts to help rehabilitate and reintegrate people back into the community, this is often delivered within a climate of fear and control, and solutions are implemented long after the crime is committed.

References

Barth, J., Bermetz, L., Heim, E., Trelle, S., & Tonia, T. (2013). The current prevalence of child sexual abuse worldwide: A systematic review and meta-analysis. *International Journal of Public Health*, *58*(3), 469–483.

Beech, A., Craig, L. A., & Browne, K. (2009a). *Assessment and treatment of sex offenders: A handbook*. Chichester: John Wiley & Sons Ltd.

Beech, A. R., Craig, L. A., & Browne, K. D. (2009b). Overview. In A. R. Beech, L. A. Craig, & K. D. Browne (Eds.), *Assessment and treatment of sex offenders: A handbook* (pp. 1–12). West Sussex: Wiley-Blackwell.

Beyrer, C. (2014). Pushback: The current wave of anti-homosexuality laws and impacts on health. *PLoS Med*, *11*(6), e1001658.

Boer, D. P. (Ed.). (2017). *The Wiley handbook on the theories, assessment and treatment of sexual offending*. West Sussex: Wiley-Blackwell.

Brown, J. M., & Walklate, S. L. (2012). *Handbook on sexual violence*. Oxon: Routledge.

Browne, A., & Finkelhor, D. (1986). Impact of child sexual abuse: A review of the research. *Psychological Bulletin*, *99*(1), 66.

Browne, K. D. (2009). Working to prevent sexual abuse in the family. In A. R. Beech, L. A. Craig, & K. D. Browne (Eds.), *Assessment and treatment of sex offenders: A handbook* (pp. 491–514). West Sussex: Wiley-Blackwell.

Burke, R. H. (2014). *An introduction to criminological theory* (4th ed.). Oxon: Routledge.

Cohen, S. (1972). *Folk devils moral panics*. Cornwall: MacFibbon and Kee Ltd.

Craig, L. A., Browne, K. D., & Beech, A. R. (2008). *Assessing risk in sex offenders: A practitioner's guide*. Chichester: John Wiley & Sons Inc.

Criminal Justice and Immigration Act (2008).

Cross, S. (2005). Paedophiles in the community: Inter-agency conflict, news leaks and the local press. *Crime, Media, Culture*, *1*(3), 284–300.

Domestic Abuse Bill (2019).

Dube, S. R., Anda, R. F., Whitfield, C. L., Brown, D. W., Felitti, V. J., Dong, M., & Giles, W. H. (2005). Long-term consequences of childhood sexual abuse by gender of victim. *American Journal of Preventive Medicine*, *28*(5), 430–438.

Elkin, M. (2018). *Sexual offending: Victimisation and the path through the criminal justice system*. London. Retrieved from www.ons.gov.uk/peoplepopulationandcommunity/crimeandjustice/articles/sexualoffendingvictimisationandthepaththroughthecriminaljusticesystem/2018-12-13#toc

Fang, X., Fry, D. A., Ji, K., Finkelhor, D., Chen, J., Lannen, P., & Dunne, M. P. (2015). The burden of child maltreatment in China: A systematic review. *Bulletin of the World Health Organization*, *93*, 176–185.

Fearon, J., & Hoeffler, A. (2014). *Benefits and costs of the conflict and violence targets for the post-2015 development agenda*. Conflict and violence assessment paper. Copenhagen: Copenhagen Consensus Center.

Fergusson, D. M., McLeod, G. F., & Horwood, L. J. (2013). Childhood sexual abuse and adult developmental outcomes: Findings from a 30-year longitudinal study in New Zealand. *Child Abuse & Neglect*, *37*(9), 664–674.

Finkelhor, D. (1984). *Child sexual abuse: New theory and research*. New York: Free Press.

Finkelhor, D., Ormrod, R. K., & Turner, H. A. (2007). Re-victimization patterns in a national longitudinal sample of children and youth. *Child Abuse & Neglect*, *31*(5), 479–502.

Finkelhor, D., Ormrod, R. K., Turner, H. A., & Hamby, S. L. (2005). The victimization of children and youth: A comprehensive, national survey. *Child Maltreatment*, *10*(1), 5–25.

Fisher, B. S., Daigle, L. E., Cullen, F. T., & Turner, M. G. (2003). Reporting sexual victimization to the police and others: Results from a national-level study of college women. *Criminal Justice and Behavior*, *30*(1), 6–38.

Garcia-Moreno, C., Guedes, A., & Knerr, W. (2012). Understanding and addressing violence against women: Sexual violence. *World Health Organization*. Retrieved from http://apps.who.int/iris/bitstream/10665/77434/1/WHO_RHR_12.37_eng.pdf

Hanvey, S., Wilson, C., & Philpot, T. (2011). *A community-based approach to the reduction of sexual reoffending: Circles of support and accountability*. London: Jessica Kingsley Publishers.

Harrison, K. (2011). *Dangerousness, risk and the governance of serious sexual and violent offenders*. Oxon: Routledge.

Hébert, M., Langevin, R., & Daigneault, I. (2016). The association between peer victimization, PTSD, and dissociation in child victims of sexual abuse [Research Support, Non-U S Gov't]. *Journal of Affective Disorders*, *193*, 227–232.

Hébert, M., Lavoie, F., & Blais, M. (2014). Post traumatic stress disorder/PTSD in adolescent victims of sexual abuse: Resilience and social support as protection factors. *Ciência & Saúde Coletiva*, *19*, 685–694.

Hsiao, C., Fry, D., Ward, C. L., Ganz, G., Casey, T., Zheng, X., & Fang, X. (2018). Violence against children in South Africa: The cost of inaction to society and the economy. *BMJ Global Health*, *3*(1), e000573.

Jay, A. (2014). *Independent inquiry into child sexual exploitation in Rotherham 1997–2013*. Rotherham: Rotherham Metropolitan Borough Council. Retrieved from www.rotherham.gov.uk/downloads/file/1407/independent_inquiry_cse_in_rotherham

Laws, D. R., & Ward, T. (2011). *Desistance from sex offending: Alternatives to throwing away the keys*. New York: Guilford Press.

Lipscombe, S. (2012). *Sarah's law: The child sex offender disclosure scheme*. House of Commons Library. Retrieved from www.insidetime.org/resources/Parliament/Sarahs-Law_SN01692_06-03-12.pdf

Lockmuller, M., Fisher, D., & Beech, A. R. (2008). Sexual offenders with mental health problems: Epidemiology, assessment and treatment. In K. Soothill, P. Rogers, & M. Dolan (Eds.), *Handbook of forensic mental health* (pp. 446–479). Devon: Willan Cullompton.

Lyon, T. D., Stolzenberg, S. N., & McWilliams, K. (2017). Wrongful acquittals of sexual abuse. *Journal of Interpersonal Violence*, *32*(6), 805–825.

Marshall, W. L., Marshall, L. E., Serran, G. A., & O'Brien, M. D. (2011). *Rehabilitating sexual offenders: A strength-based approach*. Washington, DC: American Psychological Association.

Maruna, S., Lebel, T., Mitchell, N., & Naples, M. (2004). Pygmalion in the reintegration process: Desistance from crime through the looking glass. *Psychology, Crime & Law*, *10*(3), 271–281.

McGregor, J. (2011). The legal heritage of the crime of rape. In J. M. Brown & S. L. Walklate (Eds.), *Handbook on sexual violence* (pp. 69–89). Oxon: Routledge.

Morabito, M. S., Pattavina, A., & Williams, L. M. (2016). It all just piles up challenges to victim credibility accumulate to influence sexual assault case processing. *Journal of Interpersonal Violence*, *35*(15), 3131–3170.

Office for National Statistics. (2018). *Sexual offences in England and Wales: Year ending March 2017*. London. Retrieved from www.ons.gov.uk/peoplepopulationandcommunity/crimeandjustice/articles/sexualoffencesinenglandandwales/yearendingmarch2017

O'Neal, E. N., Tellis, K., & Spohn, C. (2015). Prosecuting intimate partner sexual assault: Legal and extra-legal factors that influence charging decisions. *Violence Against Women*, *21*(10), 1237–1258.

Peterson, C., Kearns, M. C., McIntosh, W. L., Estefan, L. F., Nicolaidis, C., McCollister, K. E., . . . Florence, C. (2018). Lifetime economic burden of intimate partner violence among US adults. *American Journal of Preventive Medicine*, *55*(4), 433–444.

Protection of Children Act (1978).

Seigfried, K. C., Lovely, R. W., & Rogers, M. K. (2008). Self-reported online child pornography behavior: A psychological analysis. *International Journal of Cyber Criminology*, *2*(1), 286.

Seto, M. C., Hermann, C. A., Kjellgren, C., Priebe, G., Svedin, C. G., & Långström, N. (2015). Viewing child pornography: Prevalence and correlates in a representative community sample of young Swedish men. *Archives of Sexual Behavior*, *44*(1), 67–79.

Sexual Offences Act (2003).

Sigurdardottir, S., Halldorsdottir, S., & Bender, S. S. (2014). Consequences of childhood sexual abuse for health and well-being: Gender similarities and differences. *Scandinavian Journal of Social Medicine*, *42*(3), 278–286.

Smallbone, S., Marshall, W. L., & Wortley, R. (2013). *Preventing child sexual abuse: Evidence, policy and practice*. Devon: Routledge.

Smith, C. P., & Freyd, J. J. (2014). Institutional betrayal. *American Psychologist*, *69*(6), 575.

Spencer, D. (2009). Sex offender as homo sacer. *Punishment & Society*, *11*(2), 219–240.

Spohn, C., Tellis, K., & O'Neal, E. (2013). Policing and prosecuting sexual assault: Assessing the pathwys to justice. In H. Johnson, B. S. Fisher, & V. Jaquier (Eds.), *Critical issues on violence against women: International perspectives and promising strategies* (pp. 93–103). Oxon: Routledge.

Stoltenborgh, M., Bakermans-Kranenburg, M. J., Alink, L. R., & IJzendoorn, M. H. (2015). The prevalence of child maltreatment across the globe: Review of a series of meta-analyses. *Child Abuse Review*, *24*(1), 37–50.

Stolzenberg, S. N., & Lyon, T. D. (2014). Evidence summarized in Attorneys' closing arguments predicts acquittals in criminal trials of child sexual abuse. *Child Maltreatment*, *19*(2), 119–129.

United Nations Office on Drugs and Crime. (2017). *Total number of police-recorded sexual offences*. Retrieved from https://data.unodc.org/#state:2

Ward, T., & Beech, A. R. (2017). The integrated theory of sexual offending – revised: A multifield perspective. In D. P. Boer (Ed.), *The Wiley handbook on the theories, assessment and treatment of sexual offending* (pp. 123–137). West Sussex: Wiley-Blackwell.

Ward, T., & Brown, B. (2004). The good lives model and conceptual issues in offender rehabilitation. *Psychology, Crime & Law*, *10*(3), 243–257, https://doi.org/10.1080/10683160410001662744

Ward, T., Polaschek, D. L., & Beech, A. R. (2006). *Theories of sexual offending*. Chichester: John Wiley & Sons Ltd.

Wilcox, D., Garrett, T., & Harkins, L. (2015). *Sex offender treatment: A case study approach to issues and interventions*. West Sussex: Wiley-Blackwell.

Wortley, R., & Smallbone, S. (2006). Applying situational principles to sexual offenses against children. *Crime Prevention Studies*, *19*, 7.

Ybarra, M. L., & Mitchell, K. J. (2013). Prevalence rates of male and female sexual violence perpetrators in a national sample of adolescents. *JAMA Pediatrics*, *167*(12), 1125–1134.

2 Current approaches to sentencing and management

Introduction

According to data from Crime Survey for England and Wales (Elkin, 2018), approximately 700,000 people (aged 16–59) experienced sexual assault during 2017. This equates to an estimated 2.1% of the adult population. Police-recorded crime for the same period equated to 150,847 allegations of abuse, which included assaults against children. Thus, reporting rates are marginal when compared to actual rates. Even after an allegation is made to the police, further attrition is experienced. In 2017, of the 150,847 reports of abuse, only 5% (6,960) resulted in a conviction (Elkin, 2018). This attrition results from varying and complex factors, including under-resourced police and CPS investigators, victims withdrawing allegations, evidential challenges such as not finding a suspect or lack of physical evidence, or the CPS deciding not to prosecute.

Consequently, when discussing the sentencing and management of people convicted of sexual offending, we are mindful that the content of this chapter relates to only a very small minority of perpetrators of abuse. Clearly, within our current legal systems, much work is needed to reduce the rates of attrition of those alleging abuse, to allow justice to take its course, and to ensure that those who need help and treatment to prevent further harm can access this support. However, far greater work is needed to prevent these offences from occurring in the first place. The scope of this text unfortunately prevents further exploration of this problem and is limited to those with actual convictions. Thus for ease of discussion, the English and Welsh criminal justice process will be used to explore the sentencing and management of those convicted of sexual abuse. While there will be some policy and practice differences across European, North American, Canadian, and Australasian countries, in the main, approaches are similar.

Statutory response

When sentencing those convicted of criminal acts according to the Criminal Justice Act (c.44) 2003, judges and magistrates must have regard for the following five principles of sentencing: a) The punishment of offenders; b) The reduction of crime (including reduction by deterrence); c) The reform and rehabilitation of offenders; d) The protection of the public; and e) The making of reparation by offenders to persons affected by their offences. In addition to this, in England and Wales at least, judges and magistrates are also guided by a framework that outlines each offence and appropriate sentence required. Guidelines require them to consider a range of factors, including the type of offence committed, the harm caused, culpability of the perpetrator, any aggravating and mitigating factors, and any plea of guilt. After considering these factors, a sentence is determined. In order that judges and magistrates can fully appreciate the extent of these factors, they will often defer to specialists who can assess the risk and needs of the defendant. Assessments are varied and can be carried out by a range of professionals, including probation officers, psychologists, psychiatrists, and medical health practitioners. While judges and magistrates have a range of sentence contexts to which they can order offenders, including prisons, hospitals, and the community, in all sexual offence cases across England and Wales, offenders are subject to a notification order and for those whose offences are against a child, may be barred from working with children and/or vulnerable adults (Sexual Offences Definitive Guideline, 2013).

Criminal justice responses to those convicted of sexual offending

The criminal justice system, like any public institution, is subject to public scrutiny and is thus under extraordinary pressure to respond appropriately to social issues such as crime. In the case of responding to those accused of sexual offending, this pressure is often driven by socially constructed notions of danger, risk, and harm. Indeed, the idea of 'danger' or 'dangerous offender' is a subjective, non-scientific label. It is a normative category, not a scientific one (Ward, 2016). Historically, such labels and constructions have been used to describe whole groups of people including refugees, immigrants, young people, mods and rockers, gay people, and the lower classes (Harrison, 2011). While undoubtedly some people will be a danger to others, legislators, with little empirical evidence of their effectiveness, have developed policies that adversely affect all individuals convicted of crimes based on a subjective notion of danger and fear (Levenson, Brannon, Fortney, & Baker, 2007). As a result, measures tend to be more punitive and controlling (Thomas, 2010). This chapter details the range of sanctions and management strategies available. It is worth noting that the examples of legislation and services that follow are drawn from within the UK, although they reflect most Western criminal justice strategies.

Sanctions given to those prosecuted for sexual offending

In England and Wales, a range of guidelines are available for magistrates and judges to inform sentencing decisions for those convicted of sexual offences. There are several unique provisions made for those convicted of sexual offences, which will be briefly described here. It is not our intention to debate the worth or effectiveness of these sanctions, as there are several existing comprehensive summaries and analyses available on these issues. For some excellent examples, see Harrison (2011), Levenson and D'Amora (2007), Tewksbury (2005), and Thomas (2010).

Imprisonment

Effective from 2014, the Sentencing Council's Definitive Guidelines for Sexual Offences (2013) are used in courts across England and Wales to provide parameters for sentencing adult sexual offenders. The guidelines detail categories and starting points for sentencing and explain how to apply aggravating and mitigating factors before determining the final sentence. The document provides sentencing guidance for 52 sexual offences; we have provided a sample of these in Table 2.1 and the offence range available to judges and magistrates.

Community sentence

In addition to prison sentences, a range of community options are also available. These can be applied to suspended sentences, licence conditions, and stand-alone community sentences. Various requirements are available and depending on the needs of the offender and severity and likelihood of further offending, more than one requirement can be added to the sentence. As set out in the Criminal Justice Act, 2003, there are 12 options available to judges and magistrates. These

Table 2.1 Sample of sentence ranges for convicted sexual offenders (+18 years)

Offence	*If triable on indictment*	*Offence range*
Rape	Triable only on indictment Maximum: Life imprisonment	4–19 years' custody
Assault by penetration	Triable only on indictment Maximum: Life imprisonment	Community order – 19 years' custody
Sexual assault	Triable either way Maximum: 10 years' custody	Community order – 7 years' custody
Assault of a child under 13 by penetration	Triable only on indictment Maximum: Life imprisonment	2–19 years' custody
Meeting a child following sexual grooming	Triable either way Maximum: 10 years' custody	1–7 years' custody
Possession of indecent photograph of child	Triable either way Maximum: 5 years' custody	Community order – 3 years' custody
Indecent photographs of children	Triable either way Maximum: 10 years' custody	Community order – 9 years' custody
Exposure	Triable either way Maximum: 2 years' custody	Fine – 1 year's custody

include unpaid work; specified activity; accredited programme; prohibited activity; curfew; exclusion; residence; mental health treatment; drug rehabilitation requirement (DDR); alcohol treatment; attendance centre; and the supervision requirement. Most sentences will include a supervision condition as a minimum. For those convicted of a sexual offence, there are further requirements applied as a result of The Sexual Offences Act, 2003; The Violent Crime Reduction Act, 2006; The Offender Management Act, 2007; and The Criminal Justice and Immigration Act, 2008, which are detailed briefly here. Again, it is not our intention to outline the efficacy or effectiveness of such conditions in this text; other scholars have done this with greater proficiency than we have scope to do so here, which we recommend as further reading on this matter.

- **Registration**. All those convicted of a sexual offence must register their personal details and notify the police of any changes to their circumstance (Brain, 2010) within three days of conviction, release from prison, or at the review period. Failure to do so can result in a recall to prison or the prosecution of further crimes. Registration includes the requirement for people to provide details of their intention to travel abroad and be subject to unannounced home visits to verify the address; registrants must provide fingerprints and a photograph on registration. In a Home Office Review (2007) led by John Reid, the then Home Secretary, it was recommended that DNA, email addresses, passports, and bank details should be collected, and a note taken of any children under 18 living at the same address, and if the registrant intends to travel abroad for any period of time. Furthermore, any escalation in risk is to be reported to the police (Thomas, 2010). The period in which a person is required to register for depends on the sentence given. Those serving a life sentence, an Indeterminate Public Protection (IPP) sentence, or a sentence of more than 30 months are required to register with the authorities for an indefinite period. Those sentenced to imprisonment between six months but less than 30 months are required to register for ten years. For those with a term of imprisonment for less than six months, the registration period is seven years and those serving a community order are required to register for the period of the supervision requirement. As a result of a Supreme Court ruling that determined that the Sexual Offences Act, 2003 breached Article 8 of the European Convention of Human Rights (Gillespie, 2010), those on a lifelong registration can request to have their registration requirement reviewed after 15 years.
- **Polygraph testing**. The use of mandatory polygraph testing is relatively new in the UK. Under legislation initially laid out in the Offender Management Act, 2007, compulsory polygraph testing was launched in 2014 following evaluation of a number of pilot studies, for example Gannon et al. (2014), Grubin (2010), and Grubin et al. (2014). Mandatory testing requires adults convicted of a sexual offence and sentenced to one year or more, who are assessed as 'high risk,' to take part in a polygraph test; this forms part of their licence conditions. Failure to comply or disclosure of an offence or escalation

of risk could result in further prosecution and recall to prison. A return to custody will not, however, result from the findings of a polygraph alone. Those mandated are asked a set of questions related to their licence conditions and risk behaviours, while at the same time having their physiological responses measured, such as heart rate, breathing, and skin conductivity. The polygraph is argued not to be a lie detector that aims to trick and catch people out, but instead a 'truth facilitator' that is used to create a climate of disclosure and openness (Gannon et al., 2014). For a useful review of the efficacy and utility of polygraph, please see Elliott and Vollm (2016).

- **Electronic or satellite tracking/monitoring systems**. Electronic tagging requires the person to wear an ankle bracelet, which is connected to a box linked to the telephone line in their home. The system is usually connected by a private service provider. The tag cannot track the person's whereabouts outside of the home and can only alert the authorities if the device is not connected to the system at the allocated time (Harrison, 2011). Also available are satellite tracking systems that provide a continuous recording of the person's whereabouts. Thus, there is the option of using one of these two forms of tracking: one that is passive and provide a historic recording and report of the person's positions, as well as one that is active and can provide a 'live' update of the person's location, or for those identified as very high risk, can alert authorities if the person enters into a restricted area, such as a school or a park. A pilot of the GPS scheme in eight English police force areas was undertaken during 2016, and results found the process to support effective management of people in the community in terms of rehabilitating, facilitating risk management, informing decisions regarding recall, and providing evidence to counter claims of the person being part of a new crime (Kerr, Roberts, Davies, & Pullerits, 2019).
- **Community notification**. Following the murder of Sarah Payne in 2000 by Roy Whiting (who was known to authorities and had convictions for sexual offending), a general public led campaign (driven by the popular press) called for the creation of "Sarah's Law" (Hanvey, Wilson, & Philpot, 2011), a law mirroring one in the US. In the US, all who are convicted of sexual offences have their details publicly available as a result of a change in legislation in 1994 known as Megan's Law. While the UK government did not establish Sarah's Law, similar to Megan's Law they began a notification pilot in 2010 (The Child Sex Offender (CSO) Disclosure Scheme Guidance Document, 2010). The pilot scheme, now extending across all police areas in England, Wales, and Scotland, allows people to enquire if an individual has a previous conviction of sexual or violent offences. There are strict requirements from those requesting information. They must provide documents and personal identification, for example. They must also name the person they request the information of, the person of concern must have contact or access to children, and the person requesting the information will only be given details if the individual of concern meets certain risk criteria (Kemshall & Weaver, 2012). The number of people requesting disclosures was greatly underestimated,

as found in the pilot study in 2010, which resulted in only 54% (*n*=315) of enquiries resulting in actual applications. Of those applications only 7% received a full disclosure (Kemshall & Wood, 2010). Even with evidence of low public interest, the government rolled out the scheme nationally, arguably providing symbolic reassurances to the public and potentially reducing anxiety about the management of people convicted of sexual offending (Kemshall & Weaver, 2012).

- **Sexual Harm Prevention Order**. A Sexual Harm Prevention Order (SHPO), previously known as a Sexual Offences Prevention Order (SOPO), can only be issued by the courts to a person already convicted/cautioned of a sexual offence, under the Sexual Offences Act, 2003. According to the 2017 Sentencing Council guidelines, the order is a prohibitive one: a SHPO should prevent further harm, it must be proportionate, and it must be able to be policed effectively. The order may be issued to prevent certain types of employment or voluntary opportunities, such as scout leader, or prevent activities or behaviours, such as accessing the Internet. SHPOs are set for fixed periods of time but not less than five years (Magistrates' Court Sentencing Guidelines, 2017). The number of SOPOs/SHPOs has seen a 298% increase since 2006. In the 2006–2007 reporting year, 1,114 SOPOs were imposed and 5,551 were imposed in 2017–2018 across England and Wales (Multi-Agency Public Protection Arrangements Annual Report 2017/18, 2018).

Multi-Agency Public Protection Arrangements

To manage people convicted of sexual offending, in the UK at least, a multi-agency approach is adopted. The Criminal Justice Act, 2003 legislated for the police, prison, and probation services to act as responsible authorities under Multi-Agency Public Protection Arrangements (MAPPA). At the time of writing, MAPPA has statutory responsibility to protect the public in a coordinated manner across 42 criminal justice areas in England and Wales. In addition to responsible authorities, other agencies have a duty to cooperate with the responsible authority, depending on need. This includes agencies that deal with housing, welfare, education, and employment. Each criminal justice area is governed by a strategic management board that monitors performance, measures compliance, and produces an annual MAPPA report.

MAPPA boards manage three categories of offenders (Wood, Kemshall, Maguire, Hudson, & Mackenzie, 2007): Category 1 includes all registered sex offenders (RSOs); Category 2 includes serious, violent offenders and those who have been sentenced to 12 months or more in custody or detained under the Mental Health Act, 1983; and Category 3 includes other dangerous offenders who are capable of causing serious harm and thus require multiagency management. Where the offender is in their sentence dictates the lead agency. For example, the prison service will have statutory authority and responsibility to manage the person in prison. On release, that responsibility usually passes on to the probation service. If a person is assessed as requiring an ordinary level of agency management, that is if the risk can be managed by the lead agency with information being shared and disclosed between agencies as necessary, the person will be managed at MAPPA level one. In cases assessed as posing a high or very high risk of serious harm and where multiagency management adds value to the lead agencies' management of this risk, an active multiagency management approach will be adopted, and the person will be managed at level two. For those who meet the criteria for level two but require significant resource allocation, or perhaps have public interest considerations, active enhanced multiagency approach at level three is applied (MAPPA Guidance, 2012).

In determining the categorisation of risks and needs, the MAPPA boards use the following risk assessment tools: the Active Risk Management System (ARMS); Structured Assessment of Risk and Need (SARN); Offender Assessment System (OASys); and Risk Matrix 2000 (RM2000). These will be discussed further in Chapter 3 of this book. Offenders are categorised into low risk (current evidence does not indicate a likelihood of serious harm); medium risk (their identifiable indicators of serious harm the offender has the potential to cause harm but is unlikely to do so unless there is a change in circumstances); high risk (their identifiable indicators of risk of serious harm the potential events could happen at any time and the impact would be serious); and very high (there is an imminent risk of serious harm and the potential event is more likely than not to happen imminently and the impact would be serious).

Following risk assessment, all MAPPA clients are provided a risk management plan (RMP) that will address the identified risks and protective factors from the risk assessment. The RMP is monitored and reviewed regularly and updated when changes occur. Each RMP must contain content that, at a minimum, outlines the supervision requirements of the client (e.g. number of home visits, number of office-based attendance), monitoring and control strategies (e.g. licence conditions, polygraph expectations), interventions and treatment plans (e.g. offender behaviour programmes, drug and alcohol treatment), victim safety (safety planning, safeguarding, children services contacts), and contingency plans (e.g. a 'what if?' scenario, changing situation, deterioration of lifestyle).

As of March 2018, there were 80,983 people being managed under MAPPA (Multi-Agency Public Protection Arrangements Annual Report 2017/18, 2018), the majority of whom (*n*=58,637) are RSOs. Of these RSOs, 57,989 (99%) are being managed at an ordinary level of agency management, level one, with 1% being managed at level two (*n*=601), and only 0.08% (*n*=47) managed at level three. Since 2006–2007, there has been a 7% increase in the number of RSOs, and since 2009, a consistent 5% annual increase has been experienced in the number of RSOs. A breakdown comparing the sentencing outcomes for MAPPA Category 1 clients between 2006–2007 and 2017–2018 is detailed in Table 2.2.

Responsible authorities

The three agencies responsible for managing people convicted of sexual offending include the prison service, the police, and the probation service. One of the

Table 2.2 Comparison between 2006–2007 and 2017–2018 outcomes for MAPPA Category 1 clients

Outcomes	*2006–2007*	*2017–2018*
MAPPA eligible RSOs	30,416	58,637
Breach of notification requirement	1,552	1,950
Restrictive Orders imposed:		
• Sexual Offences Prevention Orders (SOPOs), Sexual Harm Prevention Orders (SHPOs)	1,114	5,551
• Notification Orders (NOs)	62	97
• Foreign Travel Orders (FTOs)	3	11
Breach of SOPO/SHPO returned to custody*	89	42
Breach of licence returned to custody*	-	390
Charged with Serious Further Offence	-	92

* Level 2 and 3 clients only

shared frameworks used to manage clients is sentence planning. This final section summaries sentence planning, as well as the role, responsibilities, and activities of each agency when supervising these clients.

Sentence planning

The goal and aims of sentence planning or risk management planning are shared across responsible authorities. For prison and probation officers, OASys and ARMS are used to formulate a sentence plan and for the police, ARMS is the key tool. Each client will have a sentence plan that is updated and adapted as they move through their prison and community sentence. The lead agency is responsible for the completion, update, and review of the sentence plan, as well as the sharing of the plan (or sections of it) with appropriate bodies and professionals.

Sentence/risk management plans are developed following a comprehensive risk and need assessment (see Chapter 3 for more details) of the client. They serve to detail the plan and strategy of the agency to manage the client throughout their prison or community sentence. Thus, the sentence/risk management plan must be based on rigorous assessment, respond to the changing needs of the client, and focus on factors that are related to sexual offending. Sentence/risk management plans must detail what is to be achieved during the sentence and how.

Supervising officers must make plans for the whole of the client's sentence, and work in collaboration with them to develop a meaningful plan. As detailed in Prison Service Instruction 19/2014 (Sentence planning, 2014, p. 5), the plan should detail the following:

- The overall outcomes to be achieved through the plan;
- The activity needed to achieve the intended outcomes and expected timescales;
- How the activity will be delivered to meet needs of individual offender;

- What is expected of the offender in terms of the objectives they are aiming to achieve in support of an action or outcome; and
- Who will have overall responsibility for the continued review and updating of the plan as it is delivered.

Plans must be realistic and achievable, and goals and objectives must be specific, measurable, achievable, realistic, and time-bound (SMART). Indeed, plans should be written in such a manner that a new supervising officer, in the absence of a lead officer, could make immediate sense and follow the plan with the client. Thus, a simple list of activities or interventions the client should achieve is insufficient. The assessor must provide justification for the intervention, detailing how achieving this might reduce the client's risk. Staff members should be named, and their contact details provided.

A responsive approach to plans must be adopted. In addition to regular review, plans must be updated considering significant changes in the client's life – for example, moving to a new house, the breakdown of a relationship, leaving prison, and/or getting a job. Such factors are related to offending, and therefore impact risk assessment and subsequent plan of action. Sentence/risk management plans are documents that provide senior management and MAPPA boards the information needed when strategically managing clients in the community. Thus, poorly completed plans serve to impede the safe management of clients. Robust and up to date sentence/risk management plans arguably provide assessors evidence to demonstrate defensible decision making in the event of a further offence. However, little work has been undertaken to evaluate the quality of sentence and risk management plans of clients convicted of sexual offending. In the few studies that have been undertaken, several issues have arisen, including poor risk assessments contributing to inadequate risk management strategies (Kewley, Osman, & McGuinness, 2019), overbearing plans in which controls were the dominant management strategy (Kewley, Beech, Harkins, & Bonsall, 2015), and under-resourcing and poor training of assessors, resulting in them feeling ill equipped to carry out risk management planning on those convicted of sexual offending (Kewley, 2017a).

Managing those with sexual offences in prison

Across England and Wales, as of June 2018, approximately 19% of the prison population (n=13,580) were serving a prison sentence for a sexual offence (Her Majesty's Inspectorate of Probation, 2019). While some are detained in secure hospitals, the majority of those convicted of sexual offences are held in one of the 121 prisons across England and Wales (87 of which are resettlement prisons, in which 'through the gate' services were implemented as a result of the 2013 "Transforming Rehabilitation" agenda and Offender Rehabilitation Act, 2014). A prison can be a dangerous and hostile place for those convicted of sexual offending (Levins, 2014). As such, prisoners are offered Rule 45 status, which facilitates segregation away from the main prison population. Most prisoners convicted of sexual offending are thus housed in specialist wings or vulnerable prisoner units. Some prisons are reserved specifically for those convicted of sexual offences (e.g. HMP Whatton, HMP Usk, HMP Stafford, HMP Rye Hill, and HMP Littlehey). However, the aims and goals of all prisons are the same, regardless of the population housed. Thus the expectations of prisoners, including those convicted of sexual offences, are to engage positively with the prison regime, including engaging in rehabilitation activities (such as education, training, and employment), address risks related to offending behaviour (such as offender behaviour programmes and drug and alcohol treatment), and prepare for release and resettlement (including housing and employment). Much of their prison sentence, from a structural perspective at least, parallels that of the general prison population. While in prison, they are required to work through a sentence plan with their supervising officer (and other relevant professionals).

In a recent joint inspection of the management and supervision of men convicted of sexual offences, HM Inspectorate of Probation and HM Inspectorate of Prison (2019) found significant problems with management and supervision in prison. They found poor risk assessment and planning across the sample of five establishments, including missing data, out-of-date plans, variable quality of assessments, and assessments lacking links to offending risks. In terms of preparation for release, inspectors found poor connections between community officers and the client, with some not having a named officer for release. Caseloads of prison officers were high, with some not knowing who were on their caseload. Thus, when planning for release, many cases were inadequately prepared for release. Inspectors concluded "much of the work delivered to sexual offenders in custody was poor" (p. 32).

Managing those with sexual offences on probation

All people convicted of a sexual offence and subject to licence conditions or a community order are managed under the National Probation Service (NPS), rather than privately contracted community rehabilitation companies. As of March 2018, the NPS was managing 106,819 cases in the community, of which 55% (*n*=58, 637) were registered sexual offenders. A dedicated probation officer is responsible for managing these clients, while reporting to the local MAPPA board that has the ultimate oversight and management of the case. In many NPS areas specialist officers hold these cases, and in some areas, specialist teams or units co-locate with the police and other agencies to manage this population as effectively as possible.

In the 2019 joint inspection, findings were more positive than that of prison colleagues: inspectors found NPS staff to be assessing and planning cases to a much higher degree of accuracy, quality, and timeliness. There were some areas needing improvement; for example, NPS staff needed to focus their energies on engaging clients with interventions and activities most likely to reduce sexual offending, although access to programmes was acknowledged as a challenge.

Managing those with sexual offences by the police

Those convicted of sexual offences are managed by specialist officers dedicated to carry a caseload of RSOs. There were 58,637 RSOs across England and Wales at the end of March 2018 (Multi-Agency Public Protection Arrangements Annual Report 2017/18, 2018). MOSOVO (Management of Sexual or Violent Offenders) officers work in conjunction with multi-agency arrangements to manage Category 1 clients living in the community. Where the police is the lead agency, in cases where licence or community order requirements have been served, MOSOVO officers manage the notification requirements of the case. Management of these cases require MOSOVO officers to ensure clients register and comply with notification requirements. They are also responsible for assessing the client for risks, visiting the client's registered address, and reviewing and maintaining records. Officers are also responsible for the management of the case in terms of following up on any breach or investigating suspicions of further crime.

Due to the rising numbers of RSOs, budget cuts to the police, and the introduction of the Active Risk Management System (ARMS) to assess and develop risk management plans for each client, MOSOVO officers and teams have faced significant challenges. For discussions and further analysis of some of these problems see Kewley (2017b) and Kewley et al. (2019).

Conclusion

Outlined in this chapter are the current approaches adopted by the criminal justice system in relation to the management and control of those prosecuted and convicted of sexual offences. As detailed in Chapter 1, the scope of sexual harm and abuse reaches far beyond those convicted and sentenced, and as such, the role of criminal justice agencies is to work with a relatively small population of people who have sexually harmed others. Current criminal justice approaches therefore work in a reactive and post hoc manner to sexual abuse, through the management of this small number of perpetrators. While they do work to help prevent reoffending and further harm, they are not resourced to prevent the abuse from occurring in the first place (strategies and approaches to prevent sexual abuse, beyond statutory criminal justice services, are discussed in detail in Chapter 5). In its current state, although sentencing principles require courts to consider the rehabilitation and restoration of the person, for those convicted of sexual offending, sentencing and management strategies tend to be dominated by approaches that punish and control, running counter to the notion of a positive criminology framework.

References

Brain, T. (2010). *A history of policing in England and Wales from 1974: A turbulent journey*. Oxford: Oxford University Press.

The Child Sex Offender (CSO) Disclosure Scheme Guidance Document. (2010). London: Home Office. Retrieved from www.gov.uk/government/publications/child-sex-offender-disclosure-scheme-guidance

Criminal Justice Act (2003).

The Criminal Justice and Immigration Act (2008).

Elkin, M. (2018). *Sexual offending: Victimisation and the path through the criminal justice system*. London. Retrieved from www.ons.gov.uk/peoplepopulationandcommunity/crimeandjustice/articles/sexualoffendingvictimisationandthepaththroughthecriminaljusticesystem/2018-12-13#toc

Elliott, E., & Vollm, B. (2016). The utility of post-conviction polygraph testing among sexual offenders. *Sexual Abuse: A Journal of Research and Treatment*, https://doi.org/10.1177/1079063216667922

Gannon, T. A., Wood, J. L., Pina, A., Tyler, N., Barnoux, M. F., & Vasquez, E. A. (2014). An evaluation of mandatory polygraph testing for sexual offenders in the United Kingdom. *Sexual Abuse*, *26*(2), 178–203.

Gillespie, A. A. (2010). Indeterminate notification requirements: The final answer? R (on the application of F and Thompson) v secretary of state for the home department [2010] UKSC 17. *The Journal of Criminal Law*, *74*(4), 304–309.

Grubin, D. (2010). A trial of voluntary polygraphy testing in 10 English probation areas. *Sexual Abuse*, *22*(3), 266–278.

Grubin, D., Joyce, A., Holden, E. J., Janssen, D. F., Pfäfflin, F., & Rehder, U. H. (2014). Polygraph testing of "low risk" offenders arrested for downloading indecent images of children. *Sexual Offender Treatment*, *9*(1).

Hanvey, S., Wilson, C., & Philpot, T. (2011). *A community-based approach to the reduction of sexual reoffending: Circles of support and accountability*. London: Jessica Kingsley Publishers.

Harrison, K. (2011). *Dangerousness, risk and the governance of serious sexual and violent offenders*. Oxon: Routledge.

Kemshall, H., & Weaver, B. (2012). The sex offender public disclosure pilots in England and Scotland: Lessons for "marketing strategies" and risk communication with the public. *Criminology & Criminal Justice*, *12*(5), 549–565.

Kemshall, H., & Wood, J. (2010). *Child sex offender review (CSOR) public disclosure pilots: A process evaluation* (2nd ed.). London: Home Office. Research Report 32. Retrieved from https://assets.publishing.service.gov.uk/government/uploads/system/uploads/attachment_data/file/214959/horr32c.pdf

Kerr, J., Roberts, E., Davies, M., & Pullerits, M. (2019). *Process evaluation of the global positioning system (GPS) electronic monitoring pilot: Qualitative findings*. London: Ministry of Justice Analytical. Retrieved from https://assets.publishing.service.gov.uk/government/uploads/system/uploads/attachment_data/file/779199/gps-location-monitoring-pilot-process-evaluation.pdf

Kewley, S. (2017a). Policing people with sexual convictions using strengths based approaches. *Journal of Criminal Psychology*, *7*(3), 168–182.

Kewley, S. (2017b). Policing registered sex offenders. *The Journal of Forensic Practice*, *19*(4), 296–300.

Kewley, S., Beech, A. R., Harkins, L., & Bonsall, H. (2015). Effective risk management planning for those convicted of sexual offending. *Journal of Aggression, Conflict and Peace Research*, *7*(4), 237–257.

Kewley, S., Osman, S., & McGuinness, Á. (2019). How well do police specialists risk assess registered sexual offenders? *Journal of Sexual Aggression*. Retrieved from www.tandfonline.com/doi/abs/10.1080/13552600.2019.1628315?journalCode=tjsa20

Levenson, J. S., Brannon, Y., Fortney, T., & Baker, J. (2007). Public perceptions about sex offenders and community protection policies. *Analyses of Social Issues and Public Policy*, *7*(1), 137–161.

Levenson, J. S., & D'Amora, D. A. (2007). Social policies designed to prevent sexual violence: The emperor's new clothes? *Criminal Justice Policy Review*, *18*(2), 168–199.

Levins, A. (2014). Living among sex offenders identity, safety and relationships at Whatton prison. *The Howard League for Penal Reform*. Retrieved from https://howardleague.org/wp-content/uploads/2016/03/Living-among-sex-offenders.pdf

Magistrates' Court Sentencing Guidelines. (2017). Explanatory materials. *Sexual Harm Prevention Orders*, 22. Retrieved from www.sentencingcouncil.org.uk/explanatory-material/magistrates-court/item/ancillary-orders/22-sexual-harm-prevention-orders/

Her Majesty's Inspectorate of Probation. (2019). *Management and supervision of men convicted of sexual offences: A thematic inspection by HM inspectorate of probation and HM inspectorate of prisons*. London: Her Majesty's Inspectorate of Probation. Retrieved from www.justiceinspectorates.gov.uk/hmiprobation/

Mental Health Act (1983).

Ministry of Justice, National Offender Mangement Service. MAPPA Guidance 2012 Version 4. Retreived from www.justice.gov.uk/downloads/offenders/mappa/mappa-guidance-2012-part1.pdf

Multi-Agency Public Protection Arrangements Annual Report 2017/18. (2018). London: Retrieved from https://assets.publishing.service.gov.uk/government/uploads/system/uploads/attachment_data/file/751006/mappa-annual-report-2017-18.pdf.

The Offender Management Act (2007).

Offender Rehabilitation Act (2014).

Reid, J. (2007). *Review of the protection of children from sex offenders*. London. Retrieved from http://webarchive.nationalarchives.gov.uk/20100413151441/http:/www.homeoffice.gov.uk/documents/CSOR/chid-sex-offender-review-1306072835.pdf?view=Binary

Sentence planning. (2014). *PSI 19.2014*. Summary. National Offender Managment Service, NOMS Agency Board.

Sexual Offences Act (2003).

Sexual offences definitive guideline. (2013). Retrieved from www.sentencingcouncil.org.uk/wp-content/uploads/Sexual-offences-definitive-guideline-Web.pdf

Tewksbury, R. (2005). Collateral consequences of sex offender registration. *Journal of Contemporary Criminal Justice*, *21*(1), 67–81.

Thomas, T. (2010). The sex offender register, community notification and some reflections on privacy. In K. Harrison (Ed.), *Managing High-risk Sex Offenders in the Community: Risk Management, Treatment and Social Responsibility* (pp. 61–78). Portland: Wilan Publishing.

Transforming rehabilitation: A strategy for reform. Response to Consultation CP(R)16/2013. (2013). London. Retrieved from https://assets.publishing.service.gov.uk/government/uploads/system/uploads/attachment_data/file/228744/8619.pdf

The Violent Crime Reduction Act (2006).

Ward, T. (2016). Prediction and agency: The role of protective factors in correctional rehabilitation and desistance. *Aggression and Violent Behavior*, *32*, 19–28.

Wood, J., Kemshall, H., Maguire, M., Hudson, K., & Mackenzie, G. (Eds.). (2007). *The operation and experience of multi-agency public protection arrangements (MAPPA)*. Retrieved from https://s3.amazonaws.com/academia.edu.documents/44822334/MAPPA1207.pdf?response-content-disposition=inline%3B%20filename%3DThe_operation_and_experience_of_Multi-Ag.pdf&X-Amz-Algorithm=AWS4-HMAC-SHA256&X-Amz-Credential=AKIAIWOWYYGZ2Y53UL3A%2F20200207%2Fus-east-1%2Fs3%2Faws4_request&X-Amz-Date=20200207T134114Z&X-Amz-Expires=3600&X-Amz-SignedHeaders=host&X-Amz-Signature=215f9c1d3373483affbcba6cab13cc78903daff724d6e5d1e8f380d4e18d3496. Leicester: Home Office.

3 Current approaches to the assessment of sexual offending

Assessment

While the primary purpose of assessment, from a sentencing perspective, is for assessors to advise on the likelihood of future offending, a secondary purpose is to identify both the risks and needs a person presents, so that courts can issue appropriate sentences, treatment pathways, and management strategies. Risk assessment tools must therefore reflect contemporary empirical knowledge and effectiveness to ensure that sentencing, treatment, and management of cases are appropriately issued. The development of these assessments can be traced through at least four generational periods. The first generation assessments relied on professionals using their own judgement, knowledge, and experience to assess the risk an individual posed; such assessments were often based on instinct and previous experiences (Hanson & Morton-Bourgon, 2009). This approach was soon superseded when during the 1970s a second generation of assessment saw a more evidence-based approach develop. This approach gave less attention to clinical assessments and more emphasis on evidence-based judgement linked to certain types of offending behaviours. However, these tools used to measure risk relied on historical and static items, which prevented the assessment of the dynamic nature of clients and their problems (Hanson & Bussiere, 1998). Thus, the development of a third-generation assessment responded to these limitations and tools included items that allowed for dynamic changes in a person's life (Beggs & Grace, 2010). While static items remained, items such as peer association, employment, and substance use were included to acknowledge any positive or negative changes in a person's life that might influence their offending behaviour. Finally, the fourth generation assessments consider management and interventions applied to offenders during and post sentence. These assessments tend to include a range of dynamic risk factors, strengths, needs, and responsivity of the offender (Andrews, Bonta, & Wormith, 2004). It is possible to add a fifth generation to this list, as now assessment tools attempt to incorporate not only actuarial and dynamic factors linked to offending but also what protective factors might help strengthen a person's resolve to desist from crime (de Vries Robbé, Mann, Maruna, & Thornton, 2015).

Risk prediction is of course an imperfect science and prone to many methodological problems. There are problems with consistency. For example across

England and Wales alone, there are several different risk prediction/assessment tools. These vary in terms of the variables measured, the methods used to carry out the assessment, and the reliability of the tool itself. Often agencies use varying tools, making comparisons across services a challenge. Likewise, people facing conviction may have engaged in a plea-bargaining process or indeed their convictions do not reflect the actual offence; therefore, assessors are not necessarily assessing 'true' risk. Given the variety in recidivism definitions, the notion of 'risk' is also problematic. This can cause challenges for practitioners and sentencers when interpreting or comparing risk predictions (Craig & Beech, 2010). Finally, the expectations of criminal justice agencies and practitioners to predict future human behaviour is, of course, great. This expectation is indeed problematic, as it is impossible to predict the future, and arguably, where this process is relied upon, it is harmful, as human error is inevitable. The consequences of underestimating the risk a person presents can result in catastrophic outcomes for victims, their families, and society. Likewise, overestimating risks can create excessive sanctions, costly and unnecessary treatment, excessive prison sentences, or people being refused parole.

While assessment for risk prediction is a key part of the process of sentencing offenders, so too is the requirement for assessments to determine the needs of people being assessed, and identification of appropriate strategies to manage identified risks and needs. There are several approaches used to assess the risk posed by those convicted of sexual offending. Some of these include: a) Actuarial assessment, whereby risk scales are statistically driven and predict future behaviour based on empirically tested factors. These assessments tend to classify individuals into categories of low, medium, and (very) high risk of sexual reconviction; b) Unguided clinical judgement, whereby assessors use material from case files to determine their own clinical judgement; c) Structured clinical judgement, whereby assessors use tools guided by theory and empirical evidence related to risk of reconviction. Assessors use this as the framework in which to generate their own clinical judgement based on case file data; and (d) A clinically adjusted actuarial approach: a combination of approach a) with c). Assessors usually begin with an actuarial assessment and then adjust the result depending on their clinical judgement of the case material (Craig, Beech, & Harkins, 2009).

Actuarial

Actuarial assessments have been recognised as being the most reliable when it comes to predicting future recidivism (Helmus, Hanson, & Morton-Bourgon, 2011) and far more reliable than clinical judgement alone (Hanson & Bussière, 1996; Hanson & Morton-Bourgon, 2009). Actuarial assessments are in the main made up of static factors known to be related to general and sexual recidivism (Cortoni, 2009). Static factors include, for example, age, marital status, lifestyle instability, risk taking, substance use, engaging in antisocial behaviour, and having a history of violence (Hanson & Bussiere, 1998). Such factors tend to be historic and therefore unchangeable. Several actuarial assessment tools continue to be developed and tested. Some of the most commonly used risk scales and the items that aim to predict sexual recidivism are detailed in Table 3.1, but for a more detailed analysis of the predictive strength of some of these tools, please see Craig, Browne, and Beech (2008).

While actuarial tools continue to be used, tested, and developed, there are criticisms reported in the literature, and caution is advised regarding reliance on these tools alone (Werth, 2019). First, Craig et al. (2009) discuss how official recidivism data, as a measure of further abuse, is a problem as this does not necessarily reflect true recidivism. Second, many actuarial tools classify people by characteristics of populations; this becomes a challenge when individuals do not fit into these classifications, such as women or people with intellectual disability. Third, actuarial tools tend to project risk into the long-term future. While this is a reasonable strategy from a methodological point of view, most clinicians and practitioners deal with the immanence of risk, and often need shorter-term predictions. From a clinical perspective, actuarial tools are therefore not meaningful when dealing with individual clients and when attempting to develop treatment and/or management plans (Hannah-Moffat, 2015).

Dynamic risk assessment

In light of some of the limitations experienced by practitioners using actuarial assessment tools, a new generation of dynamic approaches to risk assessment was developed. It is perhaps important to note that while there is significant value in dynamic assessment tools, actuarial tools continue to be the most effective way to predict longer term recidivism. Again it is not our intention to give an in-depth discussion of dynamic risk assessment, as there are authors who have dedicated texts to this issue and can provide greater insight, like Craig et al. (2008), Beech, Craig, and Browne (2009), and Boer, Eher, Craig, Miner, and Pfäfflin (2011). As already noted, different agencies across different regions choose to use different assessment tools. Therefore, even when providing an overview of the current assessment landscape within England and Wales, a diverse number of tools are used. For example (at the time of writing), officers in Her Majesty's Prison and Probation Service (HMPPS) use a combination of tools including the Offender Assessment System (OASys), along with the Risk Matrix 2000 (RM2000), and for those engaging in treatment, they also use the Structured Assessment of Risk and Need (SARN); whereas across police forces in England and Wales, a combination of RM2000 and the Active Risk Management System (ARMS) are used. In forensic hospital settings a combination of diagnostic tools, such as the International Statistical Classification of Diseases and Related Health Problems (ICD–10) or Diagnostic and Statistical Manual of Mental Disorders, 5th edition (DSM–5) (American Psychiatric Association, 2013), along with tools such as the Risk for Sexual Violence Protocol (RSVP),

Table 3.1 Actuarial risk scales detailing author and actuarial items

Risk scale	*Author*	*Number of items*	*List of actuarial items*
Sexual Offender Risk Appraisal Guide (SORAG)	Quinsey, Harris, Rice, and Cormier (1998)	14	• Lived with biological parents to age 16 • Elementary school maladjustment (Thornton, 1997; Hanson, 1997, 1999; Helmus, Hanson, Thornton, Babchishin, & Harris, 2012) • History of alcohol problems (parental alcoholism, teenage alcohol problem, adult alcohol problem, alcohol involved in a prior offense, alcohol involved in index offense) • Never married • Nonviolent criminal history score (calculated from the Cormier-Lang system; Quinsey et al., 1998) • Violent criminal history score (calculated from the Cormier-Lang system) • Prior hands-on sex offence convictions • Female victims under 14 years old exclusively (reverse scored) • Failure on prior conditional release • Young age at index offense • Meets DSM-III (American Psychiatric Association, 1980) criteria for a personality disorder • Meets DSM-III criteria for schizophrenia (reverse scored) • Any deviant phallometric test results • Psychopathy Checklist-Revised score (PCLR)
Structured Anchored Clinical Judgement Scale (SACJ)	Thornton (1997) and Grubin (1998)	9	• Past sexual offences (aggravating factor – any noncontact offences) • Age • Victim gender (aggravating factor – male)

Risk scale	*Author*	*Number of items*	*List of actuarial items*
			• Relationship to victim (aggravating factor – stranger) • Substance abuse • Ever been in care • Never married • Deviant sexual arousal • Score of 25+ on the PCLR
Rapid Risk Assessment for Sex Offence Recidivism (RRASOR)	Hanson (1997) and Hanson and Thornton (2000)	7	• Male victims • Unrelated victims • Stranger victims • Prior sexual offences • Prior nonsexual offences • Aged between 18–24 years • Never married
Static-99	Hanson and Thornton (1999) and Helmus, Thornton, Hanson, and Babchishin (2012)	10	• Prior sex offenses • Prior sentencing dates • Noncontact sex offense convictions • Nonsexual violent index offense convictions • Prior nonsexual violent convictions • Unrelated victim • Stranger victim • Male victim • Young age at first time; at risk for recidivism • Never married
Static-2002	Hanson and Thornton (2003)	13	• Age at release • Prior sexual offending sentencing • Juvenile arrests for sexual offence • Rate of sexual offending • Convictions for non-contact sexual offences • Male victim • Two or more victims under 12 years, one unrelated • Unrelated to victim • Stranger victim • Sentencing occasions • Breach • Years free prior to index offence • Convictions for non-sexual violence

(*Continued*)

Table 3.1 (Continued)

Risk scale	*Author*	*Number of items*	*List of actuarial items*
Risk matrix 2000	Thornton (2007)	9	• Age at commencement of risk • Sexual appearances • Criminal appearances • Sexual offences against a male • Sexual offence against a stranger • Single • Noncontact sex offence • Violence appearances • Any burglaries
Minnesota Sex Offender Screening Tool-Revised (MnSOST-R)	Epperson, Kaul, and Hesselton (2000)	9	• Male victims • Never married • Noncontact sex offences • Stranger victims • Current sex offence • Prior sex offence • Current nonsexual violence • Prior nonsexual violence • 4+ sentencing dates
Juvenile Sex Offender Assessment Protocol (J-SOAP)	Prentky and Righthand (2003)	16	• Prior legally charged sex offences • Number of sexual abuse victims • Male child victim • Duration of sex offence history • Degree of planning in sexual offences • Sexualised aggression • Sexual drive and preoccupation • Sexual victimisation history • Caregiver consistency • Pervasive anger • School behaviour problems • History of conduct disorder before age ten • Juvenile antisocial behaviour between the ages of 10 and 17 • Ever charged or arrested before the age of 16 • Multiple types of offences • History of physical assault and/or exposure to family violence

are used. Given the additional complexity of private prisons and hospitals, there is likely to be a greater variance in assessments used. Table 3.2 provides a summary of several dynamic risk assessment tools, providing an overview of the various domains and factors assessed.

In a series of recent papers, Ward and colleagues have questioned the utility of using dynamic risk factors to explain offending behaviour (Heffernan & Ward, 2017; Ward, 2016; Ward & Fortune, 2016). More specifically, they argue that: a) The concept of dynamic risk factors has not been well defined and as a consequence it is unclear whether it is a scientific (explanatory or classificatory) or normative concept; b) Relatedly, there is a lack of clarity on whether dynamic risk factors refer to causal processes or are best viewed as predictive constructs; and finally c) Because of these problems, no one is sure how best to integrate them into case formulation and treatment. In short, they lack coherence, specificity, and precision, and are heavily value laden.

In addition to the use of structured assessment tools that include both actuarial and clinical judgement, there are other approaches to risk assessment. For the purpose of this chapter we focus on the following: case formulation, psychometrics, phallometry, and polygraph.

Case formulation

Case formulation "is the preparation of an evidence-based explanation of a person's difficulties – their form, their origins, and their development and maintenance over time" (Hart, Sturmey, Logan, & McMurran, 2011, p. 118). Case formulation is intended to provide an assessment to inform a tailored, individualised treatment plan, and therefore is ideal for people with complex needs who may have not responded to treatment/or have unusual characteristics. Case formulation is both a process and a product. The process of systematically gathering and testing against theory allows the clinician to gain a deeper understanding of their client's psychological vulnerabilities and problems. Using case formulation or functional analysis allows the clinician to investigate the antecedents, behaviours, and consequences of the offence (Beech, Fisher, & Thornton, 2003). The process explores, tests, and documents the possible causes of client's sexual offending, along with how these manifests into behaviours. Case formulation thus focusses both on managing risk and promoting well-being and requires a systematic and integrated approach (Yates & Ward, 2008). The product of case formulation includes a framework for treatment or a plan to deal with future scenarios; it provides a rich understanding of the individual client's needs, their unique characteristics, and justification for bespoke treatment targets.

Ward, Nathan, Drake, Lee, and Pathé (2000) note three key challenges facing those completing case formulations. First, the task of completing a comprehensive case formulation is extremely time consuming. Second, one of the main aims of case formulation is to determine potential treatment targets. Considering most treatment programmes being delivered are in manual-based formats, there appears little utility in spending time developing an individualised treatment plan

Table 3.2 Dynamic risk tools detailing author, domains, and factors assessed

Risk tool	*Author*	*Number of domains*	*Domains and factors assessed*
Structured Assessment of Risk and Need (SARN)	Webster et al. (2006)	4	• Sexual interest (sexual preoccupation, preferring sex to include violence or force, sexual preference of children, other offence related sexual interests, specifically paraphilias) • Distorted attitudes (adversarial sexual attitudes, child abuse supportive beliefs, sexual entitlement, rape supportive beliefs, women are deceitful beliefs) • Socio-effective functioning (grievance mentality, inadequacy, lack of emotional intimacy, distorted intimacy balance) • Self-management (lifestyle impulsiveness/impulsive on stable lifestyle, poor problem-solving, poor emotional control)
STABLE 2007	Hanson and Harris (2007b)	13	• Significant social influences • Emotional identification with children • Hostility toward women • General social rejection • Lack of concern for others • Impulsivity • Poor problem-solving skills • Negative emotions • Sex drive • Preoccupations • Sex of coping • Deviant sexual preference • Cooperation with supervision
ACUTE 2007	Hanson and Harris (2007a)	7	• Victim access • Emotional collapse • Collapse of social support • Hostility • Substance abuse • Sexual preoccupations • Rejection of supervision
The Sexual Violence Risk-20 (SVR-20)	Boer et al. (1997)	3	• Psychological adjustment (sexual deviance, victim of child abuse, psychopathy, major mental illness, substance use, suicidal ideation, relationship problems, employment problems, past nonsexual violent offences, past supervision failure)

Risk tool	*Author*	*Number of domains*	*Domains and factors assessed*
			• History of sexual offences (high-density, multiple types, physical harm, weapons threats, escalation in frequency or severity, extreme minimisation denial, attitudes that support or condone) • Future plans (lacks realistic plans, negative attitude toward intervention)
Risk for Sexual Violence Protocol (RSVP)	Hart et al. (2003)	5	• History of sexual violence (chronicity, diversity, escalation, physical coercion, psychological coercion in sexual violence) • Psychological adjustment (extreme minimisation or denial, attitudes that support or condone violence, problems with self-awareness, problems with stressful coping, problems resulting from child abuse) • Mental disorder (sexual deviance, psychopathy, major mental illness, substance use, violence or suicidal ideation) • Social adjustment (problems with intimate relationships, non-intimate relationships, employment, nonsexual criminality) • Manageability (problems with planning, treatment, supervision)
Historical Clinical Risk Management-20 (HCR-20)	Douglas et al. (2014)	3	• Historical problems with violence, relationships, employment, substance use, mental disorder, personality disorder, traumatic experiences, violent attitudes, treatment or supervision responses • Recent problems including insight, violent ideation, symptoms of a major mental disorder, instability, treatment or supervision response • Future problems with professional services, living situation, personal support, treatment and supervision response, stress or coping

(*Continued*)

Table 3.2 (Continued)

Risk tool	*Author*	*Number of domains*	*Domains and factors assessed*
The Structured Assessment of Protective Factors for Violent Risk (SAPROF)	de Vries Robbé et al. (2013)	3	(The SAPROF is carried out in conjunction with the HCR-20) • Internal factors (intelligence, secure attachment in childhood, empathy, coping, self-control) • Motivational factors (work, leisure activities, financial management, motivation to treatment, attitudes toward authority, life goals, medication) • External factors (social network, intimate relationship, professional care, living circumstances, external control)
Structured Risk Assessment (SRA)	Thornton (2002)	4	• Sexual interests (offence related sexual fantasy, sexual preoccupation) • Distorted attitudes (beliefs that give permission about offending, sexuality, or victims, cognitive distortions) • Social and emotional functioning (negative effect, e.g. anger, anxiety, depression, low self-esteem, emotional loneliness, use of avoidance focussed coping strategies) • Self-management (poor planning, impulsivity, antisocial, chaotic lifestyle)
Active Risk Management System (ARMS)	Blandford and Kewley (2017)	12	• Opportunity • Sexual preoccupation • Offence-related sexual interests • Emotional congruence with children • Poor self-management • Hostile orientation • Negative social influences • Positive social influences • Commitment to desist • An intimate relationship • Employment and positive routine • Social investment (giving something back)

that is unlikely to be addressed using prescribed treatment programmes. The final issue noted by Ward and colleagues is that due to the highly subjective nature of this activity, clinicians are at risk of cognitive bias when designing individual case formulations. One reason for this final issue may lie in the lack of professional training in case formulation. Not all clinicians are competent or even trained in carrying out this type of assessment (Hart et al., 2011).

Psychometrics

Psychometric tests within a forensic context are usually administered to clients in a one-to-one, private setting, or for those within the prison setting, are often completed within groups. The administration of tests requires conditions that allow the person the ability to read, consider, and complete the tests. Furthermore, these should be in line with ethical codes of conduct, and only trained and qualified administrators ought to carry out the process (Miller & Lovler, 2016). Ideally, tests can provide assessors with a psychological profile of a person at a moment in time, identify treatment targets for individuals, and measure change. They are, therefore, useful when measuring the effectiveness of an intervention and should be administered both before and after the intervention, but only as part of a larger assessment and not in isolation to determine outcomes of an intervention.

The principles of psychometric testing require tests to be a) Standardised; b) Reliable; c) Valid; and d) Predicting future behaviour (Fernandez, 2009). There is a vast array of psychometric tests available for clinicians to use when assessing the needs and potential risks of a client with a history of sexual offending. Again, it is not our intention to discuss these in depth; many texts do this. One useful chapter that summarises measures used and their predictive accuracy can be found in Craig and Beech (2009). By way of a brief summary, we note here some tests traditionally used across England and Wales. Specialised sexual offending tests include the Multiphasic Sex Inventory (MSI) (the MSI is a 300-item self-report questionnaire with six scales including validity scales, accountability scales, sexual deviance scales, paraphilias, sexual dysfunction scales, and the sex knowledge and beliefs scale. More general psychological instruments include personality tests that measure personality disorders such as the Psychopathy Checklist-Revised PCL-R (Hare, 1991), the Minnesota Multiphasic Personality Inventory-2 (MMPI-2) (Butcher, Dahlstrom, Graham, Tellegen, & Kaemmer, 1989), and Special Hospitals Assessment of Personality and Socialisation (SHAPS) (Blackburn, 1982). Tests also examine the construct of sexual deviancy, using, for example, a Sex Offender Treatment Evaluation Project (STEP) (Beech, Beckett, & Fisher, 1998) and the Initial Deviance Assessment (IDA) (Thornton, 2002).

There are some limitations and challenges when using psychometric tests. One of the key issues is that of standardisation. A common problem in the sexual offending domain is that tests lack standardisation, that is it is difficult to know how deviant individuals are when compared to the general population because a normal sample is difficult to generate. A further problem with psychometrics is the self-reporting nature, risking socially desirable responses (Stevens,

Tan, & Grace, 2016). Tests such as Locus of Control, Empathy, and Prosocial Attitudes have been criticised for being easily manipulated, in that the person being tested can deceive or present themselves in a more positive light (Craig & Beech, 2009). While there are several challenges to the use of psychometric tests, they continue to inform assessment and thus treatment pathways for clients convicted of sexual offending.

Phallometry

Phallometry, also known as penile plethysmography, is used to assess sexually deviant preferences by measuring changes in penile circumference or volume when individuals are given visual or audio stimulation. Female responses are measured using vaginal probes or changes in the temperature of the labia. For a summary of the different devices and techniques used to measure erectile responses, please see an insightful paper by Marshall (2013). The stimulus sets used in phallometry assessment protocols are typically divided into categories based on ages, gender, and sexual activities, with the most valid tests measuring a history and persistence of sexual offending against children (McPhail et al., 2019).

There are several challenges faced by these tests, the first being an issue of standardisation (McPhail et al., 2019). Phallometric testing varies between laboratories, including the use of different stimulus sets and varying methods of collecting data, making it very difficult to compare results. At present there is not one means of identifying what a particular level of erectile response means and how this might compare to 'normal' responses (Laws, 2009). Likewise, it is unclear how to interpret different erectile responses to non-deviant stimuli, a greater response to non-deviant stimuli, or of course no response to either stimulus at all (Marshall, 2013). Considering this standardisation challenge, caution should be used when using phallometry results. Phallometric assessment is most likely to be helpful with people who have a documented and fully disclosed history of deviant sexual interests in children. However, tests should only be used as a contribution within the context of a comprehensive clinical assessment.

The second challenge to phallometric testing is ethical in nature (Laws, 2009). Inappropriate use of the phallometric testing occurs when a) assessors use responses as evidence that a person has committed a sexual offence, b) the assessment is the single means used to determine a person's sentence or release from prison, c) it is used as a screening tool when searching for a particular offender, and d) when there are questions relating to the kind of material used to produce simulation (McPhail et al., 2019), such as the use of naked images of children as well as the use of criminal images of child abuse (Fernandez, 2009). Such ethical dilemmas relate not only to the reproduction of sexual abuse and revictimisation of the child, but also exposing people to images of sexual abuse has the potential to cause harm, both for clients and of course the assessor present during the assessment.

Third, there are risks of clients faking responses (Fernandez, 2009). Like all assessment, subjects can manipulate their responses without the assessor being able to control it. Phallometric tests are equally vulnerable to this validity problem. Several studies have demonstrated that participants were able to control their arousal responses to stimuli and therefore present an under or overstimulated response to a range of stimuli. Thus, the ability to understand which responses are fake is difficult (Marshall & Fernandez, 2000).

Polygraph

The polygraph, commonly but incorrectly known as the lie detector test, has been a staple tool used in the US for several decades as part of both investigation and management of people with sexual convictions. In the UK, however, polygraph use has only recently been implemented across the HMPPS, following the introduction of legislation in the Offender Management Act, 2007 (Marshall & Thomas, 2015; Wilcox & Donathy, 2014). In the UK, tests are not used in an investigative capacity. Instead they are used to inform treatment and assist supervision (Grubin, 1998; Grubin, Kamenskov, Dwyer, & Stephenson, 2019).

The HMPPS across England and Wales uses mandatory polygraph testing for those who present the greatest risk of reoffending, and support formal offender management processes (Gannon, Wood, Pina, Vasquez, & Fraser, 2012). Of note is that the police in England and Wales, who also have responsibility for the management of those with sexual convictions, do not yet have legislative support to use the polygraph without the consent of the client. They, therefore, can only use the test on a voluntary basis when managing clients. Even so, there appear to be conflicting messages regarding the purpose of the tool within the police, with one police area seeing it as a tool for supervision, another as a tool for investigation, and a third for testing people arrested on suspicion of possessing indecent images of children (Marshall & Thomas, 2015).

The polygraph tool measures and records the breathing rate, cardiovascular activity, and perspiration rate of a client during a set period in which they are ask several questions that are both related and unrelated to problematic and criminal behaviour (Cross & Saxe, 2001). The physiological responses, when measured against control questions, are said to indicate the degree to which the person is being truthful or not in response to the questions asked. Polygraph tests used to test people with sexual convictions are known as Post-Conviction Sex Offender Testing (PCSOT) (Grubin, 2008). These are tests carried out only on those with a conviction for a sexual offence. Tests include four types of questions, those that elicit a) sexual history disclosure, b) maintenance, c) denial of index offence disclosure, and d) specific issues. Test results form part of an overall assessment and should be used as part of a range of tools used to help determine treatment pathways and supervise the client.

The accuracy of polygraph testing has been the topic of much academic debate. For useful discussions on these issues, see Gannon, Beech, and Ward (2008) and Cross and Saxe (2001). Those disputing the accuracy of polygraph argue there is a lack of theoretical support, that empirical studies are undermined by serious methodological limitations, and that the use of confession as a measure of the truth is problematic, given some of the ethical and practical applications of the tool itself. However, there are also several empirical studies that demonstrate the effectiveness of the tool, and findings include increased rates at which clients disclose, greater insight into behaviour (scale/number and types of previous offences), detail of sexual fantasy, and clients' engagement in risk behaviours or preoccupation with masturbation (Madsen, Parsons, & Grubin, 2004). In a large study examining the use of PCSOT in ten probation services across England over six months, Grubin (2006) found that 70% of new disclosures made had a direct impact on treatment or supervision plans, compared to 14% of clients not polygraphed. With some limitations to this study, a further evaluation was undertaken by Gannon, Wood, Pina, Vasquez, and Fraser (2012), who also found support for the polygraph and a similar trajectory. Although not quite as remarkable as the 70% figure, they found clients who were periodically examined using the polygraph were twice as likely to make significant disclosures when compared to the control group. Whether clients tell the truth and do not give false disclosures is still a concern. However, in two separate studies, less than 10% of clients acknowledged giving a false test (Grubin & Madsen, 2006; Kokish, Levenson, & Blasingame, 2005), suggesting that the majority of clients appear in the main to be truthful with their disclosure.

There remain some uncertainties regarding polygraph testing and its outcomes. While there is clear guidance that states a person will not be convicted solely on the evidence gathered from a polygraph test, there is still a lack of clarity regarding what action should be taken when a new offence or new victims are identified (Marshall & Thomas, 2015).

Conclusion

This chapter has outlined the current state and use of several assessment tools and approaches used to assess people convicted of sexual offences across England and Wales, ahead of sentencing, treatment, and management. The expectation on criminal justice practitioners to carry out consistently accurate risk prediction is unrealistic, and arguably unfair. In their hands are a range of contemporary and well tested tools that ought to guide their professional judgement and practice. Yet as noted, while confidence is high in terms of the reliability of some static actuarial risk assessment tools, for individual treatment planning, these tools are perhaps less useful. Dynamic and protective factors appear to offer more promise for individual treatment planning, yet the theoretical underpinnings of dynamic factors are themselves questionable, and until research is carried out to empirically test the causal or predictive value of dynamic factors, the development of dynamic tools is perhaps futile. Within a culture and climate in which risk remains deficit focussed, research examining dynamic and protective factors has been lethargic. This text thus hopes to help support and encourage strengths-based interest in a positive criminology movement that might examine and test these factors. Clearer definition and empirical testing of these factors are important so that appropriate risk assessment tools can be developed and criminal justice practitioners can engage with effective and meaningful tools to help protect those at risk of victimisation as well as help support people with criminal histories to live a life free from crime.

References

American Psychiatric Association (Ed.). (1980). *Quick reference to the diagnostic criteria from DSM-III*. Washington, DC: American Psychiatric Association.

American Psychiatric Association. (2013). *Diagnostic and statistical manual of mental disorders* (5th ed.). Washington, DC: American Psychiatric Association.

Andrews, D. A., Bonta, J., & Wormith, J. S. (2004). *The level of service/case management inventory (LS/CMI)*. Toronto: Multi-Health Systems.

Beech, A. R., Beckett, R. C., & Fisher, D. (1998). *STEP 3: An evaluation of the prison sex offender treatment programme*. London: Home Office.

Beech, A. R., Craig, L. A., & Browne, K. (2009). *Assessment and treatment of sex offenders: A handbook*. Chichester: John Wiley & Sons Ltd.

Beech, A. R., Fisher, D. D., & Thornton, D. (2003). Risk assessment of sex offenders. *Professional Psychology: Research and Practice*, *34*(4), 339.

Beggs, S. M., & Grace, R. C. (2010). Assessment of dynamic risk factors: An independent validation study of the violence risk scale: Sexual offender version. *Sexual Abuse*, *22*(2), 234–251.

Blackburn, R. (1982). *The special hospitals assessment of personality and socialisation*. Unpublished manuscript, Park Lane Hospital, Liverpool.

Blandford, M., & Kewley, S. (2017). The development of the active risk management system. *Journal of Criminal Psychology*, *7*(3), 155–167.

Boer, D. P., Eher, R., Craig, L. A., Miner, M. H., & Pfäfflin, F. (2011). *International perspectives on the assessment and treatment of sexual offenders: Theory, practice and research*. West Sussex: Wiley Blckwell.

Boer, D. P., Hart, S., Kropp, P., & Webster, C. (1997). *Manual for the sexual violence risk-20*. Burnaby: The Mental Health. Law, & Policy Institute, Simon Fraser University.

Butcher, J. N., Dahlstrom, W., Graham, J., Tellegen, A., & Kaemmer, B. (1989). *Minnesota multiphasic personality inventory-2 (MMPI-2): Manual for administration and scoring*. Minneapolis: University of Minnesota Press.

Cortoni, F. (2009). Factors associated with sexual recidivism. In A. R. Beech, L. A. Craig, & K. D. Browne (Eds.), *Assessment and treatment of sexual offenders: A handbook* (pp. 39–52). Chichester: John Wiley & Sons Ltd.

Craig, L. A., & Beech, A. R. (2009). Psychometric assessment of sexual deviance. In A. R. Beech, L. A. Craig, & K. Browne (Eds.), *Assessment and treatment of sex offenders: A handbook*. Chichester: John Wiley & Sons Ltd.

Craig, L. A., & Beech, A. R. (2010). Towards a guide to best practice in conducting actuarial risk assessments with sex offenders. *Aggression and Violent Behavior*, *15*(4), 278–293.

Craig, L. A., Beech, A. R., & Harkins, L. (2009). The predictive accuracy of risk factors and frameworks. In A. R. Beech, L. A. Craig, & K. D. Browne (Eds.), *Assessment and treatment of sex offenders: A handbook* (pp. 53–74). Chichester: Wiley and Sons.

Craig, L. A., Browne, K. D., & Beech, A. R. (2008). *Assessing risk in sex offenders: A practitioner's guide*. Chichester: John Wiley & Sons Inc.

Cross, T. P., & Saxe, L. (2001). Polygraph testing and sexual abuse: The lure of the magic lasso. *Child Maltreatment*, *6*(3), 195–206.

de Vries Robbé, M., de Vogel, V., & Douglas, K. S. (2013). Risk factors and protective factors: A two-sided dynamic approach to violence risk assessment. *Journal of Forensic Psychiatry & Psychology, 24*(4), 440–457.

de Vries Robbé, M., Mann, R. E., Maruna, S., & Thornton, D. (2015). An exploration of protective factors supporting desistance from sexual offending. *Sexual Abuse: Journal of Research and Treatment, 27*(1), 16–33.

Douglas, K. S., Hart, S. D., Webster, C. D., Belfrage, H., Guy, L. S., & Wilson, C. M. (2014). Historical-clinical-risk management-20, version 3 (HCR-20V3): Development and overview. *International Journal of Forensic Mental Health, 13*(2), 93–108.

Epperson, D. L., Kaul, J. D., & Hesselton, D. S. (2000). *Minnesota sex offender screening tool, revised (MnSOST-R): Development, performance, and recommended risk level cut scores*. Iowa: MN Department of Corrections.

Fernandez, Y. (2009). The standardisation of phallometry. In A. Beech, L. A. Craig, & K. Browne (Eds.), *Assessment and treatment of sex offenders: A handbook*. Chichester: John Wiley & Sons Ltd.

Gannon, T. A., Beech, A. R., & Ward, T. (2008). Does the polygraph lead to better risk prediction for sexual offenders? *Aggression and Violent Behavior, 13*(1), 29–44.

Gannon, T. A., Wood, J., Pina, A., Vasquez, E., & Fraser, I. (2012). The evaluation of the mandatory polygraph pilot. *Ministry of Justice Research Series, 14*, 12.

Grubin, D. (1998). *Sex offending against children: Understanding the risk* (vol. 99). London: Home Office, Policing and Reducing Crime Unit, Research, Development and Statistics Directorate.

Grubin, D. (2006). *Polygraph pilot study: Final report*. London: Home Office. Retrieved January 1, 2012.

Grubin, D. (2008). The case for polygraph testing of sex offenders. *Legal and Criminological Psychology, 13*(2), 177–189.

Grubin, D., Kamenskov, M., Dwyer, R. G., & Stephenson, T. (2019). Post-conviction polygraph testing of sex offenders. *International Review of Psychiatry, 31*(2), 141–148.

Grubin, D., & Madsen, L. (2006). Accuracy and utility of post-conviction polygraph testing of sex offenders. *The British Journal of Psychiatry, 188*(5), 479–483.

Hannah-Moffat, K. (2015). The uncertainties of risk assessment: Partiality, transparency, and just decisions. *Federal Sentencing Reporter, 27*(4), 244–247.

Hanson, R. K. (1997). *The development of a brief actuarial risk scale for sexual offense recidivism*. Ottawa: Solicitor General of Canada.

Hanson, R. K., & Bussière, M. T. (1996). *Predictors of sexual offender recidivism: A meta-analysis 1996–04*. Ottawa: Department of the Solicitor General of Canada.

Hanson, R. K., & Bussiere, M. T. (1998). Predicting relapse: A meta-analysis of sexual offender recidivism studies. *Journal of Consulting and Clinical Psychology, 66*(2), 348–362.

Hanson, R. K., & Harris, A. (2007a). *ACUTE-2007*. Unpublished manuscript. Department of the Solicitor General Canada. Retrieved from the authors at Andrew.Harris@PSEPC-SPPCC.GC.CA.

Hanson, R. K., & Harris, A. (2007b). *STABLE-2007*. Unpublished manuscript. Department of the Solicitor General of Canada. Retrieved from the authors at Andrew.Harris@PSEPC-SPPCC.GC.CA.

Hanson, R. K., & Morton-Bourgon, K. E. (2009). The accuracy of recidivism risk assessments for sexual offenders: A meta-analysis of 118 prediction studies. *Psychological Assessment, 21*(1), 1–21.

Hanson, R. K., & Thornton, D. (1999). *Static 99: Improving actuarial risk assessments for sex offenders* (vol. 2). Ottawa: Solicitor General of Canada.

Hanson, R. K., & Thornton, D. (2000). Improving risk assessments for sex offenders: A comparison of three actuarial scales. *Law and Human Behavior, 24*(1), 119–136.

Hanson, R. K., & Thornton, D. (2003). *Notes on the development of static-2002: 2003–01*. Canada. Retrieved from www.publicsafety.gc.ca/cnt/rsrcs/pblctns/nts-dvlpmnt-sttc/nts-dvlpmnt-sttc-eng.pdf

Hare, R. D. (1991). *The hare psychopathy checklist-revised*. Toronto: Multi-Health Systems, Incorporated.

Hart, S., Kropp, P., Laws, D., Klaver, J., Logan, C., & Watt, K. (2003). *The risk for sexual violence protocol (RSVP)*. Burnaby: Mental Health, Law and Policy Institute of Simon Fraser University, Pacific Psychological Assessment Corporation & British Columbia Institute Against Family Violence.

Hart, S., Sturmey, P., Logan, C., & McMurran, M. (2011). Forensic case formulation. *International Journal of Forensic Mental Health, 10*(2), 118–126.

Heffernan, R., & Ward, T. (2017). A comprehensive theory of dynamic risk and protective factors. *Aggression and Violent Behavior, 37*, 129–141.

Helmus, L., Hanson, R. K., & Morton-Bourgon, K. (2011). International comparisons of the vailidity of actuarial risk tools for sexual offenders, with focus on static-99. In D. P. Boer, R. Eher, L. A. Craig, M. H. Miner & F. Pfäfflin (Eds.), *International perspectives on the assessment and treatment of sexual offenders: Theory, practice and research* (pp. 57–83). West Sussex: John Wiley & Sons.

Helmus, L., Hanson, R. K., Thornton, D., Babchishin, K. M., & Harris, A. J. (2012). Absolute recidivism rates predicted by static-99R and static-2002R sex offender risk assessment tools vary across samples: A meta-analysis. *Criminal Justice and Behavior, 39*(9), 1148–1171.

Helmus, L., Thornton, D., Hanson, R. K., & Babchishin, K. M. (2012). Improving the predictive accuracy of Static-99 and Static-2002 with older sex offenders: Revised age weights. *Sexual Abuse. A Journal of Research and Treatment, 24*(1), 64–101.

International Statistical Classification of Diseases and Related Health Problems (2nd ed., vol. 3). (2004). Geneva: World Health Organization. Retrieved from www.who.int/classifications/icd/en/

Kokish, R., Levenson, J. S., & Blasingame, G. D. (2005). Post-conviction sex offender polygraph examination: Client-reported perceptions of utility and accuracy. *Sexual Abuse: A Journal of Research and Treatment, 17*(2), 211–221.

Laws, D. R. (2009). Penile plethysmography: Strengths, limitations, innovations. In D. Thornton & D. R. Laws (Eds.), *Cognitive approaches to the assessment of sexual interest in sexual offenders* (pp. 7–30). Chichester: John Wiley & Sons.

Madsen, L., Parsons, S., & Grubin, D. (2004). A preliminary study of the contribution of periodic polygraph testing to the treatment and supervision of sex offenders. *Journal of Forensic Psychiatry & Psychology, 15*(4), 682–695.

Marshall, D., & Thomas, T. (2015). Polygraphs and sex offenders: The truth is out there. *Probation Journal, 62*(2), 128–139.

Marshall, W. L. (2013). Phallometric assessments of sexual interests: An update. *Current Psychiatry Reports, 16*(1), 428.

Marshall, W. L., & Fernandez, Y. M. (2000). Phallometric testing with sexual offenders: Limits to its value. *Clinical Psychology Review, 20*(7), 807–822.

McPhail, I. V., Hermann, C. A., Fernane, S., Fernandez, Y. M., Nunes, K. L., & Cantor, J. M. (2019). Validity in phallometric testing for sexual interests in children: A meta-analytic review. *Assessment, 26*(3), 535–551.

Miller, L. A., & Lovler, R. L. (2016). *Foundations of psychological testing: A practical approach* (5th ed.). London: Sage.

Prentky, R., & Righthand, S. (2003). *Juvenile sex offender assessment protocol-II (J-SOAP-II) manual*. Washington, DC: US Department of Justice, Office of Justice Programs, Office of Juvenile Justice and Delinquency Prevention.

Quinsey, V. L., Harris, G. T., Rice, M. E., & Cormier, C. A. (1998). *Violent offenders: Appraising and managing risk*. Washington, DC: American Pscyhological Association.

Stevens, C. D., Tan, L., & Grace, R. C. (2016). Socially desirable responding and psychometric assessment of dynamic risk in sexual offenders against children. *Psychology, Crime & Law*, *22*(5), 420–434.

Thornton, D. (1997). *Structured anchored clinical judgement*. Paper presented at the NOTA Annual Conference, Southampton.

Thornton, D. (2002). Constructing and testing a framework for dynamic risk assessment. *Sexual Abuse: A Journal of Research and Treatment*, *14*(2), 139–153.

Thornton, D. (2007). *Scoring guide for risk matrix 2000.9/SVC*. Retrieved from www.birmingham.ac.uk/Documents/college-les/psych/RM2000scoringinstructions.pdf

Ward, T. (2016). Dynamic risk factors: Scientific kinds or predictive constructs. *Psychology, Crime & Law*, *22*(1–2), 2–16.

Ward, T., & Fortune, C.-A. (2016). The role of dynamic risk factors in the explanation of offending. *Aggression and Violent Behavior*, *29*, 79–88.

Ward, T., Nathan, P., Drake, C. R., Lee, J. K., & Pathé, M. (2000). The role of formulation-based treatment for sexual offenders. *Behaviour Change*, *17*(4), 251–264.

Webster, S. D., Mann, R. E., Carter, A. J., Long, J., Milner, R. J., O Brien, M. D., . . . Ray, N. L. (2006). Inter-rater reliability of dynamic risk assessment with sexual offenders. *Psychology, Crime & Law*, *12*(4), 439–452.

Werth, R. (2019). Risk and punishment: The recent history and uncertain future of actuarial, algorithmic, and "evidence-based" penal techniques. *Sociology Compass*, *13*(2), e12659.

Wilcox, D. T., & Donathy, M. L. (2014). British experiences of polygraph testing sexual offenders an update. *European Polygraph*, *8*(1), 23–28.

Yates, P., & Ward, T. (2008). Good lives, self-regulation, and risk management: An integrated model of sexual offender assessment and treatment. *Sexual Abuse in Australia and New Zealand*, *1*(1), 2–19.

4 Current approaches to the treatment of sexual offending

Treatment

It is not our aim to give a detailed review of the treatment available for those convicted of sexual offending. There are several excellent texts dedicated to this topic, including Beech, Craig, and Browne (2009), Marshall, Marshall, Serran, and O'Brien (2011), and finally Wilcox, Garrett, and Harkins (2015), who provide a case study approach to applying interventions and the issues related to unique client populations and contexts. Instead, this chapter aims to summarise, in brief, the current treatment landscape for those incarcerated, living in the community, or receiving treatment within a secure hospital setting following a conviction for sexual offending. First, we summarise the chronology and trace the development of current treatment strategies.

Laws and Marshall (2003) provide a detailed history of the treatment of sexual offenders from the mid-1800s to 1969. They highlight John B. Watson's influence on forensic psychology in the field of behaviourism, and that of Alfred Kinsey in his descriptive taxonomic approach. Although not widely used, traces of Watson's behaviourism can be found in early sexual offending treatment interventions through operant conditioning principles as detailed by B. F. Skinner (Skinner, 1938, 1963), though Pavlovian classical conditioning became more mainstream. Likewise, the influence of Kinsey in his development and exploration of human sexuality (Kinsey, Pomeroy, Martin, & Sloan, 1948) played an important role during a time when little attention was given to the exploration of human sexuality in the field. Laws and Marshall (2003) signal the early emergence of cognitive behavioural treatment (Tolman, 1932) and treatment theories (Guthrie, 1935), later developed by Bandura (1969) and Marshall (1996).

Behavioural therapy emerged as a treatment option designed to tackle clients with sexually deviant interests or unusual sexual behaviours. At the time, these included homosexuality, transvestism, and fetishisms. Treatments ranged from aversion therapy where noxious gases or chemicals were inhaled or injected while clients watched target sexual images and activities. Likewise, electric shock treatment was administered while clients observed deviant material. Most of this work targeted homosexual clients to change sexual preference, though evidence finds these types of aversion therapies ineffective in changing sexual behaviours/interests in the long term (Cantor, 2018).

Penile plethysmography (PPG) emerged in the late 1950s (see Chapter 3 regarding phallometry's use in assessment) and was used to measure the effects of behaviour modification treatment. The assumption of treatment was that through abstinence or a reduction in a behaviour, eventually changes in sexual interest and preferences would occur (McGuire, Carlisle, & Young, 1964) and could be observed through PPG. While PPG remains a popular and effective measurement tool, the literature highlights issues regarding lack of standardisation, the problem of participants faking responses, and ethical concerns regarding the subject of the stimuli and its use on adolescents (Coric et al., 2005).

Marshall and Laws (2003) detail two significant changes in offender treatment post 1970 – the use of cognitive processes to support behavioural change and greater clarity of treatment programmes. Cognitive psychology also began to play a role in the treatment of people convicted of sexual offending (Kazdin, 1978; Neisser, 1976). Indeed, by focussing on cognitive processes such as memory, beliefs, and thoughts, the field of cognitive behavioural therapy emerged. Likewise, treatment programmes also started to focus on victim empathy and the self-esteem of the client. Marshall and Laws (2003) highlight the shift in which treatment focussed on meeting the needs of clients in more prosocial ways. Helping clients to improve social skills as well as tackle deviant sexual preferences became equally as important. Key thinkers in this area include Barlow (1974) and Marshall (1971).

The 1980s saw the emergence of the Relapse Prevention Model (Laws, 1989; Pithers, Marques, Gibat, & Marlatt, 1983). This treatment approach enabled clinicians and clients to focus on triggers and areas of risk that may help develop strategies by which clients could avoid or mitigate potential risks – the idea being that clients could live in the world amongst risk, but live offence free. Social learning theories (Bandura, 1978) provided further explanation of some inappropriate behaviours presented by clients with convictions for sexual offending.

More recent-day treatment programmes, as Marshall and Laws (2003) highlight, have developed a greater integrated theoretical explanation of sexual offending. Indeed, statutory led programmes began to expand treatment targets of clients that included "sexual preferences, sex education, empathy, social skills (including a greater emphasis on relationship skills), self-esteem, substance abuse, anger management, and, of course, relapse prevention" (Marshall & Laws, 2003, p. 102). The 1990s saw the greatest surge in treatment programmes, with a shift away from relapse prevention (Marshall & Laws, 2003) and towards a self-regulation model (Ward & Hudson, 2000). In addition, the criminal justice system faced significant criticism for failing offender rehabilitation and following a surge of activities, thus emerged a body of work known as 'what works.' This movement saw significant activity to empirically test the effectiveness of rehabilitation interventions and the impact on recidivism. For an account of the historical process of the what works movement, see McGuire (2003). This movement was broader than that of sexual offender treatment alone, as it aimed to address all offender behaviour interventions.

One of the most significant drivers of research during the 1990s was the intention to develop our understanding and application of the theoretical explanations of rehabilitation. These include strategies of clinicians' style and characteristics, as well as identifying which treatment targets need to be addressed. Some of the conditions found to aid successful treatment emerged from the works of Andrews and Bonta (1994) and their Risk-Need-Responsivity (RNR) approach, and the Good Lives Model (GLM), first developed by Ward and Stewart (2003). The RNR approach indicates that treatment should target empirically known factors related to recidivism (risk), that interventions should address the individual and unique needs of clients (needs), and that treatment should respond to individual learning styles and cultural context in which clients exist (responsivity). To strengthen and complement an RNR approach, the GLM enables clinicians to take a strengths-based approach by framing treatment in a way that helps clients to develop and build opportunity and capacity to achieve life goals, thereby reducing risk. In addition, for the two most recent decades, see public health approaches with particular focus on tertiary prevention programmes (Laws, 2000; McMahon, 2000), as well as those with greater attention to desistance related factors (Laws & Ward, 2011; Ward & Laws, 2010).

Current interventions

Offender behaviour programmes

One of the strategies used globally to reduce the risk of recidivism in those convicted of a sexual offence is sexual offender treatment programmes (SOTPs). In correctional services at least, SOTPs are arguably the most common primary intervention. While the effectiveness of such treatment appears encouraging, SOTPs in the field of what works generate considerable debate (Maguire, Grubin, Losel, & Raynor, 2010). Establishing the effectiveness of SOTPs is a thorny issue, with several methodological challenges. Schmucker and Lösel (2017) highlight how measuring the effectiveness of an intervention is complicated by at least five issues: a) Sexual offending is heterogenous; b) Offender typologies are varied; c) The causality of sexual offending is unclear; d) Treatment approaches vary; and e) The follow up period is lengthy and the generation of control groups present ethical/design issues. As a result of these issues, there are fewer evaluations of the effectiveness of SOTPs compared to more general offending programmes.

Historically, SOTPs have been mandatory for those who are convicted of a sexual offence, who acknowledge they committed the offence, and who meet other inclusion criteria. SOTPs are delivered in a prison or community context (usually a probation or health facility), usually on a weekly basis, over a set period. There are some treatment provisions where clients can access support or treatment outside of the criminal justice system on a voluntary basis. There is usually a fee for treatment, however, and it is likely more akin to one-to-one therapy rather than correctional services group treatment, although this is not always the case

(Eldridge & Findlater, 2009). Despite some operational differences, the components of SOTPs are similar across most geographical and organisational boundaries. In terms of these components, specific focus on programmes delivered across England and Wales will follow in the next section, along with a summary of what we know regarding their effectiveness.

Components of SOTPs

In the treatment of adult males convicted of sexual offending, SOTPs have been influenced by several important bodies of work. Certainly, the two dominant forces shaping and underpinning SOTPs include the work of Andrews and Bonta (2016), particularly their Risk-Need-Responsivity principles, and Ward and Stewart's (2003) Good Lives Model. Recently, the importance of promoting the desistance process in people with convictions by helping to develop social capital (Farmer, McAlinden, & Maruna, 2015) and integrated models of change that incorporate responses addressing bio-psycho-social causes of sexual offending that have since emerged (Carter & Mann, 2016) have begun to permeate treatment models. Aspects that help therapists deliver treatment effectively, such as motivational interviewing (Miller & Rollnick, 2002) and characteristics of therapists' style (Marshall, 2005), continue to inform what and how treatment should be delivered.

To provide an outline of SOTPs, focus on treatment administered by Her Majesty's Prison and Probation Service (HMPPS) across England and Wales features here. Accredited SOTPs have been delivered across the estate since the 1990s. These programmes included a higher intensity core programme, lower intensity rolling programme, and a follow on booster programme, delivered according to people's risk and need, as determined by the Risk Matrix 2000 risk classification (Völlm, Craissati, Grubin, & Skett, 2019). However, in light of emerging literature and evidence, in particular from the Mews, Di Bella, and Purver (2017) study, which suggested prison core SOTPs did not reduce sexual offending, a new suite of programmes was developed, implemented, and rolled out across the country in 2016 (Wilkinson & Powis, 2019) and SOTPs were replaced. Given that these changes affect only those correctional services that deliver SOTPs, individual therapists and other treatment providers offering treatment outside of the legal framework are not included in this discussion.

The new 2016–2017 roll out of programmes Horizon and Kaizen are conceivably evidenced informed, rather than evidenced based (McCartan, Hoggett, & Kemshall, 2018), and see inclusion into treatment for the first time in England and Wales of those who are maintaining their innocence or are not yet treatment ready. Treatment is delivered in group sessions (males only) and in a one-to-one format, and treatment is designed in such a way that a continuation of treatment can be maintained and provided both in prisons and in the community.

The Horizon programme is offered to those who present a medium (and above) risk, offering around 60 hours of treatment. Treatment targets are more broadly criminogenic factors (McCartan et al., 2018), such as offence supportive attitudes, problem solving, self-control, and intimacy. The programme incorporates aspects of healthy sexual functioning and helps clients develop their social capital. A 50-hour version of the Horizon programme is available for those convicted of an Internet-only sexual offence. This is only provided in the community, and not at the prison. The Kaizen programme, on the other hand, is targeted at people with high and very high risks and needs and delivers intensive treatment of over 160 hours. This programme targets specific sexual offending risk related factors such as offence supportive attitudes, offence related sexual interests, and grievance thinking. An additional Healthy Sexual programme of up to 30 (1–2 hour) sessions can also be provided if needed. To support group programme work, offender managers use a flexible toolkit called 'New Me MOT.' This provision supports the maintenance and ongoing application of new skills while living in the community and dealing with everyday challenges. Unlike previous SOTPs in which victim empathy and offence responsibility were key treatment targets, this new suite of treatments aims to develop new skills, foster the desistance process (Maruna & Mann, 2019), and support clients affected by their own childhood trauma (Williams & Carter, 2018).

As noted earlier, this new suite of programmes has been developed and informed by the what works movement, but at the time of writing, the programmes themselves are yet to face full evaluation. The extant literature, however, does provide insight and evidence to support their effectiveness. Indeed, several key meta-analyses find positive support for such offender behaviour treatment programmes. In terms of sexual offender behaviour programmes specifically, Hanson et al. (2002) combined 43 studies and found reduced sexual recidivism rates in those who engaged in treatment compared to those who did not (12.3% treated vs. 16.8% untreated). Likewise, meta-analysis by Lösel and Schmucker (2005; Schmucker & Lösel, 2015, 2017) also indicated that treated populations recidivated less than those untreated. In their 2005 review of 69 studies (including both biological and psychological interventions), significant reduction in recidivism was observed in the treated sample (11.1% treated vs. 17.5% untreated). The 2015 and 2017 studies, although utilising a smaller sample, including fewer biological studies due to a stricter inclusion criterion, still found a significant difference, with treated populations recidivating at a reduced rate compared to those without treatment (10.1% treated vs. 13.7% untreated).

Although not a meta-analysis, one large single study found negative effects for those engaging in treatment (Mews et al., 2017). The findings of this study have generated, in equal measure, international interest and concern. The study examined the recidivism rates of 15,781 men who had completed an SOTP core programme in prison in England and Wales between 2001 and 2012. They found, when compared to an untreated group of men matching 87 variables, that sexual recidivism rates for the treated group was greater than that of the untreated group (10% treated vs. 8% untreated). While these findings are highly significant and should not be overlooked, Gannon, Olver, Mallion, and James (2019) note that the single study nature of these findings, along with them only including prison treatment, mean they need to be included into a meta-analysis review first.

Thus, Gannon et al. (2019) carried out, arguably, the most comprehensive and extensive meta-analysis examining the effectiveness of violent treatment programmes to date, including data from the Mews et al. (2017) study. Gannon and colleagues included 68 sources (70 studies detailed) in their review, all of which examined the treatment of sexual, domestic, and general violence. Their examination reaches beyond our present interest in sexual violence treatment, but for the purpose of this chapter, we will focus only on the sexual offender treatment findings. Gannon and colleagues found support for previous meta-analysis findings in that there was a significant reduction in recidivism in the population who had completed a treatment programme, when compared to those who had not (9.5% treated vs. 14.1% untreated). Furthermore, Gannon and colleagues found that when a qualified psychologist was consistently present during the treatment process, recidivism was further reduced; group based treatment outperformed individual treatment, as did treatment programmes in which elements of behavioural modification were included; polygraph testing did not assist in the reduction of further offences; and programmes delivered in New Zealand, Australia, and Canada outperformed all other countries to a considerable extent.

While the findings of these meta-analyses are encouraging for SOTPs, it is worth noting that meta-analysis as a method is not without its limitations, and, of course, critics (Eysenck, 1995; Rosenthal & DiMatteo, 2001). Indeed, Schmucker and Lösel (2017) highlight methodological weaknesses in this approach indicating that many of the studies included in the review combined different offence types, included a range of treatment modalities, had small sample sizes, faced issues of attrition, had diverse follow-up periods, and were at times poorly controlled studies. Gannon et al. (2019) noted similar concerns with their approach but were able to control for the quality of individual studies and quality of recidivism variables, which they found had little impact on the recidivism reduction.

Pharmacology

There are at least three areas of problematic sexual thoughts or behaviours in which pharmacological options are a consideration. These include deviant sexual interest, hypersexual cognition, and hypersexual behaviour (Winder et al., 2019). In England and Wales, the piloting of the use of pharmacological treatment or the Medical Management of Sexual Arousal (MMSA) was first established between a partnership with HMPPS and NHS in 2007 (Winder et al., 2018). The prescription of medical interventions to manage future risk, as opposed to managing a client's health need, does, however, present challenges for health practitioners (Völlm et al., 2019), in particular the risk to health practitioners being perceived as managers of risk and somewhat responsible when prescription fails to prevent further offending. Apart from this one concern, the efficacy of MMSA in the reduction of reoffending remains unclear (Khan et al., 2015).

There are three classes of medication used in the prescription of MMSA, including antiandrogens (AAs), gonadotropin releasing hormone (GnRH) agonists, and selective serotonin reuptake inhibitors (SSRIs). AAs and GnRHs work by reducing testosterone or blocking/suppressing the effects of testosterone; this in turn aims to reduce the client's sex drive or frequency of sexual fantasy. SSRIs help with problems such as mood dysregulation, rumination, pre-occupation, and compulsion. For symptoms sexual in nature, they help reduce the frequency and intensity of fantasy, rumination, and compulsion to act and therefore serve as a mood stabiliser (Winder et al., 2019). A graded prescription strategy is usually adopted, with SSRIs being prescribed in the first instance, followed by testosterone lowering medication, if symptoms are not managed effectively by SSRIs. There are exceptions regarding when AAs or GnRHs may be prescribed in the first instance, for example in cases where sexual behaviours or drive is so distressing that the client is unable to function (Völlm et al., 2019). However, in all cases, treatment should include access to concurrent psychological intervention. As with all medication, there are risks and side effects for the client. In one review, Lewis, Grubin, Ross, and Das (2017) found GnRH caused adverse side effects in all studies included in the review. Most common were hot flushes, weight gain, problems gaining erections or pain with erections, reduced body hair, and depression. Less common side effects included asthenia, myalgia, nausea, blood pressure changes, increased liver markers, back pain, and a reduction in bone density. Also, effects on fertility were found, including reduced sperm count, motility, and morphology up to a period of 24 months post treatment.

In relation to the effectiveness of MMSAs, this area is somewhat debated. On the one hand, if a person's distress and impairment is reduced through prescribing of such medication, arguably the MMSA is effective. However, the aim of MMSAs is not only to help a client manage biological symptoms, but also to prevent further offending. The effectiveness of MMSAs in preventing reoffending is, however, unknown. This is due in part to a lack of research in this area, as well as methodological weakness. Where studies have been undertaken, poor design has resulted in findings not being included into meta-analysis or larger reviews. This problem is shown in a 2015 review of the literature where Khan and colleagues found only seven studies fitting their criteria for review, all of whom were over 20 years old. They aimed to examine cases where antilibidinal medications were used to prevent further sexual offending, and they required the study design to incorporate a comparison group (either the use of a placebo, or not included in treatment or given just standard treatment without medication). One of the studies examined the use of antipsychotic medication in the prevention of sexual offending, and the remaining six tested three testosterone suppressants (cyproterone acetate, ethinyl oestradiol, and medroxyprogesterone acetate). Authors were unable to carry out a meta-analysis due to the poor quality of evidence and heterogeneity of interventions, comparators, and research design. As such, the authors could not conclude the extent to which pharmacological interventions reduce sexual recidivism.

Following the work of Khan et al. (2015), Winder and colleagues have engaged in programmes of evaluation to examine this issue (Winder et al., 2019) and address the significant gap in our understanding and knowledge. In an examination of 127 men incarcerated for sexual offending and diagnosed with hypersexual disorder, Winder et al. (2018) examined the effects of SSRIs and AAs. They found their sample to experience reduced pre-occupation and sexual behaviours within one month of prescription, and a continued decrease in symptoms at three- and six-month intervals. The decrease in symptoms levelled out for those taking SSRIs, but the decline continued for those prescribed with AAs. While sexual hypersexual disorder symptoms were reduced in this sample, the MMSA is arguably effective in reducing symptoms. However, its effectiveness in reducing sexual reoffending is yet to be tested.

Conclusion

This chapter provided a summary and overview of both historical and current approaches used to treat and work with those convicted of sexual offending. It provided a synopsis of early (and rather dubious) treatment strategies, including aversion therapy and electric shock treatment, moving on to the more legitimate and contemporary treatment such as cognitive and relapse prevention approaches. To contextualise these interventions, this chapter included a short summary of approaches to treatment, such as the 'what works' movement, Risk-Need-Responsivity, and the Good Life Model. The chapter reported on the notion that current treatment approaches are primarily heavily influenced by medicalised models in which people with sexual convictions are 'treated' and have rehabilitation done 'to them.' They experience significant methodological challenges, for which researchers are yet to unify and develop agreed strategies of inquiry. A further problem with the current paradigm is the timing of such interventions – provision of treatment occurs post offence, and even then it is only available in certain criminal justice contexts and conditions. An ideological shift towards working with people with sexual preferences, interests, and behaviours is needed. The shift needs to occur so that people are prevented from harming others in the first place; arguably, treatment post hoc is too late. Positive criminological approaches might provide some direction and value, and are thus worthy of further exploration.

References

Andrews, D. A., & Bonta, J. (1994). *The psycholoqy of criminal conduct*. Cincinnati: Anderson Publishing Co.

Andrews, D. A., & Bonta, J. (2016). *The psychology of criminal conduct* (5th ed.). New York: Routledge.

Bandura, A. (1969). Social-learning theory of identificatory processes. In *Handbook of socialization theory and research* (pp. 213, 262). Chicago: Rand McNally.

Bandura, A. (1978). Social learning theory of aggression. *Journal of Communication, 28*(3), 12–29.

Barlow, D. H. (1974). The treatment of sexual deviation: Towards a comprehensive behavioral approach. In *Innovative treatment methods in psychopathology* (pp. 121–147). New York: Wiley-Blackwell.

Beech, A., Craig, L. A., & Browne, K. (2009). *Assessment and treatment of sex offenders: A handbook*. Chichester: John Wiley & Sons Ltd.

Cantor, J. M. (2018). Can pedophiles change? *Current Sexual Health Reports, 10*(4), 203–206.

Carter, A. J., & Mann, R. E. (2016). Organizing principles for an integrated model of change for the treatment of sexual offending. In D. P. Boer (Ed.), *The Wiley handbook on the theories, assessment and treatment of sexual offending* (pp. 359–381). West Sussex: Wiley-Blackwell.

Coric, V., Feuerstein, S., Fortunati, F., Southwick, S., Temporini, H., & Morgan, C. A. (2005). Assessing sex offenders. *Psychiatry MMC, 2*(11), 26–29.

Eldridge, H., & Findlater, D. (2009). A community residential treatment approach for sexual abusers: A description of the Lucy faithfull foundation's Wolvercote clinic and related projects. In *Assessment and treatment of sex offenders: A handbook* (pp. 349–366). West Sussex: Wiley-Blackwell.

Eysenck, H. (1995). Meta-analysis or best-evidence synthesis? *Journal of Evaluation in Clinical Practice, 1*(1), 29–36.

Farmer, M., McAlinden, A.-M., & Maruna, S. (2015). Understanding desistance from sexual offending: A thematic review of research findings. *Probation Journal, 62*(4), 320–335.

Gannon, T. A., Olver, M. E., Mallion, J. S., & James, M. (2019). Does specialized psychological treatment for offending reduce recidivism? A meta-analysis examining staff and program variables as predictors of treatment effectiveness. *Clinical Psychology Review, 73*, doi:10.1016/j.cpr.2019.101752

Guthrie, E. R. (1935). *Psychology of learning*. Oxford: Harper.

Hanson, R., Gordon, A., Harris, A., Marques, J., Murphy, W., Quinsey, V., & Setc, M. (2002). First report of the collaborative outcome data project on the effectiveness of psychological treatment for sex offenders. *Sexual Abuse: A Journal of Research and Treatment, 14*(2), 169–194.

Kazdin, A. E. (1978). *History of behavior modification: Experimental foundations of contemporary research*. Baltimore: University Park Press.

Khan, O., Ferriter, M., Huband, N., Powney, M. J., Dennis, J. A., & Duggan, C. (2015). Pharmacological interventions for those who have sexually offended or are at risk of offending. *Cochrane Database of Systematic Reviews, 2*.

Kinsey, A. C., Pomeroy, W. B., Martin, C. E., & Sloan, S. (1948). *Sexual behavior in the human male* (vol. 1). Philadelphia, PA: Saunders.

Laws, D. (1989). *Relapse prevention with sex offenders*. New York: Guilford Press.

Laws, D. R. (2000). Sexual offending as a public health problem: A North American perspective. *Journal of Sexual Aggression, 5*(1), 30–44.

Laws, D. R., & Marshall, W. L. (2003). A brief history of behavioral and cognitive behavioral approaches to sexual offenders: Part 1. Early developments. *Sexual Abuse, 15*(2), 75–92.

Laws, D. R., & Ward, T. (2011). *Desistance from sex offending: Alternatives to throwing away the keys*. New York: Guilford Press.

Lewis, A., Grubin, D., Ross, C. C., & Das, M. (2017). Gonadotrophin-releasing hormone agonist treatment for sexual offenders: A systematic review. *Journal of Psychopharmacology, 31*(10), 1281–1293.

Lösel, F., & Schmucker, M. (2005). The effectiveness of treatment for sexual offenders: A comprehensive meta-analysis. *Journal of Experimental Criminology, 1*(1), 117–146.

Maguire, M., Grubin, D., Losel, F., & Raynor, P. (2010). "What works" and the correctional services accreditation panel: Taking stock from an inside perspective. *Criminology and Criminal Justice, 10*(1), 37.

Marshall, W. L. (1971). A combined treatment method for certain sexual deviations. *Behaviour Research and Therapy*, *9*(3), 293–294.

Marshall, W. L. (1996). The sexual offender: Monster, victim, or everyman? *Sexual Abuse: A Journal of Research and Treatment*, *8*(4), 317–335.

Marshall, W. L. (2005). Therapist style in sexual offender treatment: Influence on indices of change. *Sexual Abuse*, *17*(2), 109–116.

Marshall, W. L., & Laws, D. R. (2003). A brief history of behavioral and cognitive behavioral approaches to sexual offender treatment: Part 2. The modern era. *Sexual Abuse*, *15*(2), 93–120.

Marshall, W. L., Marshall, L. E., Serran, G. A., & O'Brien, M. D. (2011). *Rehabilitating sexual offenders: A strength-based approach*. Washington, DC: American Psychological Association.

Maruna, S., & Mann, R. (2019). Reconciling "Desistance" and "What Works." *HM Inspectorate of Probation Academic Insights 2019/1*. Retrieved from www.justiceinspectorates.gov.uk/hmiprobation/wp-content/uploads/sites/5/2019/02/Academic-Insights-Maruna-and-Mann-Feb-19-final.pdf

McCartan, K., Hoggett, J., & Kemshall, H. (2018). Risk assessment and management of individual's convicted of a sexual offence in the UK. *Sex Offender Treatment*, *13*(1–2), 1–8.

McGuire, R. J. (2003). *Offender rehabilitation and treatment: Effective programmes and policies to reduce re-offending*. West Sussex: John Wiley & Sons.

McGuire, R. J., Carlisle, J. M. U., & Young, B. G. (1964). Sexual deviations as conditioned behaviour: A hypothesis. *Behaviour Research and Therapy*, *2*(2–4), 185–190.

McMahon, P. M. (2000). The public health approach to the prevention of sexual violence. *Sexual Abuse: A Journal of Research and Treatment*, *12*(1), 27–36.

Mews, A., Di Bella, L., & Purver, M. (2017). *Impact evaluation of the prison-based core sex offender treatment program*. London. Retrieved from https://assets.publishing.service.gov.uk/government/uploads/system/uploads/attachment_data/file/623876/sotp-report-web-.pdf

Miller, W., & Rollnick, S. (2002). *Motivational interviewing: Preparing people for change Guilford* (2nd ed.). New York: Guilford Press.

Neisser, U. (1976). *Cognition and reality: Principles and implications of cognitive psychology*. New York: WH Freeman, Times Books, Henry Holt & Co.

Pithers, W. D., Marques, J. K., Gibat, C. C., & Marlatt, G. A. (1983). Relapse prevention with sexual aggressives: A self-control model of treatment and maintenance of change. *The sexual aggressor: Current perspectives on treatment* (pp. 214–239). New York: Van Nostrand Reinhold.

Rosenthal, R., & DiMatteo, M. (2001). Meta-analysis: Recent developments in quantiative methods for literautre reviews. *Annual Review Psychology*, *52*, 59–82.

Schmucker, M., & Lösel, F. (2015). The effects of sexual offender treatment on recidivism: An international meta-analysis of sound quality evaluations. *Journal of Experimental Criminology*, *11*(4), 597–630.

Schmucker, M., & Lösel, F. (2017). Sexual offender treatment for reducing recidivism among convicted sex offenders: A systematic review and meta-analysis. *Campbell Systematic Reviews*, *13*(1), 1–75.

Skinner, B. F. (1938). *The behaviour of organisms*. Nueva York: Appleton-Century-Crofts.

Skinner, B. F. (1963). Operant behavior. *American Psychologist*, *18*(8), 503–515.

Tolman, E. (1932). *Purposive behavior in animals and men*. Oxford: Appleton-Century.

Völlm, B., Craissati, J., Grubin, D., & Skett, S. (2019). Learning from research: Adapting interventions for sexual offending to improve outcomes. *Criminal Behaviour and Mental Health, 29*(4), 227–238.

Ward, T., & Hudson, S. M. (2000). A self-regulation model of relapse prevention. In *Remaking relapse prevention with sex offenders: A sourcebook* (pp. 79–101). Thousand Oaks, CA: Sage.

Ward, T., & Laws, D. R. (2010). Desistance from sex offending: Motivating change, enriching practice. *International Journal of Forensic Mental Health, 9*(1), 11–23.

Ward, T., & Stewart, C. A. (2003). The treatment of sex offenders: Risk management and good lives. *Professional Psychology: Research and Practice, 34*(4), 353–360.

Wilcox, D., Garrett, T., & Harkins, L. (2015). *Sex offender treatment: A case study approach to issues and interventions*. Chichester, West Sussex: Wiley-Blackwell.

Wilkinson, K., & Powis, B. (2019). *A process study of the horizon programme*. Retrieved from https://assets.publishing.service.gov.uk/government/uploads/system/uploads/attachment_data/file/769540/process-study-horizon-programme.pdf

Williams, F., & Carter, A. J. (2018). Engaging with forensic populations: A biologically informed approach. In A. R. Beech, A. J. Carter, R. E. Mann & P. Rotshtein (Eds.), *The Wiley Blackwell handbook of forensic neuroscience* (vol. 1, pp. 575–599). West Sussex: John Wiley & Sons.

Winder, B., Fedoroff, J. P., Grubin, D., Klapilová, K., Kamenskov, M., Tucker, D., . . . Vvedensky, G. E. (2019). The pharmacologic treatment of problematic sexual interests, paraphilic disorders, and sexual preoccupation in adult men who have committed a sexual offence. *International Review of Psychiatry, 31*(2), 159–168.

Winder, B., Lievesley, R., Elliott, H., Hocken, K., Faulkner, J., Norman, C., & Kaul, A. (2018). Evaluation of the use of pharmacological treatment with prisoners experiencing high levels of hypersexual disorder. *The Journal of Forensic Psychiatry & Psychology, 29*(1), 53–71.

5 Prevention strategies of sexual harm

Prevention approaches are categorised and explained on three levels: primary, secondary, and tertiary (McMahon, 2000). Primary prevention aims to prevent violence from occurring in the first place; approaches tend to be universal, targeting broad and general populations. Secondary approaches work with groups or individuals who present with particular risk factors or characteristics that might place them at increased risk of victimising others or being vulnerable to victimisation themselves. The tertiary approach adopts strategies for perpetrators or victims already known to the criminal justice or health and care systems; prevention activities therefore centre on stopping violence from re-occurring, rather than preventing it from occurring in the first place.

While a considerable amount of work has begun evaluating and implementing prevention strategies, the extent to which these strategies are effective in terms of eradicating sexual harm is unclear. Starfield, Hyde, Gérvas, and Heath (2008) detail some of the significant drifts in policy, including a preoccupation with identifying and addressing independent risk factors, a failure to consider the client's perspective, a failure to set priorities that address the inequalities in populations, addressing and improving health in general rather than focussing on specific elements in people's lives, and measuring the performance in practitioners that are easily measurable but failing to measures life improvements (Ataguba & Mooney, 2010; Starfield et al., 2008).

Considering these issues, it is perhaps unsurprising to note that our understanding of the effectiveness of sexual harm prevention interventions is, at best, patchy. We briefly outline some of the current prevention strategies aimed to tackle sexual abuse and this chapter is thus divided into the three prevention approaches: primary, secondary, and tertiary.

Primary prevention

Primary prevention strategies, in the context of sexual violence, aim to prevent violence and harm from occurring in the first place. True primary prevention strategies ought not to target victims or harm reduction, as at that stage, the crime has been committed. Instead, its aim is to target potential perpetrators of sexual violence and interference before they offend (Rothman, 2016). The primary prevention literature provides many examples of the criticisms detailed by Starfield et al. (2008) in that much of the work focusses on single factor risks and limited empirical evidence demonstrating effectiveness and changes following the implementation of a programme. DeGue et al. (2014) note how literature reviews of prevention programmes primarily tend to simply document and describe the programmes on offer. However, in their systematic review of 140 primary prevention strategies, DeGue and colleagues critiqued the methodological rigour of prevention programmes, finding only three deemed methodologically sound and able to demonstrate rigour and thus included into their review. These three studies were *Safe Dates* (Foshee et al., 2004); *Shifting Boundaries* (Taylor, Stein, Mumford, & Woods, 2013); and the *1994 Violence against Women Act Funding* (Boba & Lilley, 2009). Each study reported behavioural outcomes in terms of a change in sexual violence. The remaining 137 studies, however, failed in differing degrees to demonstrate enough rigour to be included in the review.

While this review is helpful in providing us with an overview of which primary prevention programmes are effective, the studies reviewed highlight the criticism raised by Starfield et al. (2008). Each of the three programmes, on their own, work to tackle very specific elements of sexual violence and in a particular context, for example dating violence, sexual harassment, and rates of rape. The *Safe Dates* prevention programme was curriculum focussed and delivered in schools to children in the eighth and ninth grade in the US. Ten sessions focussed on aspects such as the consequences of dating violence, conflict management, and gender stereotypes. Researchers followed students over four years and found reductions in dating sexual violence. Likewise, the *Shifting Boundaries* intervention also worked in schools, with sixth and seventh grade students, who were followed up at a six-month point. This intervention involved more environmental and awareness raising tactics, and so included activities such as building based restraining orders, poster campaigns, and hot-spot mapping. This intervention took place over a six- to ten-week period, after which researchers found a reduction in sexual harassment and peer sexual violence. In the final study found to be effective by DeGue et al. (2014), the *1994 Violence against Women Act Funding*, the intervention was a funding stream issued by the US Department of Justice to provide grants to programmes aimed to improve enforcement, victim advocacy, and state level capacity between the years of 1997 and 2002. Reports from police areas found reductions in annual rape rates in areas where funding had been allocated.

The Violence Prevention Information System (Violence studies, 2019), a collation of internationally published scientific data on all aspects of interpersonal violence, found only 22 'effective' primary prevention interventions seeking to prevent sexual violence (for a discussion on the methodological approach used to selecting studies for inclusion in the repository, see Butler et al. (2017)). These 22 primary prevention studies are divided into two categories: communication and relationship skills training (of which there are two studies) and rape-awareness and knowledge school programmes (of which there are 20). For the communication and relationship skills training category, only one systematic review found gender-transformative interventions effective. These interventions aim to move the social norms of masculinity to a more gender equitable position. Such interventions worked with heterosexually active men and were found to serve as a protective factor against partner violence and reduce the spread of STI/HIV infections (Dworkin, Treves-Kagan, & Lippman, 2013). In a meta-analysis (categorised under the rape-awareness and knowledge school programmes), Flores and Hartlaub (1998) found that programmes that focus on human sexuality and were delivered in workshops or as video interventions appeared to be successful at reducing rape myth acceptance. However, as with DeGue et al's. (2014) systematic review, it is not clear if these interventions have any long-term effects on changing behaviours. Indeed, in one of the meta-analysis of the rape education programme, Brecklin and Forde (2001) found that attitudinal change was short term and even declined over time.

In their paper on preventing intimate partner violence from a primary prevention perspective, Harvey, Garcia-Moreno, and Butchart (2007) draw on an ecological model (Krug, Mercy, Dahlberg, & Zwi, 2002) to understand intimate partner sexual violence.

An ecological model of violence (see Figure 5.1) suggests that there are both individual and societal factors relating to a person's behaviour; thus when

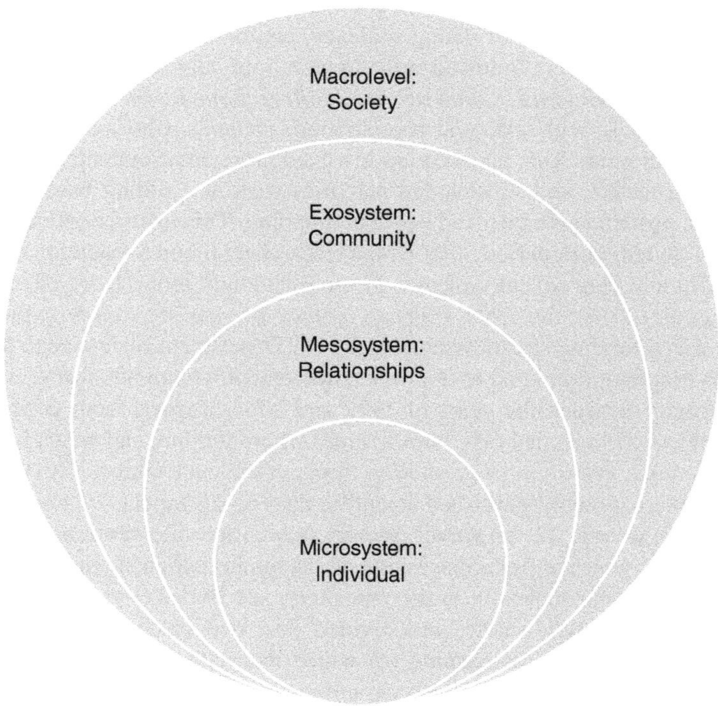

Figure 5.1 Ecological model of violence

targeting a universal population, a multilevel approach is required. The model postulates that for us to understand and help prevent sexual abuse, all ecological factors need to be considered and addressed. The first level in the model is that of the microsystem and individual. These include the genetic, historical, and educational factors within the person; second are the mesosystem factors, which include the nature of intimate and close relationships both past and present; the third detail exosystem factors, which include the types of relationships outside of an intimate relationship, such as work colleagues, school friends, and wider community friendships; and finally the macro level or societal factor that refers to the messages and norms presented throughout society in which violence is either supported or condoned.

In 2012, the UK government provided some guidance for policy makers and commissioners to use when developing strategies to tackle violence (Bellis, Hughes, Perkins, & Bennett, 2012). To a great extent, the report recognises the need for a more ecological approach to violence by recognising a broader range of types of violence, such as sexual violence, youth violence, elder abuse, violence against health service staff, intimate partner violence, and so on. The paper proposes a public health approach and from a primary prevention perspective call for decision makers to consider the following types of programmes: parenting programmes that help support families including home visits by nurse practitioners, developing life skills in children and young people through bullying prevention programmes, and academic enrichment programmes and Sure Start Children's Centres for pre-school children and their families. The UK government also set out to work with high risk youths and gangs through therapies, family interventions, and mentoring programmes. They also sought to reduce the availability of alcohol through controlling of sales and prices and deliver community interventions, including environmental re-designs of areas at risk of violence. Finally, they aim to change social norms that support violence through media campaigns and legislation to demonstrate to people that violence is unacceptable. While this report offers a comprehensive example of what the WHO would indicate as an effective ecological approach to prevent violence and sexual violence, this is all it does. At the time of writing, it is unclear if commissioners have adopted any of the interventions outlined in the report, let alone measured what effect these might have had on reducing sexual violence.

Even with what appears to be government support of a strategy that adopts a multi-layered, ecological response to sexual violence, very few initiatives have emerged. Instead, single factor interventions are more common, and while these might be useful to the individual, they only address one element of sexual violence. We know that numerous theories, both single and multi-factorial, explain sexually harmful behaviour (as outlined in Chapter 2). Primary prevention strategies are therefore also required to be multi-factorial and ecological in their design. Focussing only on the identification of risk factors is no longer useful. Nation et al. (2003) reviewed prevention interventions and found nine common principles required for any prevention programme to be successful in their effectiveness. Each of these nine principles are listed and briefly detailed in Table 5.1.

Table 5.1 Characteristics of effective prevention programmes

Principle related to effective prevention programmes	*Description*
Comprehensive	This characteristic relates to the idea that interventions are delivered in a multi-layered manner. In addition to more than one programme intervention being delivered to prevent a behaviour, these are also best delivered in a number of settings and contexts.
Varied teaching methods	To support changing behaviour, teaching methods must vary to meet the needs of those receiving the intervention. As such, skills practice, knowledge development, discussion, hands on experience, etc., must be adopted.
Sufficient dosage	The intensity of the intervention dosage must be measured in both quality and quantity of contact hours. Where need is greater, a higher dosage of treatment is needed.
Theory driven	This characteristic highlights the need for scientific justification for the intervention, rather than anecdotal evidence. Theories that explain both aetiology and the mechanism of intervention were the most successful.
Positive relationships	In child interventions, the quality of the relationships between the parent or caregiver was essential. Fostering a strong positive relationship alongside the intervention or as part of it was strongly related to positive outcomes.
Appropriately timed	Timing is critical in that programmes that were designed to capitalise on specific developmental points in a child's life were most successful. The age and development point of the child must be considered, and materials tailored accordingly.
Socio-culturally relevant	Programmes must be culturally, religiously, and socially relevant to communities. A tailoring of interventions is therefore required. For more unique communities, a further bespoke model must be developed to meet the needs of individuals within communities.
Outcome evaluation	Interventions with strong evaluation strategies are the most effective. This is because they work towards robust evidence-based models and engage in a process of review and re-development.
Well-trained staff	Interventions are most effective when staff are well trained, sensitive, and competent at delivering the material. Staff ought to be well supported and be provided supervision also.

Missing from this list of characteristics is the need to focus interventions and strategies on universal elements of prevention. An ecological approach adopts a wider perspective on the issue and requires us to consider the needs of the individual at the centre of wider ecosystem (McKenzie, 1924). While the individual at the centre of the ecosystem must be considered, that is factors such as the person's personality, personal history, attitude towards change and so on must be looked at, as they are critical for the success of any intervention programme, the need to extend beyond the individual is important too. As humans we do not function in isolation. Therefore, focussing interventions on individuals can only limit the opportunity to make a real and long-lasting change. We survive within families, friendships, communities, and wider cultures. Prevention strategies recognise and include these structures. Thus, just as the microsystem requires attention, so too do the meso, eco, and macro levels. For example, when considering primary approaches to prevention that are ecological in nature, it is important to understand causal factors that might explain why people abuse others. When attempting to understand why people sexually abuse women and children, feminist perspectives provide an excellent base to understand the individual within an ecological framework (Purvis & Ward, 2006). This is because the individual perspective is as important as the cultural and community context. Sexual abuse is symptomatic of wider inequalities in our society. Perpetrators of sexual abuse, in the main, perpetrate violence to exert power and control over another person. This sense of entitlement is fuelled, in part, by patriarchal and misogynistic cultures and social structures within our culture. Prevention strategies ought to tackle these inequalities not by focussing on the individual but on the inequalities experienced by women, children, and those marginalised in society, including those from non-white communities, people with disabilities, and LGBT communities.

Secondary prevention

Secondary prevention approaches aim to work with groups or individuals who present particular risk factors or characteristics that are known to place them at an increased risk of both victimising others and being vulnerable to victimisation themselves. Factors known to be related to sexual violence are complex; they vary at different points in the life course and at different levels throughout society, within smaller communities, in intimate relationships, and within the individual. Thus, being able to identify and target specific groups at specific points in time is an enormous task.

To catalogue known risk factors of violence (including sexual abuse and violence), the UK Department of Health produced a report to support policy makers and providers of prevention interventions by providing a summary of known risk factors. For the full report see Bellis et al. (2012). But for a list of examples of factors see Table 5.2.

In comparison to programmes targeting primary and tertiary levels, secondary prevention interventions aimed at tackling those vulnerable to sexual abuse are relatively limited, particularly in terms of programmes available and evaluations of effectiveness (McCartan, Merdian, Perkins, & Kettleborough, 2017). This was found in our brief review of the literature in preparation for this chapter. Only a small number of studies detailing and evaluating secondary interventions over the last two decades were found, and are briefly summarised here.

Table 5.2 Risk factors for violence

Risk group	*Examples of risk factors*
Vulnerable to child abuse	• Unplanned pregnancy • Single parent household • Young, poor parents • Socially isolated parents • Parental alcohol consumption and drug use • Domestic violence in the home • Child disability or illness • Child behavioural problems
Vulnerable to perpetrate violence in adulthood	• Emotional, physical, or sexual abuse • Emotional or physical neglect • Violence against household members • Living with household members who were substance abusers, mentally ill, suicidal, or imprisoned • Having one or no parents, or experiencing parental separation or divorce • Bullying, or exposure to community or collective violence
Vulnerable to violence as a youth	• Male gender • Neglect and abuse in childhood • Personality traits, e.g. hyperactivity/conduct disorder • Poor family functioning • Domestic violence in the home • Delinquent peers and gang involvement • Living in a high crime area • Alcohol consumption • Social inequality
Vulnerable to intimate partner and sexual violence	• Female gender • Younger age • Lower household income • Being single, co-habiting, separated, or divorced • Living in areas of high physical disorder • Alcohol consumption (perpetrators and victims) • Controlling and jealous partner • Childhood abuse (perpetrators and victims) • Gender inequality • Cultural norms tolerant of violence
Vulnerable to elder abuse	• High levels of dependence • Mental and cognitive disorders • Carer alcohol consumption and drug use • Carer financial problems • Carer burnout • Social isolation • Lack of social support • Age discrimination

In the US as part of an education programme, young males between the ages of 11 and 14 received education awareness training by trained coaches in schools (Abebe et al., 2017). The programme, called the Adolescent Relationship Abuse and Sexual Violence Prevention programme, was evaluated using a randomised control trial (RCT) with *n*=973 participants. It was found to be effective in reducing the number of sexual violence incidences, increasing students' knowledge, and increasing bystander responses. Another educational programme known as Stewards of Children considered the change in reporting rates in adults of children they perceived to be at risk of harm (Letourneau, Nietert, & Rheingold, 2016). While the study did not evaluate changes in abusive behaviour, they did observe an increase in the rates of reporting by adults of suspected child abuse. Thus, the assumption follows that rates of harm were reduced by statutory services acting upon allegations made.

In their review of the literature of prevention interventions in Aboriginal communities, Shea, Nahwegahbow, and Andersson (2010) found support for the Ngati Porou Community Injury Prevention Project, where education sessions, information packs, and training were given to 'at risk' families. They found both a reduction of violence and an increased awareness of what constitutes violent behaviours in the family following the intervention. However, in two RCT studies, a) the Hawaii Healthy Start Programme in which families at risk received targeted home visits in which emotional support, parenting training, and education was provided, and b) Healthy Families Alaska, which promotes positive parenting, child health, and development advice, authors found they did not reduce either sexual or generalised violence or harm. They did find support for the First Nations youth programme in which adolescents with a history of maltreatment were provided education on dating violence, dealing with conflict, healthy relationship skills, and communication skills. This programme targeted 14- to 16-year-olds and through an RCT, a reduction in violence and an increase in emotional security was found.

Finally, in one US programme that delivered cognitive behavioural therapy to victims of interpersonal violence with post-traumatic stress disorder (PTSD), Iverson et al. (2011) found violence (after six months of treatment) was reduced. This was found to be through empowering women and reducing their symptoms of depression and PTSD. Women who completed the treatment self-reported fewer violent assaults than those who did not.

Although limited in numbers, there are some examples of prevention programmes targeting potential sexual abusers before they abuse, that is people living with sexually deviant interests. This population, if we assume they have never offended, will not be known to authorities. Thus, making an intervention available and accessible to them without identifying them is essential. A German campaign that began in 2005, the Prevention Project Dunkelfeld (PPD), delivered a media campaign targeting those with sexual interests in children, offering them a confidential and anonymous telephone help line and treatment (Beier, Ahlers et al., 2009). This unique prevention intervention specifically targeted, through an active high-profile media campaign, those who self-identify as being sexually attracted to children and are at risk of causing harm. Unique to this project is the fact that it targeted and successfully engaged people already known to correctional services but also those who had never been convicted of an offence, yet self-identified as being at risk of harmful behaviour (Beier, Ahlers, et al., 2009). PPD offers a range of treatment interventions including group and one-to-one work. This includes cognitive behavioural therapy, built on the underlying principles of relapse prevention, self-regulation, and the Good Lives Model. In addition to group work, interventions also include pharmacological strategies. While the key aim of the PPD is to prevent sexual harm, other treatment targets include motivating change, self-monitoring, helping clients deal with sexualised coping strategies, sexual functioning, attachments, challenging attitudes that support abuse, empathy, and relapse prevention. Treatment includes goal setting with the aim of supporting clients to live meaningful lives, free from the desire to sexually offend. A study that followed 69 participants who had engaged in PPD for 12 months found encouraging post-treatment outcomes, including "reduced loneliness, reduced emotion orientated coping, fewer emotional victim empathy deficits, fewer CSA supportive attitudes, fewer coping self-efficacy deficits and less sexual preoccupation" (Beier et al., 2015, p. 9). A similar intervention was delivered in the UK and Ireland called Stop it Now!, offering confidential advice and support to those at risk of perpetrating sexual abuse. Reviews of both campaigns report positive outcomes with users of the service, who self-report changes in their behaviour in that either at the point of crisis they chose not to offend, or in the more longer term, they felt more in control of their lives and were able to better cope with difficult situations (Beier, Neutze, et al., 2009; Brown et al., 2014).

Tertiary prevention

Tertiary prevention in the field of sexual offender focussed interventions is probably the most resourced and researched area of the public health model. Tertiary prevention aims to target specific individuals with known criminogenic factors specifically related to the likelihood of future sexual harm. This includes those already convicted of sexual offending. While much is known of such prevention strategies, very little is understood of those who may present a risk but have not yet entered the criminal justice system. A brief summary of tertiary prevention programme for those already convicted is provided here and includes the role of registration, notification, pharmacology, offender behaviour programmes, and initiatives such as Circles of Support and Accountability (COSA).

Registry and notification

Most people convicted of a sexual offence in England and Wales are either given a community sentence or following a period of imprisonment are eventually released into the community. This group is primarily initially managed by the National Probation Service. Either within three days of release from prison or at the start of the community order, people are required to register at a police station.

Registry and notification require people to provide copies of personal documentation, such as passport details, National Insurance number, confirmation of current address, details of any other adults or children living at the address, and bank and credit card details. It is usual for registry and notification to take place every 12 months; if there is a change in the person's circumstances within this period, they have three days in which to notify the police of these changes (Guidance on Part 2 of the Sexual Offences Act, 2003, 2018).

Other requirements detailed by the Sexual Offences Act, 2003 may be more specific to an individuals' licence or probation order – the courts will determine these – but commonly they include restrictions on the use of the Internet, on travelling to particular geographical locations, on travelling outside of the UK, and on contact with a particular person. Likewise, there are requirements to take particular action, such as engaging in polygraph testing, informing the supervising officer of the start of new relationships, or notifying the police or supervising officer if they stay at another address for seven nights or more in the 12-month period. Failure to adhere to registration or notification requirements can result in the person being returned to prison or further orders being added to their current conditions.

Notifications and requirements are legislative requirements that aid the management of clients as well as serve to prevent further offending. The effectiveness of this strategy as prevention is, however, largely unknown. Instead, it serves more as an information source for law enforcers (Harris, Levenson, Lobanov-Rostovsky, & Walfield, 2018). It is argued that many unintended consequences to such requirements are experienced. As Levenson, Ackerman, Socia, and Harris (2015) note, there are requirements that prevent clients from living in certain areas, cause housing and homelessness issues. Likewise, people required to move to new areas often become displaced from family and friends and face isolation and loneliness (Levenson & Hern, 2007). With notification action from criminal justice professionals, family members of the convicted person can become targets for abuse and isolation from the local community (Levenson & Tewksbury, 2009). The result of the many barriers to reintegration may well elevate risk factors known to be related to sexual reoffending, and inadvertently place members of the public at an increased risk, rather than prevent further harm. Thus, neoliberal claims that registration and notification strategies prevent harm is yet to be empirically tested. Instead, these mechanisms appear to serve as mere administrative controls.

Pharmacology

The range of pharmacological treatment approaches used to treat people convicted of sexual offending vary from country to country and state to state. Pharmacological treatment strategies include the administration and use of hormonal and non-hormonal drugs to reduce sexual drive or sexual arousal in this population (Hill, Briken, Kraus, Strohm, & Berner, 2003). Treatments include drugs known as antiandrogens, such as Cyproterone acetate, that reduce testosterone (Lippi & van

Staden, 2017) and agents that stabilise mood, such as Fluoxetine and Paroxetine (Winder, Skett, Hocken, & Kaul, 2016). The effectiveness of these treatments are, however, unclear due to a limited number of studies as well as a range of negative side effects reported by those using these medications (Turner, Petermann, Harrison, Krueger, & Briken, 2017). To understand the scope and scale of the use of these pharmacological approaches, Turner et al. (2017) carried out a systematic review of the literature. They found between 10% and 15% of clients using this treatment reported a reduction in deviant sexual fantasy. As the legal framework and regulatory bodies supporting such treatment are either absent or lack clarity regarding the use of this treatment as such, ethical concerns emerge, such as patient consent, knowledge of likely side effects and risks, and the requirements to engage in treatment being voluntary. Despite this, several reviews suggest that pharmacological treatment is effective in helping to reduce sexual urges and preoccupations (Khan et al., 2015).

In the UK, a pilot trial of the use of pharmacological treatment, termed Medication to Manage Sexual Arousal (MMSA), began in 2007. In an evaluation of this implementation, Winder et al. (2018) examined 100 adult males using either antiandrogen or mood stabilising medications to reduce sexual preoccupation and hyper-sexual behaviour. Results demonstrated a reduction in both sexual preoccupation and hypersexual behaviour just one month after commencement of treatment. While these results are encouraging, more longitudinal research is certainly needed to examine recidivism rates and behaviours outside of the prison environment.

Behaviour programmes

Over the last three decades, cognitive behavioural offender behaviour programmes have developed. These programmes were discussed in the previous chapter, but we note them here once more in the context of tertiary prevention. Cognitive behavioural treatment requires clients to engage actively in programmes designed to help address deficits that contribute to offending behaviour. As such, clients engage in activities that aim to increase self-awareness, develop and learn new skills, and have an opportunity to practice skills in a safe learning environment (Brown, 2011). The principles of cognitive behavioural offender behaviour programmes have traditionally derived from Andrews and Bonta's (1994) Risk-Need-Responsivity (RNR) principles. The RNR requires treatment programmes to address the specific risk a person presents, by administering an appropriate 'treatment dosage.' The person's criminogenic needs must be met and that treatment must be delivered in such a way that an individual participant's learning and development needs are met.

Western correctional approaches to offender behaviour programmes have adopted an accreditation approach whereby offender treatment programmes adhere to what works principles (Cullen & Gilbert, 1982; Gendreau & Ross, 1983) to ensure that only effective and evidence-based treatment programmes are delivered. Accredited programmes therefore require a sound underlying theoretical base, a model of change that is empirically tested, and the application of the programme that ensures programme integrity (Brown, 2011).

Across England and Wales, a suite of interventions is available across prisons and community establishments for those convicted of sexual offending (Wilkinson & Powis, 2019). These include programmes designed specifically for those assessed as having a high risk of reoffending, those having committed Internet offences only, juveniles or females only, people with intellectual disabilities, people with personality disorders, and people who have been through the main treatment programmes but wish to maintain treatment gains. Most programmes are based on group work, but for specialist populations, such as women, treatment is likely to be delivered on a one-to-one basis. It is not our intention to review or provide an in-depth history of the development of these programmes. Please see Wilcox, Garrett, and Harkins (2015) for an excellent collection of chapters that highlight the challenges of correctional treatment programmes including some of the ethical, responsivity, and specialisation issues.

One of the recent changes in the theoretical underpinnings of accredited programmes has been the significant influence of the Good Lives Model (GLM) (Ward & Stewart, 2003). The GLM enables treatment providers and clients to build upon already existing capabilities and strengths, rather than focus on deficits and risks alone. This has enabled a more ethically sound and holistic approach to treatment. The GLM argues that as humans we all strive to achieve goals in life, such as inner peace, knowledge, agency, and meaningful relationships. Thus, practitioners assist clients to achieve goals by developing strategies and providing and facilitating participants with opportunities to achieve goals. Consequently, working towards a good life by default helps prevent people from offending by helping them to achieve life goals through appropriate and healthy means. The GLM therefore supports and complements the principles of the RNR model.

The primary goal of cognitive behavioural treatment programmes is to reduce recidivism, and thus prevent further offences from occurring. While secondary goals exist, for example helping clients to manage problematic emotions more effectively, the bottom line is that interventions must reduce recidivism. Our understanding of how effective cognitive behavioural treatment programmes are in reducing recidivism is an area of great debate (Gannon, Olver, Mallion, & James, 2019). Initial reviews, such as by Furby, Weinrott, and Blackshaw (1989), found no evidence that clinical treatment reduced the rates of further recidivism. However, they found almost all studies in their review to have methodological problems, making interpretation and appropriateness analysis difficult. In a later meta-analysis, Hanson, Bourgon, Helmus, and Hodgson (2009) found that when adhering strictly to rehabilitation principles, correctional treatment programmes were more effective for treated offenders than non-treated sexual offenders. Hanson et al. (2009) found that 19.2% of those who had not engaged in treatment went on to further offend, compared to 10.9% of the treated population.

In a more recent meta-analysis, Schmucker and Lösel (2015) found that recidivism rates for those who had engaged in treatment were less than those who did not. However, treatment was more effective for those treated in the community than those in prison. Importantly, those who were deemed as low risk showed no treatment effect at all. In a review of prison-based sexual offender treatment programmes in the UK, Mews, Di Bella, and Purver (2017) found that recidivism rates for untreated participants were significantly less than those who had engaged in treatment (10% treated vs. 8.0% untreated). Likewise, for those who went on to reoffend with noncontact sexual offences, recidivism rates again were unfavourable for those who had been through treatment, with 4.4% recidivism rates, compared to 2.9% recidivism rates for those who have not undergone treatment. In the most recent meta-analysis where 68 studies and 55,604 individuals who had sexually offended were included, Gannon et al. (2019) found recidivism in 13.4% of treated individuals compared to 19.4% across all sexual, domestic violence, and generalised violence programmes.

These mixed results understandably cause concern. Indeed, it is argued that the effectiveness of such programmes is quite poor. This is clearly unacceptable; Oberlader, Schmidt, and Banse (2018) summarise that future studies therefore need to include the use of random controlled trials, the ability to test theory and implementation across different treatment settings, and the need to broaden and agree with some consistency on what our understanding of effectiveness actually means.

Non-statutory interventions

Outside of statutory services there are very few tertiary prevention interventions. One intervention that has garnered interest and attention is Circles of Support and Accountability (COSA). The foundations of COSA, also known as Circles, are built upon the concept of restorative justice. COSA was founded in the early 1990s by a faith-based community in Canada in response to the release of a person deemed at high risk of reoffending but who had no social networks or support on release from prison (Hanvey, Wilson, & Philpot, 2011). The community actively sought to support and help reintegrate this person back into the community, with great success. In the early 2000s COSA became part of a community response/service in some areas across England and Wales. The aim of COSA and every Circle is to reduce reoffending by adhering to three key principles: a) Providing support to the core member by reducing loneliness and isolation, modelling prosocial relationships, and demonstrating humanity and care; b) Monitoring the core members through regular meetings and reviews, thus protecting the public and helping community safety; Circle members are obliged to inform statutory authorities of any concerns of an escalation of risk; and c) Helping maintain a life free from offending; volunteers help the core member to do this by holding him or her accountable for his or her behaviour, building a relationship of trust and helping him or her maintain any treatment goals already achieved (Saunders & Wilson, 2003).

The results of evaluation of COSA are encouraging, with research demonstrating a reduction in the core member's feelings of isolation and stigmatisation and with volunteers feeling that they are able to hold core members accountable (Thomas & Thompson, 2014). In relation to a reduction in reoffending recidivism rates in Canada during a 35-month follow-up period (average) of men who had engaged in a Circle, Wilson, Cortoni, and McWhinnie (2009) found an 83% reduction in sexual recidivism and a 73% reduction in all types of violent recidivism when compared to a matched comparison group. In a UK, in a study following the delivery of one COSA over four years whereby 14 core members had engaged in the intervention, Bates, Saunders, and Wilson (2007) found that not one core member had been reconvicted for a further sexual offence. Building on this small study, an evaluation of a further 25 core members living out in the community for more than 36 months was undertaken and it was found that only one core member had a further sexual conviction for a non-contact Internet offence (Bates, Macrae, Williams, & Webb, 2012). While still a further offence, authors of the study argue it nevertheless represents a decrease in offending as his previous contact sexual offending had involved three female children. While findings from these preliminary studies are encouraging, far more work is needed to fully evaluate this intervention. Indeed, research strategies need to include designs that are longitudinal and randomised control studies, as well as to extend examination beyond that of recidivism to include psychosocial changes as well (Clarke, Brown, & Völlm, 2017).

Conclusion

Preventing sexual abuse must be tackled using a global public health approach. As discussed in this chapter, our knowledge and understanding of each of the three levels of prevention is at best patchy. By implementing primary prevention interventions that tackle single risk factors and use mainly reductive approaches, it is unsurprising that the social, political, historical, and cultural issues linked to violence remain unaddressed. Likewise, secondary interventions are also limited. Very few interventions adopt the full range of ecological and multi-layered approaches ideally required to help those known to be at risk of perpetrating harm. While some exist, such as PPD and Stop it Now!, most focus on controlling and containing people at risk of harm. Finally, while criminal justice system (CJS) approaches such as offender behaviour programmes have begun to adopt more desistance focussed approaches, such programmes tend to operate within a policy and a CJS framework that is restrictive and punitive, minimising opportunities for those convicted of sexual offending to fully function within the community post-conviction. Without a significant shift in international policy whereby sexual abuse is viewed and tackled as a public and global issue in which all factors that underpin sexual abuse are addressed, it is unlikely that much headway will be made. Thus, we propose consideration of positive criminological principles be applied to the prevention of sexual abuse to correct a criminal justice response to sexual abuse, and connect with the broader social, cultural, and political structures in our society that continue to underpin this harmful behaviour.

References

Abebe, K. Z., Jones, K. A., Ciaravino, S., Ripper, L., Paglisotti, T., Morrow, S. E., . . . Miller, E. (2017). A cluster-randomized trial of a middle school gender violence prevention program: Design, rationale, and sample characteristics. *Contemporary Clinical Trials*, *62*, 11–20.

Andrews, D., & Bonta, J. (1994). *The psycholoqy of criminal conduct*. Cincinnati: Anderson Publishing Co.

Ataguba, J. E., & Mooney, G. (2010). Building on "the concept of prevention: A good idea gone astray?" *Journal of Epidemiology and Community Health*, *65*, 116–118.

Bates, A., Macrae, R., Williams, D., & Webb, C. (2012). Ever-increasing circles: A descriptive study of Hampshire and Thames valley circles of support and accountability 2002–09. *Journal of Sexual Aggression*, *18*(3), 355–373.

Bates, A., Saunders, R., & Wilson, C. (2007). Doing something about it: A follow-up study of sex offenders participating in Thames valley circles of support and accountability. *British Journal of Community Justice*, *5*(1), 19–42.

Beier, K. M., Ahlers, C. J., Goecker, D., Neutze, J., Mundt, I. A., Hupp, E., & Schaefer, G. A. (2009). Can pedophiles be reached for primary prevention of child sexual abuse? First results of the Berlin prevention project dunkelfeld (PPD). *The Journal of Forensic Psychiatry & Psychology*, *20*(6), 851–867.

Beier, K. M., Grundmann, D., Kuhle, L. F., Scherner, G., Konrad, A., & Amelung, T. (2015). The German dunkelfeld project: A pilot study to prevent child sexual abuse and the use of child abusive images. *The Journal of Sexual Medicine*, *12*(2), 529–542.

Beier, K. M., Neutze, J., Mundt, I. A., Ahlers, C. J., Goecker, D., Konrad, A., & Schaefer, G. A. (2009). Encouraging self-identified pedophiles and hebephiles to seek professional help: First results of the prevention project dunkelfeld (PPD). *Child Abuse & Neglect*, *33*(8), 545–549.

Bellis, M. A., Hughes, K., Perkins, C., & Bennett, A. (2012). *Protecting people promoting health: A public health approach to violence prevention for England*. London: Department of Health.

Boba, R., & Lilley, D. (2009). Violence against women act (VAWA) funding: A nationwide assessment of effects on rape and assault. *Violence Against Women*, *15*(2), 168–185.

Brecklin, L. R., & Forde, D. R. (2001). A meta-analysis of rape education programs [Meta-Analysis]. *Violence and Victims*, *16*(3), 303–321.

Brown, A., Jago, N., Kerr, J., McNaughton Nicholls, C., Paskell, C., & Webster, S. (2014). Call to keep children safe from sexual abuse: A study of the use and effects of the Stop it Now! UK and Ireland Helpline. *NatCen Social Research*. Retrieved from www.basw.co.uk/resources/call-keep-children-safe-sexual-abuse-study-use-and-effects-stop-it-now-uk-and-ireland

Brown, S. (2011). An introduction to sex offender treatment programmes and their risk reduction efficacy. In K. Harrison (Ed.), *Dangerousness, risk and the governance of serious sexual and violent offenders* (1st ed., pp. 81–104). Devon: Routledge.

Butler, N., Quigg, Z., Burrows, S., Butchart, A., Mikton, C., Hughes, K., & Bellis, M. (2017). *Violence info methodology*. Retrieved from http://apps.who.int/violence-info/Violence%20Info%20Methodology%20October%202017%20-%20b13deb6.pdf

Clarke, M., Brown, S., & Völlm, B. (2017). Circles of support and accountability for sex offenders: A systematic review of outcomes. *Sexual Abuse*, *29*(5), 446–478.

Cullen, T. F., & Gilbert, E. K. (1982). *Reaffirming rehabilitation*. Cincinnati, OH: Anderson.

DeGue, S., Valle, L. A., Holt, M. K., Massetti, G. M., Matjasko, J. L., & Tharp, A. T. (2014). A systematic review of primary prevention strategies for sexual violence perpetration. *Aggression and Violent Behavior*, *19*(4), 346–362.

Dworkin, S. L., Treves-Kagan, S., & Lippman, S. A. (2013). Gender-transformative interventions to reduce HIV risks and violence with heterosexually-active men: A review of the global evidence. *AIDS and Behavior*, *17*(9), 2845–2863.

Flores, S. A., & Hartlaub, M. G. (1998). Reducing rape-myth acceptance in male college students: A meta-analysis of intervention studies. *Journal of College Student Development*, *39*(5), 438–448.

Foshee, V. A., Bauman, K. E., Ennett, S. T., Linder, G. F., Benefield, T., & Suchindran, C. (2004). Assessing the long-term effects of the safe dates program and a booster in preventing and reducing adolescent dating violence victimization and perpetration. *American Journal of Public Health*, *94*(4), 619–624.

Furby, L., Weinrott, R. M., & Blackshaw, L. (1989). Sex offender recidivism: A review. *Psychological Bulletin*, *105*(1), 3–30.

Gannon, T. A., Olver, M. E., Mallion, J. S., & James, M. (2019). Does specialized psychological treatment for offending reduce recidivism? A meta-analysis examining staff and program variables as predictors of treatment effectiveness. *Clinical Psychology Review*, doi:10.1016/j.cpr.2019.101752.

Gendreau, P., & Ross, R. R. (1983). Correctional treatment: Some recommendations for effective intervention. *Juvenile and Family Court Journal*, *34*(4), 31–39.

Guidance on part 2 of the sexual offences act 2003. (2018). London. Retrieved from www.gov.uk/government/publications/guidance-on-part-2-of-the-sexual-offences-act-2003

Hanson, R. K., Bourgon, G., Helmus, L., & Hodgson, S. (2009). The principles of effective correctional treatment also apply to sexual offenders: a meta-analysis. *Criminal Justice and Behavior*, *36*(9), 865–891.

Hanvey, S., Wilson, C., & Philpot, T. (2011). *A community-based approach to the reduction of sexual reoffending: Circles of support and accountability*. London: Jessica Kingsley Publishers.

Harris, A. J., Levenson, J. S., Lobanov-Rostovsky, C., & Walfield, S. M. (2018). Law enforcement perspectives on sex offender registration and notification: Effectiveness, challenges, and policy priorities. *Criminal Justice Policy Review*, *29*(4), 391–420.

Harvey, A., Garcia-Moreno, C., & Butchart, A. (2007). Primary prevention of intimate-partner violence and sexual violence: Background paper for WHO expert meeting May 2–3, 2007. *World Health Organisation*. Retrieved from www.who.int/violence_injury_prevention/publications/violence/IPV-SV.pdf?ua=1

Hill, A., Briken, P., Kraus, C., Strohm, K., & Berner, W. (2003). Differential pharmacological treatment of paraphilias and sex offenders. *International Journal of Offender Therapy and Comparative Criminology*, *47*(4), 407–421.

Iverson, K. M., Gradus, J. L., Resick, P. A., Suvak, M. K., Smith, K. F., & Monson, C. M. (2011). Cognitive-behavioral therapy for PTSD and depression symptoms reduces risk for future intimate partner violence among interpersonal trauma survivors. *Journal of Consulting and Clinical Psychology*, *79*(2), 193–202. doi:10.1037/a0022512

Khan, O., Ferriter, M., Huband, N., Powney, M. J., Dennis, J. A., & Duggan, C. (2015). Pharmacological interventions for those who have sexually offended or are at risk of offending. *Cochrane Database of Systematic Reviews*, *2*.

Krug, E. G., Mercy, J. A., Dahlberg, L. L., & Zwi, A. B. (2002). The world report on violence and health. *The Lancet*, *360*(9339), 1083–1088.

Letourneau, E. J., Nietert, P. J., & Rheingold, A. A. (2016). Initial assessment of stewards of children program effects on child sexual abuse reporting rates in selected South Carolina counties. *Child Maltreatment*, *21*(1), 74–79.

Levenson, J. S., Ackerman, A. R., Socia, K. M., & Harris, A. J. (2015). Where for art thou? Transient sex offenders and residence restrictions. *Criminal Justice Policy Review*, *26*(4), 319–344.

Levenson, J. S., & Hern, A. L. (2007). Sex offender residence restrictions: Unintended consequences and community reentry. *Justice Research and Policy*, *9*(1), 59–74.

Levenson, J. S., & Tewksbury, R. (2009). Collateral damage: Family members of registered sex offenders. *American Journal of Criminal Justice*, *34*(1), 54–68.

Lippi, G., & van Staden, P. J. (2017). The use of cyproterone acetate in a forensic psychiatric cohort of male sex offenders and its associations with sexual activity and sexual functioning. *South African Journal of Psychiatry*, *23*(1).

McCartan, K. F., Merdian, H. L., Perkins, D. E., & Kettleborough, D. (2017). Ethics and issues of secondary prevention efforts in child sexual abuse. *International Journal of Offender Therapy and Comparative Criminology*, 1–19.

McKenzie, R. D. (1924). The ecological approach to the study of the human community. *American Journal of Sociology*, *30*(3), 287–301.

McMahon, P. M. (2000). The public health approach to the prevention of sexual violence. *Sexual Abuse*, *12*(1), 27–36.

Mews, A., Di Bella, L., & Purver, M. (2017). *Impact evaluation of the prison-based Core Sex Offender Treatment Programme*. London: Ministry of Justice. Retrieved from https://assets.publishing.service.gov.uk/government/uploads/system/uploads/attachment_data/file/623876/sotp-report-web-.pdf

Nation, M., Crusto, C., Wandersman, A., Kumpfer, K. L., Seybolt, D., Morrissey-Kane, E., & Davino, K. (2003). What works in prevention: Principles of effective prevention programs. *American Psychologist*, *58*(6–7), 449.

Oberlader, V., Schmidt, A. F., & Banse, R. (2018). Methodische Herausforderungen in der Evaluation von Straftäterbehandlungsprogrammen. In M. Walsh, B. Pniewski, M. Kober, & A. Armborst (Eds.), *Evidenzorientierte Kriminalprävention in Deutschland: Ein Leitfaden für Politik und Praxis* (pp. 313–332). Wiesbaden: Springer Fachmedien Wiesbaden.

Purvis, M., & Ward, T. (2006). The role of culture in understanding child sexual offending: Examining feminist perspectives. *Aggression and Violent Behavior*, *11*(3), 298–312.

Rothman, D. (2016). Early detection and intervention for adolescents at risk for engaging in abusive sexual behavior: A case for prevention. In *Treatment of sex offenders* (pp. 191–222). Cham, Switzerland: Springer.

Saunders, R., & Wilson, C. (2003). Circles of support and accountability in the Thames valley: Questions and answers. *NOTA News*, *45*.

Schmucker, M., & Lösel, F. (2015). The effects of sexual offender treatment on recidivism: An international meta-analysis of sound quality evaluations. *Journal of Experimental Criminology*, *11*(4), 597–630.

Shea, B., Nahwegahbow, A., & Andersson, N. (2010). Reduction of family violence in aboriginal communities: A systematic review of interventions and approaches. *Pimatisiwin*, *8*(2), 35–60.

Starfield, B., Hyde, J., Gérvas, J., & Heath, I. (2008). The concept of prevention: A good idea gone astray? *Journal of Epidemiology & Community Health*, *62*(7), 580–583.

Taylor, B. G., Stein, N. D., Mumford, E. A., & Woods, D. (2013). Shifting boundaries: An experimental evaluation of a dating violence prevention program in middle schools. *Prevention Science*, *14*(1), 64–76.

Thomas, T., & Thompson, D. (2014). Circles of support and accountability. In P. Taylor, K. Corteen, & S. Morley (Eds.), *A companion to criminal justice, mental health and risk: Companions in criminology and criminal justice* (pp. 46–47). Bristol: Policy Press.

Turner, D., Petermann, J., Harrison, K., Krueger, R., & Briken, P. (2017). Pharmacological treatment of patients with paraphilic disorders and risk of sexual offending: An international perspective. *The World Journal of Biological Psychiatry*, 1–10.

Violence studies. (2019). Retrieved from http://apps.who.int/violence-info/studies?area=sexual-violence&aspect=prevention

Ward, T., & Stewart, C. A. (2003). The treatment of sex offenders: Risk management and good lives. *Professional Psychology: Research and Practice*, *34*(4), 353–360.

Wilcox, D., Garrett, T., & Harkins, L. (2015). *Sex offender treatment: A case study approach to issues and interventions*. Chichester: Wiley-Blackwell.

Wilkinson, K., & Powis, B. (2019). *A process study of the horizon programme*. Retrieved from https://assets.publishing.service.gov.uk/government/uploads/system/uploads/attachment_data/file/769540/process-study-horizon-programme.pdf

Wilson, R. J., Cortoni, F., & McWhinnie, A. J. (2009). Circles of support & accountability: A Canadian national replication of outcome findings. *Sexual Abuse*, *21*(4), 412–430.

Winder, B., Lievesley, R., Elliott, H., Hocken, K., Faulkner, J., Norman, C., & Kaul, A. (2018). Evaluation of the use of pharmacological treatment with prisoners experiencing high levels of hypersexual disorder. *The Journal of Forensic Psychiatry & Psychology*, *29*(1), 53–71.

Winder, B., Skett, S., Hocken, K., & Kaul, A. (2016, November 10–11). *Outcomes and lessons learnt from the national evaluation of the medication to manage sexual arousal (MMSA) programme for individuals in secure settings*. Conference contribution of 4th Health & Justice Summit, Cardiff, Wales.

6 Positive criminology as an alternative

To determine if an approach, intervention, programme, or model fits the umbrella of positive criminology, Ronel and Segev (2014) propose several criteria. The first is that an approach or intervention must result in a positive experience and be beneficial for the individual. Positive experiences are of course relative, and different groups or individuals will experience interventions quite differently. It is important, therefore, that interventions are recognised as value driven and thus at times a decision between what is perceived to be right and wrong may be required. In an example provided by Ronel and Elisha (2011), the injection of heroin will likely provide a positive experience for a heroin user, but this is known to be harmful and thus deemed wrong by others. Thus, a positive outcome for the person cannot be the main and only driver, and as such a second characteristic is that positive criminological approaches must aim to transform a person's psychological or behavioural state and also help to prevent crime (Ronel & Segev, 2015). Third, a positive criminological approach recognises and embraces the notion of integration. This is achieved through the inclusion of a range of resources including social/interpersonal, intrapersonal, and spiritual resources. Social and interpersonal integration is a critical component in the desistance process (Weaver & McNeill, 2015), as we know that addressing psychological and social needs assists the person to re-integrate. Yet positive criminology highlights the importance of developing skills that assist intrapersonal integration too. In addition to psychological and social development, positive criminological interventions must provide attention to the spiritual needs of the individual, fostering opportunities for people to grow and reach beyond a self-centred perspective. This is important not only for personal growth, but in the context of sexual violence, for helping prevent harm to others.

Positive criminology serves as a valuable criminal justice paradigm and a sound basis that researchers ought to explore. Ronel and Segev (2014) provide a useful and more detailed discussion regarding these reasons, but in short, they note that a positive criminological approach ultimately helps reduce recidivism. In the same way as adherence to Good Life Model (GLM) principles (Ward & Stewart, 2003) can encourage and support clients to develop life goals to achieve primary goods, helping them lead a positive, meaningful, and offence free life, similarly it is argued that adopting positive criminological approaches that focus on strengthening and developing an individual's psychological, social, and spiritual goals will help people truly flourish. Like the GLM, deficits and risks are by default eradicated and the desistance process is fostered.

A second interesting facet of a positive criminological approach is the opportunity it provides to work with the person as a whole, rather than as with current approaches, which focus mainly on criminogenic factors (Andrews & James, 2016). Third, positive criminology enables and encourages the individual to take ownership and responsibility for their behaviour and problems. Thus, the process is inclusive, and supports the idea of doing things 'with' a person rather than doing things 'to' them. A fourth aspect that determines an approach as a positive criminological one is that it is socially inclusive. Positive criminology supports the person within the context of a community. It recognises and responds to experiences of the individual, the victim, and the community; the latter two tend to be neglected following a conviction within current criminal justice strategies. Positive criminology also provides a spiritual platform and is the fifth reason why this paradigm has the potential to benefit individuals as they attempt to move away from crime. A spiritual approach offers people the opportunity to appreciate their place and role within the world, providing them the chance to increase feelings of belonging, respect, and hope. Finally, positive criminology serves as a role model for transformation, meaning that everyone involved in such an approach shares the same values and beliefs about the inevitability of human failure. Likewise, it models the notion that where there is acceptance and respect, humans can grow from trauma and harm, irrespective of their status as a 'victim' or 'perpetrator' of crime.

Although positive criminology is in its infancy, criminology and forensic psychology have been examining positive criminological issues for decades. As such, there are some good examples of positive criminological approaches applied across a range of criminal justice contexts. A brief commentary on some of these approaches is provided here, including prisoner education, self-help groups, therapeutic jurisprudence, strengths-based intervention programmes, restorative justice, and positive sexuality.

Prisoner education

Prisoner education is deemed a key factor in helping to reduce crime, and it thus serves to support the prison agenda of rehabilitation. While there is no causal connection between effectiveness of prison education and reduced recidivism, increased employment and positive outcomes are experienced by those engaging in these programmes (Ellison, Szifris, Horan, & Fox, 2017). Studies have found that engaging in educational programmes while in prison reduces the risk of reoffending (*Justice data lab re-offending analysis*, 2015). Indeed, for young people convicted of sexual offences, educational and employment guidance alone may help reduce their risk of further offending (van den Berg, Bijleveld, Hendriks, & Mooi-Reci, 2014). Perhaps of more importance is the opportunity for prison education to assist in personal growth and stimulation in prison. The United Nations

(1990) states that "all prisoners shall have the right to take part in cultural activities and education aimed at the full development of the human personality." Education supports the development of both social capital and improvement of prisoners' well-being (Coates, 2016). Access to basic education is essential as the prison population, when compared to the non-prison populations, may lack basic levels of education (Hawley, Murphy, & Souto-Otero, 2012), having literacy skill levels equivalent to an 11-year-old (Education and Skills Funding Agency, 2017).

Prison education is therefore critical in supporting the growth of its population. Yet resources and conditions are poor, with many establishments being overpopulated. England and Wales have the largest population of prisons across Europe, many of which are privatised (Czerniawski, 2016). While research – and indeed policy – advocates the rights of all prisoners to access basic levels of education in prison, studies suggest that less than a quarter of prisoners engage in prison education (Hawley et al., 2012). In one recent inspection of prisons across England and Wales, Her Majesty's Inspector of Prison for England and Wales (HM Inspectorate of Prisons, 2018) found decreasing levels of purposeful activities across prisons, with prisoners having fewer opportunities than before to access meaningful training and education. While inspectors found increased value in the support of peer mentoring, the overall effectiveness of education had declined to such a degree that access to basic English and math was found to be poor.

Access to educational programmes are important for personal growth and securing employment. Yet following a conviction, additional barriers, beyond that of educational attainment, are experienced. Indeed, for those with a conviction for sexual offending, the barriers are greater still (Brown, Spencer, & Deakin, 2007). Barriers to employment for those convicted of sexual offending are well documented and often unrelated to educational levels or work experience. Instead, they are a result of the stigmatision of their crime or because formal registration requirements restrict certain activities or force constant transience and homelessness (Levenson, Ackerman, Socia, & Harris, 2015). In a study of a small sample of sexual offenders, Brown et al. (2007) reported that because of participants' lack formal education, case workers encouraged them to seek out low-skilled employment. However, employers were anxious and often turned them down once the disclosure of their offence occurred. This was experienced regardless of the skills, qualifications, or experiences they had.

Providing educational and employment opportunities to those with sexual convictions is a difficult matter. However, one of the ways in which those convicted of sexual offending might access opportunities in the job market might be through self-employment or entrepreneurship opportunities. Unlike formal educational programmes that serve to provide prisoners with basic education, including literacy and numeracy, entrepreneurship educational programmes help prisoners recognise and secure future entrepreneurial opportunities. Patzelt, Williams, and Shepherd (2014) proposed that these types of educational programmes provide prisoners with skills and knowledge to explore alternative opportunities beyond traditional employment, in which barriers for ex-prisoners are so great. In a study exploring the role of these programmes, Patzelt et al. (2014) found that outcomes reached beyond exposure to an opportunity. In light of their current circumstances, people began to make greater sense of their past and future selves. This shift in agency not only helped improve the prisoners' perception of education and employment, but also helped them rediscover and rebuild a sense of self. The notion of a possible positive future self is supported by the work of Paternoster and Bushway (2009), who argued that considering ideas of a future self helps stimulate a process of desistance from crime. Educational programmes for those convicted of sexual offences, therefore, may need to reach beyond simple knowledge building, but should help to develop life skills and meaningful opportunities through entrepreneurship schemes that may give people hope of what they might become.

Self-help/peer support groups

Peer support and self-help groups respond to a diverse range of health and social needs, including patients with severe mental illness (Mahlke et al., 2017), people with cancer (McCaughan, Parahoo, Hueter, Northouse, & Bradbury, 2017), people with diabetes (Yu et al., 2018), and people with dementia (Willis, Semple, & de Waal, 2018), as well as assisting people who have experienced trauma, such as veterans reintegrating into the community (Ray, Kemp, Hubbard, & Cucciare, 2017) and those experiencing chronic pain (Finlay, Peacock, & Elander, 2018), and can help prevent exploitation of young people (Buck, Lawrence, & Ragonese, 2017). Self-help or peer-to-peer support groups are, however, different from traditional group support sessions. Traditional therapy is usually delivered by a professional or trained person who is qualified to lead treatment. In a self-help group setting, it is the group members, deemed as experts, who lead the group. It is believed that through a process of shared experiences or connection of unique characteristics, mutual understanding and growth can be experienced. Self-help groups are common in the field of addiction; the self-help model is similar to Alcoholics Anonymous (AA) and Narcotics Anonymous. While self-help groups are well established for the likes of AA, groups for a whole range of social and psychological challenges are emerging. One such group for men with a history of domestic abuse, established in Israel, was examined by Gold, Sutton, and Ronel (2017). In their study, they found that through the participation in a self-help group, the seven participants were able to recognise negative features within their own lives through the shared experiences of others. Indeed, at later points in their lives they were able to restrain and control negative behaviours after reflecting on the experiences of others in similar situations. The authors found participants as having experienced, for the first time, meaningful friendships as they connected with others. Working with others who shared similar experiences meant that participants could trust each other without feeling judged. This brought a sense of unity within the group, especially as support extended beyond the set hours of the support group. This is something that goes beyond professional therapy services, where clients are limited to allotted appointments or office hours. The self-help group model, in contrast, provides ongoing support outside of the group session.

One of the issues for those convicted of sexual offences in prison is the perception of others and their subsequent willingness to work and support this group. Relationships and support between staff and those convicted of sexual offences are found to be less supportive than between staff and non-sexual offender prisoners. Prisoners tend to seek support from those with similar conviction types (van den Berg, Beijersbergen, Nieuwbeerta, & Dirkzwager, 2018). Sexual offenders are often segregated away from the main prison, sometimes living in separate wings or in a completely separate sections of a prison that is dedicated to this group. Research finds that people with sex offences report living in constant fear (Ricciardelli & Moir, 2013) and feel like outcasts (Blagden & Pemberton, 2010). While an underlying fear and sense of isolation is experienced in prison, this is perhaps magnified when living out in the community. Registry laws arguably lead to several unintended consequences, among which Tolson and Klein (2015) report homelessness, unemployment, isolation, and stigmatisation. Any one of these issues alone is likely to impact a person's ability to reintegrate safely into the community. Therefore, the need for support from family and friends is crucial. However, for many, support is no longer available or viable, either because of isolation as a result of being physically relocated away from family and friends, or as a result of family and friends being no longer willing, or legally free, to engage with the person. Self-help groups, therefore, may provide a source of comfort, companionship, and support. For those convicted of sexual offending, self-help groups might provide a space to share the fears and frustrations only experienced by others convicted of sexual offending and thus help overcome barriers such as loneliness. One such support group in Nebraska, known as Fearless, aims to do just that (Sample, Cooley, & ten Bensel, 2018). Group members include people with convictions, their families, and friends. It was formed in response to the challenges that people required to register faced following the Adam Walsh Act, 2006. While the group initially served as a network of people reacting to legislative changes, members of the group recognised the social and emotional needs of people with convictions and their family members and the sparse support available. Thus, the group offers members peer-to-peer support, social activities, and advocacy. The peer-led group results in people feeling less isolated and frightened, and gaining friendships, employment opportunities, and improved confidence. Likewise, family members of those convicted, who also have unique needs, benefit from the support of this type of group.

The reciprocal nature of the self-help group is perhaps one of its greatest strengths. Self-help groups respond to individual needs and the wider social needs of the group. The individual gains the support of others, but this support is reciprocal, and as such, the individual extends their own support to others. The shared characteristics of users of self-help group help to break down social stigma and thus a real sense of trust and mutual appreciation is often experienced. When people face challenges such as addiction, antisocial behaviour, or deviant interests, they report feeling vulnerable, isolated, and lonely. Opportunities to share and work with others in a self-help group context can help reduce loneliness (Laudet,

Cleland, Magura, Vogel, & Knight, 2004), provide resilience and protection, and enable participants to grow from trauma (Chen & Gueta, 2015).

Although many studies examining self-help groups are found to be methodologically weak, Bagnall et al. (2015) found in their review of the prison literature that programmes delivered by peers provided greater positive effects than those that did not. It is unclear why peer support programmes provide greater effects or are as effective as those delivered by professionals. However, it appears that, in prison at least, the availability of peers is a rich resource and therefore access to support is readily available. It is also likely that peers perceive less judgement and more trust to exist between each other than them and professionals.

Therapeutic jurisprudence

Therapeutic jurisprudence (TJ) offers a range of structural and practical solutions that seek to respond to the harmful consequences of contemporary justice systems (Gal & Wexler, 2015). It does this by engaging in a critique of some of the unintended harms caused by legal structures and processes, and provides evaluation of the practice of a broad range of professionals within the criminal justice system.

TJ thus promotes alternative practice within criminal justice contexts, for example through the use of specialist courts that focus on specific issues such as drugs or violence. Such courts encourage and support the person who has committed the crime to take responsibility for their actions and future behaviours. Likewise, TJ supports and promotes behaviours of criminal justice professionals, including the use of praise, empathy, and active listening; indeed, a TJ perspective considers solutions that are strengths based, avoid harm, and divert people away from prison. TJ is equally concerned with the treatment of the victims of crime. As previously mentioned, TJ researchers recognise the limitations of current criminal justice system structures and practices in relation to the harmful effects they have on victims of crime. Thus, TJ promotes the need for reform of legal systems so that victims may have a voice and a place within the process.

Gal and Wexler (2015) highlight several connections between positive criminology and TJ. Like positive criminology, TJ aims to enhance and improve the experiences and lives of the criminal and the victim; it focusses on problem solving approaches to crime, and solutions are future and goal orientated, so that the person convicted can take and maintain responsibility with a maximum degree of autonomy. TJ is concerned with social and psychological outcomes when responding to crime and the criminal justice system. It is less interested in the delivery of punishment per se, and more interested in the resolution and restoration of people's lives after crime has been committed. Gal and Wexler (2015) argue, however, that TJ is far broader than positive criminology, noting the infancy of this new approach. They argue that TJ examines not just the role of actors in the criminal justice system but also the need for reform. In doing this, TJ arguably considers a far broader population such as policymakers, criminal justice, legal, health, and social care professionals, offenders, and victims, whereas positive criminology in its current state appears to target a bespoke group of professionals such as forensic/clinical psychologists, prison and rehabilitation personnel, and those who offend.

For people convicted of sexual offending, a TJ approach may be useful in a number of ways, including the use of appropriate sentences and restrictions, practitioner approaches, policy reform, and rehabilitation options, rather than purely punishment.

Strengths-based approaches (meditation, the arts, and psychological therapy)

There are many examples of strengths-based programmes and interventions within prison settings; one such activity is the use of meditation and mindfulness. Mindfulness-based activities are reported to reduce stress and improve health (Grossman, Niemann, Schmidt, & Walach, 2004). For incarcerated populations, yoga and meditation techniques have encouraging effects on psychological well-being and behavioural functioning (Auty, Cope, & Liebling, 2017) and for inmates with substance problems, meditation can support healthier, harm reducing behaviours (Bowen et al., 2006). The practice of *vipassana*, an ancient meditation technique, has been introduced and offered in several prisons across the world as a means of helping people to rehabilitate (Hetu, 2006), not only beyond prison but while incarcerated as well. In the examination of a *vipassana* course in one Israeli prison, Ronel, Frid, and Timor (2013) found that through the perceived altruism of volunteers who came to deliver the programme, participants felt a sense of reciprocal kindness to others. As a result, relations between prison staff and prisoners improved, to such a degree that a positive social atmosphere was created within the prison itself. The course further helped participants learn how to cope during points of crisis, and participants who were recovering from substance use were able to develop greater levels of self-control and self-respect, and learned how to overcome impulsive responses.

Like *vipassana*, arts-based therapies are prevalent in many prison institutions; therapies including drama, art, dance, poetry, and sculpture. However, one of the problems with arts-based therapies and prisoners is the limited empirical evidence. There is a surge of political and social interest in the exploration of how the arts can play a central role in the well-being and health of people more generally (Megranahan & Lynskey, 2018). Yet, in the UK, arts therapists registered with the Health and Care Professionals Council deliver only art, music, and drama therapies (Health Care and Professionals Council (HCPC) Protected Titles, 2018). For the purpose of this chapter we therefore provide examples from drama, art, and music.

In one UK intervention called Insult to Injury, the Geese Theatre Company delivered a nine-day drama-based programme to participants from six prisons who were convicted of violent and aggressive offences. Blacker, Watson, and Beech (2008) found that following engagement in the programme and when combined with cognitive behavioural therapy, participants experienced a reduction in anger. Using drama and theatrical techniques, along with cognitive behavioural anger management principles, facilitators supported participants through an exploration of their previous aggressive behaviours. Sessions were directed through processes of self-reflection, examination around masculinity, power and control, concepts of choice, and alternative actions. Moreover, participants were provided with strategies to respond appropriately to anger in the future through problem solving, positive self-talk, and anger management techniques.

In another study carried out by Orkibi, Bar, and Eliakim (2014), researchers explored the effect of drama-based group therapy on 12 participants, five with mental illness and seven without. The Amitim Programme is a group established to support people with mental illness and is sponsored by the Israel Association of Community Centres and the Ministry of Health. Researchers were interested in exploring the perceptions and levels of stigma among people without mental illness, as well as the self-esteem and self-stigma of those with mental illness. The intervention totalled 20 sessions where the group met once a week for two hours. Participants engaged in activities that allowed both people with mental illness and those without to share experiences. They found self-esteem increased for all participants with mental illness, plus their internalised self-stigma decreased. For those without mental illness, their perceptions and public stigma decreased during the intervention. Thus, it appears that by bringing different groups together and engaging in a process of drama therapy using playfulness and the opportunity to witness the experiences of others (Jones, 2007), positive effects are experienced.

In adult male prison populations, arts therapy was found to reduce depression. Gussak (2004) found those who engaged in a four-week art therapy group experienced a decrease in depressive symptoms and improvements in mood. In the follow-up study, therapy ran twice a week for eight weeks, with art activities first being introduced to the individual on a simple level, but then activities developing into more complex and group-based tasks. While there were some methodological issues, the therapy was deemed to be beneficial in terms of improving people's mood and socialisation within the prison when compared to the control group (Gussak, 2006).

Megranahan and Lynskey (2018) found music therapy had a positive impact on the treatment of those recovering from substance use. Although studies included in their review were methodologically limited (e.g. studies were single-therapy sessions or did not collect any long-term follow-up data), findings were still encouraging. In a study examining the effects of new-age, relaxing music during the counter conditioning of external substance cue conditioning, craving reactivity, craving beliefs, and depression, Stamou et al. (2017) found that by listening to new-age, relaxing music, craving responses and craving beliefs were reduced.

Beyond the arts, strengths-based psychological therapies have been delivered for several decades and are possibly best demonstrated by the work of the Rockwood Psychological Services in Ontario, Canada (Marshall, Marshall, Serran, & O'Brien, 2011). For many years, therapists have used positive psychological approaches to work with people convicted of sexual offending. Their work includes a preparatory programme, primary programme, and denier's programme. Their approach draws on the positive psychological paradigm, in order that all clients might engage more effectively in treatment by focussing on the strengths and resiliencies they might have. This work applies several models to support a positive psychological approach, including approaches such as the GLM (Ward & Stewart, 2003), discussed in earlier chapters; 'Old me' versus 'New me,' a model that draws on Haaven, Little, and Petre-Miller's (1990) work (used in earlier SOTPs), which supports clients to consider a new positive future self, new self-awareness, and knowledge; and motivational interviewing (MI), first used in the treatment of people with addictive behaviour, in which Miller and Rollnick (1991, 2002) proposed four guiding principles for therapists: Therapists must express empathy, signal discrepancy, roll with resistance, and instil hope. In addition to these four guiding MI principles, therapists must also engage in a spirit of collaboration rather than coercion, and a therapeutic alliance of support must be developed. Goals must be set jointly rather than determined and prescribed by the therapist. The therapeutic process must allow clients' own insights to emerge, and focus ought to promote the agent's own autonomy and choice to change. Rockwood Psychological Services therapists use an invitational therapeutic style (Jenkins, 1990), whereby client's issues are elicited from the client themselves, rather than through a downward process where the therapist determines treatment goals. Such an invitational response supports the MI model, whereby the relationship is a partnership and the client is the 'expert' of his or her own life. The final model adopted by the work at Rockford Psychological Services is the use of approach goals. Approach goals – in contrast to avoidance goals, whereby the client is required to avoid particular people, places, thoughts, and behaviours – allow goals to be achieved. It is thought that by encouraging people to achieve, rather than avoid, specific activities, clients are more likely to engage in treatment and be motivated to remain offence free (Mann, Webster, Schofield, & Marshall, 2004).

Restorative justice

There is no single shared or universal definition of what a restorative justice (RJ) intervention is, and as such, many variations and interpretations of RJ exist. It is claimed that RJ philosophies and principles are grounded in traditions that date back to the early Greeks, Maoris in New Zealand, and Navajos in North America (Braithwaite, 1999). In essence, RJ recognises that crime harms people, relationships, and communities, and that justice is required to heal and repair these harms as far as is possible. RJ is therefore a holistic community approach to crime and harm. It requires decisions to be made by the local community about how best to deal with crime in the local community, rather than be state determined. As such, RJ approaches incorporate voices of a wide range of actors involved in crime, including the victim, the perpetrator, the community, organisations, and so on. The purpose of involving a broad spectrum of community members is to acknowledge that crime is a social and community issue, rather than an individual problem; it is therefore the responsibility of the community to respond to individuals who commit crime, as a whole, and to share the responsibility for solving the problem, as well as being part of the solution. A community response, arguably, makes the solution more meaningful to all involved, both in providing appropriate punishment and to support the perpetrator in reintegration and reparation of the harm caused. RJ aims to be a shared and fair process; as such it adopts a humanistic and caring response towards all those who are affected by crime, including the victim, offender, and others in the community. By adopting a humanistic approach, it aims to help the victim recover and restore their dignity, giving them a sense of safety and control. For the perpetrator, the approach seeks to assist them to take responsibility and help them repair and make amends to those harmed.

The application of RJ interventions vary, but tend to fall into one of three approaches: a) RJ at a distance, where the perpetrator of a crime is made aware of the harms they have caused, done through attending a prison course or though work with an RJ facilitator; the person may then write a letter (this may never be sent) to the victim; b) A face-to-face conference which is led by a trained facilitator who works with both the victim and the perpetrator before, during, and after the meeting. During the meeting both parties have the chance to ask questions, express thoughts and feelings, and agree on a resolution to the harm caused; and c) A circle type conference, in which other members of the community/family are included; this offers support to the victim and the perpetrator.

There are several meta-analyses and systematic reviews examining the effectiveness of RJ. Victim and offender satisfaction, compliance with the restitution, and recidivism rates were all found to be more effective in cases where an RJ approach had been applied (Latimer, Dowden, & Muise, 2005). Following 12 randomised controlled trials across the UK and Australia, Sherman, Strang, Barnes et al. (2015) found a reduction in repeat offending in ten of the 12 experiments. RJ conferences were found to be more effective with prolific offenders and those engaged in violent crime but were less effective in cases of property crime. Nevertheless, it is from the perspective of the victim where the outcomes are positive. Those engaging in an RJ conference reported a reduction in a fear of further crime and feelings of satisfaction by whole process. Likewise, in a review examining the cost effectiveness of RJ, Sherman, Strang, Mayo-Wilson, Woods, and Ariel (2015) found RJ was more likely to reduce the frequency and therefore the subsequent cost of further crime.

While reports of RJ are encouraging, one criticism is that the global interpretation of RJ and its aims and philosophies have become distilled and distorted. For example, the diversity of RJ conferencing and what 'restoration' actually means has resulted in empirical claims being brought into question or at the very least being misinterpreted. Several criticisms of RJ allege that RJ erodes the legal rights of the offender; minimises crime; fails to make real change; results in discriminatory outcomes; extends police powers; causes a power imbalance between victim and offender; encourages vigilantism; lacks legitimacy; and fails to provide justice. For an excellent and detailed response to these critiques, see Morris (2002).

A further claim is that RJ is unsuitable for certain types of crime. Critics argue (see Daly and Stubbs (2006) for an excellent discussion of some of the nuanced perspectives in this debate) in domestic and/or sexual abuse cases or where power and control are motivators in the commissioning of the crime, RJ is inappropriate. Clearly, not all cases of domestic or sexual violence would be appropriate for an RJ solution. However, Wager (2015) notes that for couples who wish to continue their relationship post violence, an RJ solution provides a useful and effective platform. It does this through the adoption of a positive victimological approach (not to be confused with positive victimology). For example, the use of a public apology given during an RJ intervention can to some extent validate the experiences of the victim, thus removing the sense of responsibility s/he may have carried. Likewise, through an RJ conference, the victim, who is likely to have the support of others during the process, usually their family and friends, often report that the opportunity for them to be involved through the conference helps them re-gain their support, one reason being that previously, others may not have believed the victim.

Regarding the use of RJ for sexual crime, considerable debate exists and caution is advised (Koss, 2010). It has been argued that certain types of sexual abuse cases may be more suitable for RJ than others. For example, in cases of family sexual abuse, victims may be more vulnerable to further abuses of power and control, which may not be the case in a rape by a stranger (Keenan & Zinsstag, 2014). Hargovan (2005) argues that each case ought to be considered individually, using strict criteria for inclusion/exclusion, such as the potential for further harm to victim, the psychopathic state of offender, parties' willingness to participate, and offence history. One of the key concerns is the risk of further harm to the victim. Keenan and Zinsstag (2014) note that for victims of sexual abuse, RJ can result in positive and empowering outcomes. They summarise the literature regarding the outcomes for sexual offence victims taking part in an RJ as including positive psychological benefits as a result of having the opportunity to discuss the offence before, during, and after the RJ conference; reduced post-traumatic stress and fear; reduced feelings of blame that victims often experience through traditional legal processes; having unanswered questions answered; gaining a sense of empowerment, closure, and healing; and by receiving an apology, whether public or private, getting validation of their feelings and experiences. The outcomes for perpetrators of sexual abuse are reported as equally positive. These include the opportunity for the perpetrator to explore important feelings, demonstrate accountability and take responsibility for their behaviour, express and demonstrate remorse, demonstration of a motivation to desist, and reintegrate and connect with family members.

Central to an RJ approach is "Safety for all; Prevention of re-victimization; Redressing power imbalances; Confidentiality; Due process rights for offenders to a fair trial, to have legal counsel and not to be self-incriminating" (Keenan & Zinsstag, 2014, p. 11). Yet these principles can be compromised if practitioners engaging in RJ work with sexual victims and offenders do not have the high skill levels and expert knowledge of sexual violence and trauma (Mercer, Sten Madesen, Keenan, & Zinsstag, 2015) or where there is a drive and pressure for people to 'reconcile' but understanding of what reconciliation means is often missed. Likewise, where the apology is manipulative or disingenuous; where gender, race, or culture are not recognised or understood by the facilitator; and where the legal rights of the perpetrator are not recognised, harm to both victim and perpetrator can be significant.

In their article examining RJ practice for sexual violence in different countries, Keenan, Zinsstag, and O'Nolan (2016) found a wide variety in practice, often existing 'under the radar.' Given that there is no one clear definition (Daly, 2016), this is perhaps unsurprising. Thus, greater attention to the role and practice of RJ is needed to ensure the safe and successful application of RJ interactions in sexual abuse cases. There is a need to respond with sensitivity to the sociocultural contexts in which abuse occurs, as well as a need for RJ interventions to integrate with criminal justice systems. If RJ is to become a mainstream provision in the effort to address issues of sexual violence, then appropriate policy, practice, and guidance must be developed through learning from countries already delivering RJ interventions in cases of sexual violence.

Positive sexuality

An often-ignored issue, as highlighted by Cossins (2017), is the difference between what is deemed abnormal and what is socially acceptable. Often, this difference is socially constructed, temporal, and geographically distributed. As such, our understanding of sexuality and sexual deviance is potentially flawed, as both criminological and psychological theories are based upon social and political preference. While people who have committed harm and violence against others ought to be punished for their behaviour, religious doctrines tends to drive an ideology that interprets any sexual behaviour as negative. Indeed, such sex-negative communities often claim that all sexual acts (apart from those with the aim to procreate) is needless and risky. As such, sex-negative societies tend to adopt punitive policies (Williams, Thomas, & Prior, 2015). For example, issues such as homosexuality, masturbation, and contraception continue to divide Western society, where such practices are deemed immoral, and in some cases, continue to be illegal.

Given that "sex-negativity, breeds secrecy, which contributes to a climate where sexual assaults may be more likely to occur" (Williams, Thomas, & Prior, 2015, n.p.n.), greater sex-positivity is needed. A sex-positive society is open and honest about sex and its pleasures, as well as the risks involved. However, it does this in a way that is educational, inclusive, and empowering. When considering how a sex-positive culture might support those that have sexual interests towards children, it encourages individuals to come forward, discuss their interests, and seek support. A sex-positive culture would view the stigmatisation of people labelled a sexual deviant as unethical.

A positive sexuality framework has been proposed by researchers exploring issues of sex and sexuality (Williams, Thomas, Prior, & Walters, 2015). Their eight dimensions of a positive sexuality framework include a) Reference to strengths, happiness, and well-being; b) Individual sexuality as unique and multi-faceted; c) A need for open and honest communication; d) Humanising and inclusive; e) Encourages peace-making; f) Applies to all levels of social structure; g) Applicable to professional ethics; and h) Welcomes multiple epistemological and methodological positions. For a detailed exploration of each domain, please see Williams, Thomas, Prior, and Walters' (2015) introduction of the framework. Given the current sex-negative climate, a much broader understanding of sex and sexuality is needed, particularly when working with clients convicted of sexual offending, And particularly as the stigmatisation of people with sexual interests in children runs the risk of increasing the likelihood of recidivism (Williams, 2015). Engaging with a positive sexuality framework may enable an ethical and humane way for clinicians to engage in discussions and offer treatment that aims to help improve the health and well-being of the client while also help reduce the risk of them engaging in harmful sexual behaviours that may lead to abuse and harm.

Conclusion

There are many existing interventions and approaches that appear to fall under the criteria and umbrella of positive criminology, as set out by Ronel and Segev (2015). While these intervenions adhere to positive criminological principles in theory, they fall short in practice. With poor resources, inadequate prison conditions, and a lack of community application to many correctional activities such as education and employment, the substance of current interventions lack enough depth to truly transform people's lives. For people with sexual offending convictions, the barriers to realising opportunities as a result of engaging through these interventions are even greater than those of a general offending population. For many, this is likely a result of the stigma and labelling effect caused by policy and the legislative framework practitioners operate within. Thus, a far greater paradigm shift is needed, one that reaches beyond individual interventions. The following chapter explores this problem further by considering the application of positive criminological risk assessment approaches, specifically to those convicted of sexual offending.

References

Andrews, D. A., & James, B. (2016). *The psychology of criminal conduct* (5th ed.). New York: Routledge.

Auty, K. M., Cope, A., & Liebling, A. (2017). A systematic review and meta-analysis of yoga and mindfulness meditation in prison: Effects on psychological well-being and behavioural functioning. *International Journal of Offender Therapy and Comparative Criminology*, *61*(6), 689–710.

Bagnall, A.-M., South, J., Hulme, C., Woodall, J., Vinall-Collier, K., Raine, G., . . . Wright, N. M. (2015). A systematic review of the effectiveness and cost-effectiveness of peer education and peer support in prisons. *BMC Public Health*, *15*(1), 290.

Blacker, J., Watson, A., & Beech, A. R. (2008). A combined drama-based and CBT approach to working with self-reported anger aggression. *Criminal Behaviour and Mental Health*, *18*(2), 129–137.

Blagden, N., & Pemberton, S. (2010). The challenge in conducting qualitative research with convicted sex offenders. *The Howard Journal of Criminal Justice*, *49*(3), 269–281.

Bowen, S., Witkiewitz, K., Dillworth, T. M., Chawla, N., Simpson, T. L., Ostafin, B. D., . . . Marlatt, G. A. (2006). Mindfulness meditation and substance use in an incarcerated population. *Psychology of Addictive Behaviors*, *20*(3), 343–347.

Braithwaite, J. (1999). Restorative justice: Assessing optimistic and pessimistic accounts. *Crime and Justice*, *25*, 1–127.

Brown, K., Spencer, J., & Deakin, J. (2007). The reintegration of sex offenders: Barriers and opportunities for employment. *The Howard Journal of Criminal Justice*, *46*(1), 32–42.

Buck, G., Lawrence, A., & Ragonese, E. (2017). Exploring peer mentoring as a form of innovative practice with young people at risk of child sexual exploitation. *British Journal of Social Work*, *47*(6), 1745–1763.

Chen, G., & Gueta, K. (2015). Application of positive criminology in the 12-Step program. In N. Ronel & D. Segev (Eds.), *Positive criminology* (pp. 208–220). London: Routledge.

Coates, S. (2016). *Unlocking potential: A review of education in prison*. Ministry of Justice. Retrieved from https://assets.publishing.service.gov.uk/government/uploads/system/uploads/attachment_data/file/524013/education-review-report.pdf

Cossins, A. (2017). The sociology of sex offending: The offender, culture, and context. In D. P. Boer (Ed.), *The Wiley handbook on the theories, assessment and treatment of sexual offending* (pp. 267–288). West Sussex: Wiley-Blackwell.

Czerniawski, G. (2016). A race to the bottom – Prison education and the English and Welsh policy context. *Journal of Education Policy*, *31*(2), 198–212.

Daly, K. (2016). What is restorative justice? Fresh answers to a vexed question. *Victims & Offenders*, *11*(1), 9–29.

Daly, K., & Stubbs, J. (2006). Feminist engagement with restorative justice. *Theoretical Criminology*, *10*(1), 9–28.

Education and Skills Funding Agency. (2017). OLASS English and maths assessments: Participation 2015/16. *FE Data Library: Education and Training*. Retrieved from www.gov.uk/government/statistical-data-sets/fe-data-library-education-and-training

Ellison, M., Szifris, K., Horan, R., & Fox, C. (2017). A rapid evidence assessment of the effectiveness of prison education in reducing recidivism and increasing employment. *Probation Journal*, *64*(2), 108–128.

Finlay, K. A., Peacock, S., & Elander, J. (2018). Developing successful social support: An interpretative phenomenological analysis of mechanisms and processes in a chronic pain support group. *Psychology & Health*, *33*(7), 846–871.

Gal, T., & Wexler, D. (2015). Synergizing theraputic jurisprudence and positive criminology. In N. Ronel & D. Segev (Eds.), *Positive criminology*. New York: Routledge.

Gold, D., Sutton, A., & Ronel, N. (2017). Non-violent empowerment: Self-help group for male batterers on recovery. *Journal of Interpersonal Violence*, *32*(20), 3174–3200.

Grossman, P., Niemann, L., Schmidt, S., & Walach, H. (2004). Mindfulness-based stress reduction and health benefits: A meta-analysis. *Journal of Psychosomatic Research*, *57*(1), 35–43.

Gussak, D. (2004). Art therapy with prison inmates: A pilot study. *Arts in Psychotherapy*, *31*(4), 245–259.

Gussak, D. (2006). Effects of art therapy with prison inmates: A follow-up study. *The Arts in Psychotherapy*, *33*(3), 188–198.

Haaven, J., Little, R., & Petre-Miller, D. (1990). *Treating intellectually disabled sex offenders: A model residential program*. Orwell, VT: Safer Society Press.

Hargovan, H. (2005). Restorative justice and domestic violence: Some exploratory thoughts. *Agenda, 19*(66), 48–56.

Hawley, J., Murphy, I., & Souto-Otero, M. (2012). *Survey on prison education and training in Europe – Final report.* Order 23 of the DG Education and Culture Framework Contract 02/10-Lot July 1, 2012. Retrieved from www.epea.org/wp-content/uploads/NC3113979ENN.en_.pdf

Health Care and Professionals Council (HCPC) Protected Titles. (2018). Retreived from www.hcpc-uk.org/about-us/who-we-regulate/the-professions/

Hetu, V. (2006). Effect of vipassana on the psyche of inmates: A socio-psychological study. *Indian Journal of Criminology & Criminalistics, 27*, 48–64.

HM Inspectorate of Prisons. (2018). *HM chief inspector of prisons for England and Wales annual report 2017–18.* Retrieved from www.justiceinspectorates.gov.uk/hmiprisons/wp-content/uploads/sites/4/2018/07/6.4472_HMI-Prisons_AR-2017-18_Content_A4_Final_WEB.pdf

Jenkins, A. (1990). Invitations to responsibility: The therapeutic engagement of men who are violent and abusive. *Australian and New Zealand Journal of Family Therapy, 11*(2), 74–74.

Jones, P. (2007). *Drama as therapy volume 1: Theory, practice and research.* London: Routledge.

Justice data lab re-offending analysis: Prisoners education trust. (2015). London. Retrieved from https://assets.publishing.service.gov.uk/government/uploads/system/uploads/attachment_data/file/459470/prisoners-education-trust-report.pdf

Keenan, M., & Zinsstag, E. (2014). Restorative justice and sexual offences: Can'changing lenses' be appropriate in this case too? *Monatsschrift for Criminology, 97*(1), 93–106.

Keenan, M., Zinsstag, E., & O'Nolan, C. (2016). Sexual violence and restorative practices in Belgium, Ireland and Norway: A thematic analysis of country variations. *Restorative Justice, 4*(1), 86–114.

Koss, M. P. (2010). Restorative justice for acquaintance rape and misdemeanor sex crimes. In J. Ptacek (Ed.), *Restorative justice and violence against women* (pp. 218–238). New York: Oxford University Press.

Latimer, J., Dowden, C., & Muise, D. (2005). The effectiveness of restorative justice practices: A meta-analysis. *The Prison Journal, 85*(2), 127–144.

Laudet, A. B., Cleland, C. M., Magura, S., Vogel, H. S., & Knight, E. L. (2004). Social support mediates the effects of dual-focus mutual aid groups on abstinence from substance use. *American Journal of Community Psychology, 34*(3–4), 175–185.

Levenson, J., Ackerman, A. R., Socia, K. M., & Harris, A. J. (2015). Where for art thou? Transient sex offenders and residence restrictions. *Criminal Justice Policy Review, 26*(4), 319–344.

Mahlke, C. I., Priebe, S., Heumann, K., Daubmann, A., Wegscheider, K., & Bock, T. (2017). Effectiveness of one-to-one peer support for patients with severe mental illness – A randomised controlled trial. *European Psychiatry, 42*, 103–110.

Mann, R. E., Webster, S. D., Schofield, C., & Marshall, W. L. (2004). Approach versus avoidance goals in relapse prevention with sexual offenders. *Sexual Abuse: A Journal of Research and Treatment, 16*(1), 65–75.

Marshall, W. L., Marshall, L. E., Serran, G. A., & O'Brien, M. D. (2011). *Rehabilitating sexual offenders: A strength-based approach.* Washington: American Psychological Association.

McCaughan, E., Parahoo, K., Hueter, I., Northouse, L., & Bradbury, I. (2017). Online support groups for women with breast cancer. *Cochrane Database of Systematic Reviews, 3.*

Megranahan, K., & Lynskey, M. T. (2018). Do creative arts therapies reduce substance misuse? A systematic review. *The Arts in Psychotherapy*, *57*, 50–58.

Mercer, V., Sten Madesen, K., Keenan, M., & Zinsstag, E. (2015). *Doing restorative justice in cases of sexual violence: A practice guid*. Leuven, KU: Leuven Institute of Criminology, University of Leuven.

Miller, W., & Rollnick, S. (1991). *Motivational interviewing: Preparing people to change addictive behaviors:* New York: Guilford Press.

Miller, W., & Rollnick, S. (2002). *Motivational interviewing: Preparing people to change* (2nd ed.). New York: Guilford Press.

Morris, A. (2002). Critiquing the critics: A brief response to critics of restorative justice. *British Journal of Criminology*, *42*(3), 596–615.

Orkibi, H., Bar, N., & Eliakim, I. (2014). The effect of drama-based group therapy on aspects of mental illness stigma. *The Arts in Psychotherapy*, *41*(5), 458–466.

Paternoster, R., & Bushway, S. (2009). Desistance and the "feared self": Toward an identity theory of criminal desistance. *The Journal of Criminal Law and Criminology*, *99*(4), 1103–1156.

Patzelt, H., Williams, T. A., & Shepherd, D. A. (2014). Overcoming the walls that constrain us: The role of entrepreneurship education programs in prison. *Academy of Management Learning & Education*, *13*(4), 587–620.

Ray, J. M., Kemp, L. L., Hubbard, A., & Cucciare, M. A. (2017). Developing a peer support protocol for improving veterans' engagement to computer-delivered cognitive behavioural therapy. *Behavioural and cognitive psychotherapy*, *45*(3), 253–265.

Ricciardelli, R., & Moir, M. (2013). Stigmatized among the stigmatized: Sex offenders in Canadian penitentiaries. *Canadian Journal of Criminology and Criminal Justice*, *55*(3), 353–386. Retrieved from.

Ronel, N., & Elisha, E. (2011). A different perspective: Introducing positive criminology. *International Journal of Offender Therapy and Comparative Criminology*, *55*(2), 305–325.

Ronel, N., Frid, N., & Timor, U. (2013). The practice of positive criminology: A vipassana course in prison. *International Journal of Offender Therapy and Comparative Criminology*, *57*(2), 133–153.

Ronel, N., & Segev, D. (2014). Positive criminology in practice. *International Journal of Offender Therapy and Comparative Criminology*, *58*(11), 1389–1407.

Ronel, N., & Segev, D. (2015). *Positive criminology*. London: Routledge.

Sample, L. L., Cooley, B. N., & ten Bensel, T. (2018). Beyond circles of support: "Fearless" – An open peer-to-peer mutual support group for sex offense registrants and their family members. *International Journal of Offender Therapy and Comparative Criminology*, *62*(13), 4257–4277.

Sherman, L. W., Strang, H., Barnes, G., Woods, D. J., Bennett, S., Inkpen, N., . . . Slothower, M. (2015). Twelve experiments in restorative justice: The Jerry Lee program of randomized trials of restorative justice conferences. *Journal of Experimental Criminology*, *11*(4), 501–540.

Sherman, L. W., Strang, H., Mayo-Wilson, E., Woods, D. J., & Ariel, B. (2015). Are restorative justice conferences effective in reducing repeat offending? Findings from a campbell systematic review. *Journal of Quantitative Criminology*, *31*(1), 1–24.

Stamou, V., Clerveaux, R., Stamou, L., Le Rocheleuil, S., Berejnoi, L., Romo, L., & Graziani, P. (2017). The therapeutic contribution of music in music-assisted systematic desensitization for substance addiction treatment: A pilot study. *The Arts in Psychotherapy*, *56*, 30–44.

Tolson, D., & Klein, J. (2015). Registration, residency restrictions, and community notification: A social capital perspective on the isolation of registered sex offenders in our communities. *Journal of Human Behavior in the Social Environment*, *25*(5), 375–390.

Unitied Nations. (1990). *45/111. Basic principles for the treatment of prisoners*. Retrieved from www.un.org/ruleoflaw/blog/document/basic-principles-for-the-treatment-of-prisoners/

van den Berg, C., Beijersbergen, K., Nieuwbeerta, P., & Dirkzwager, A. (2018). Sex offenders in prison: Are they socially isolated? *Sexual Abuse*, *30*(7), 828–845.

van den Berg, C., Bijleveld, C., Hendriks, J., & Mooi-Reci, I. (2014). The juvenile sex offender: The effect of employment on offending. *Journal of Criminal Justice*, *42*(2), 145–152.

Ward, T., & Stewart, C. A. (2003). The treatment of sex offenders: Risk management and good lives. *Professional Psychology: Research and Practice*, *34*(4), 353–360.

Wager, N. (2015). Restorative justice and domestic violence. A view from a positive victimological perspective. In N. Ronel & D. Segev (Eds.), *Positive criminology* (pp. 261–275). London: Routledge.

Weaver, B., & McNeill, F. (2015). Lifelines: Desistance, social relations, and reciprocity. *Criminal Justice and Behavior*, *42*(1), 95–107.

Williams, D. J. (2015). Challenging dehumanization in US sex offender policy by listening to silenced voices. *Journal of Positive Sexuality*, *1*.

Williams, D. J., Thomas, J. N., & Prior, E. E. (2015). Moving full-speed ahead in the wrong direction? A critical examination of US sex-offender policy from a positive sexuality model. *Critical Criminology*, *23*(3), 277–294.

Williams, D. J., Thomas, J. N., Prior, E. E., & Walters, W. (2015). Introducing a multidisciplinary framework of positive sexuality. *Journal of Positive Sexuality*, *1*(6), 6–11.

Willis, E., Semple, A. C., & de Waal, H. (2018). Quantifying the benefits of peer support for people with dementia: A Social Return on Investment (SROI) study. *Dementia*, *17*(3), 266–278.

Yu, D., Graffy, J., Holman, D., Robins, P., Cai, Y., Zhao, Z., & Simmons, D. (2018). Impact of peer support on inpatient and outpatient payments among people with type 2 diabetes: A prospective cohort study. *Diabetic Medicine*, *35*(6), 789–797.

7 Current positive criminology applications in terms of assessment

Introduction

The notion of managing and assessing 'risk' and 'dangerousness' has become a central aim of Western criminal justice agencies. This need to classify is in part a result of society attempting to respond to those who do not comply with the norms within society, and thus commit crimes. As noted in previous chapters, the notion of 'crime' and therefore the laws around risk and dangerousness are socially, politically, and historically constructed. Solutions are arguably reductive, targeting and pathologising the individual. An interesting discussion between Foucault and his students is useful in highlighting how dangerousness and risk can only really be understood when, as 'assessors,' we fully understand the wider contributing factors of crime (Foucault, Simon, & Elden, 2017). In their discussion, Foucault uses the example of a woman who murdered her child. He asks his students to consider if this woman was destitute and starving, and if her child was starving to death, would her killing the child be an act of love to save the child from an inevitable slow, cruel, and painful death? He asks if in this context we would say she is dangerous. Thus, when attempting to understand risk assessment, especially within a positive criminological framework, it is essential to understand crime within its context and person's motivations. In Foucault's example, understanding the woman's context and motivation, while not condoning her actions, allows us to support her needs in a far more effective way.

We must also recognise the criminal justice regime, or "new penology" (Feeley & Simon, 1992), in which practitioners operate. Assessors as employees of criminal justice organisations inevitably perceive criminals through a particular correctional lens. The notion of risk and dangerousness is now deeply embedded within law and policy (Harrison, 2011), and is evident in correctional practice and the tools used. To support a new way of working, one that is akin to the principles of positive criminology, shifts in policy, legislation, and practice are needed. We note, in the field of risk assessment at least, that correctional practitioners are already drawing on tools to support their practice and work more positively and holistically when assessing their clients. By using strengths-based tools and holistic practice, a shift in paradigm may begin. However, for this to occur, it must do so across all aspects of the criminal justice system.

One of the many goals of criminal justice and correctional agents working with people convicted of sexual crime is to work with clients in such a way that prevents them from commissioning further sexual abuse. For practitioners and clinicians to do this effectively, they must first understand what is needed to help prevent further harm. Informed by specific agency or government policy, it is usually the role of a lead practitioner to determine the best strategy to manage the client and the risk they are perceived to pose. In cases of sexual abuse, practitioners tend to work within a multi-agency context. As such, lead practitioners will seek advice and support and be guided by the expertise and knowledge other agencies bring in the development of a strategy.

One of the ways in which practitioners can determine individual strategies for clients is to carry out a comprehensive assessment. Practitioners are often called upon to carry out assessments for court or parole boards, for external agencies responsible for the management of a case, such as (in England and Wales) Multi-Agency Public Protection Arrangements (MAPPA) boards, or, for case management purposes, practitioners can monitor the progress of the client throughout the duration of the case management period. While assessments are required for multiple purposes, they serve to determine both the risk and needs of a client, and in cases of those with sexual offences, inform appropriate treatment or management plans. A summary of current risk assessment tools is detailed in Chapter 3.

Sexual offending is multi-faceted, complex, and temporal; it is therefore likely that assessment and subsequent strategies to treat or manage an individual are likely to be as complex and dynamic as the problems that led to offending in the first place. Depending on the purpose and practitioner carrying out the assessment, subsequent plans are likely to be complex, and include details of external agency involvement, tasks and actions set by the lead practitioner for other practitioners involved in the case, and even actions for the client to achieve. These might include actions that restrict activity, such as living in a particular town, or include actions that require activity, such as the client attending an employment training appointment. When considering a positive criminological approach to assessing clients convicted of sexual offending, we propose that practitioners must continue to explore, test, and understand the risk a client presents; however, we argue that in addition to this, assessors must equally attend to the strengths the client also brings.

Considering the strengths of a person in any risk assessment is critical because even the most prolific of abusers spend periods of time when they are not offending. Marshall, Marshall, Serran, and O'Brien (2011) report on one such client, the case of John, who was convicted and referred for treatment for committing sexual offences against young boys. He kept detailed written accounts of his day-to-day activities throughout his adult life. He recorded all his activities, including going shopping, helping his mother, travelling on the bus, going to work; in fact, in these diaries he also included detailed accounts of the 420 boys he groomed and abused over a 26-year period. When his diaries were analysed, it was found that while he had engaged in a process of grooming and sexually abusing hundreds of children over a long period of time, when offending periods were put in the context of the remainder of his life, offending related activities accounted for only 8% of his time (8% includes time grooming, fantasising, and abusing children). The remaining 92% of his time was spent engaged in mundane, 'normal' day-to-day activities. While John clearly engaged in harmful behaviours that required attention and treatment, for most of his time, John was not offending or thinking about offending. It is these 'non-offending' periods that ought to be considered from a positive criminological assessment perspective. In the case of John, understanding what factors supported non-offending activities are as useful and important as those factors (risks) that drew him closer to offending.

There are several assessment tools currently available that focus on both risk as well as strengths and protective factors. Before considering these, it is worth outlining the terminology used in the risk assessment literature. The term 'strength' or 'strength-based' is used quite broadly; this has arguably led to some definitional and conceptual issues. Strengths-based, on the one hand, is usually used to define a set of actions, an approach, or a perspective for clinicians or practitioners to use when working with a client; it is a mechanism or process external to the person. In a social work context, the notion of strengths-based first appeared in the 1980s; here the aim was to help social workers frame their work with clients by helping them navigate challenges in life such as housing and employment. By using a strengths-based approach in their work, their actions became goal orientated, with clients being central and active in the development of their own care plans (Oliver & Charles, 2015). Strengths in this sense is about a process, external to the client, designed in such a way that the activities of external agents help the person grow and develop greater resilience.

More commonly, as a result of the ground-breaking work of Seligman and Csikszentmihalyi (2000), strengths are viewed as internal to the person. These are often described as character strengths and can, for example, be seen in educational literature where the development of personal individual character strengths is achieved through certain curriculum and educational programmes. For example, students are provided the opportunity to explore and develop their own character strengths, or explore the strengths of others, through characters in literature, art, or drama. The aim of such programmes is to support an educational environment that might foster improved health and well-being of students (Quinlan, Swain, Cameron, & Vella-Brodrick, 2015; White & Waters, 2015). Likewise, in the employment sector, a focus on the character strengths of individuals helps improve working environments, well-being of staff, and performance (Dubreuil, Forest, & Courcy, 2014). Strengths and strengths-based approaches are therefore a combination of internal factors, including features that are potentially psychological, neurological, and cognitive in nature, as well as external factors, including resources that are social, educational, and economic.

However, the criminology literature goes beyond the notion of strengths, using additional terms such as protective and promotive factors, and this can cause confusion. These terms are perhaps less well defined and often used interchangeably (Baglivio, Wolff, Piquero, Howell, & Greenwald, 2016; Jolliffe, Farrington, Loeber, & Pardini, 2016), and indeed, for studies examining those convicted of sexual offending, an even greater blurring of definition is apparent (de Vries Robbé, Mann, Maruna, & Thornton, 2015).

Protective factors are perhaps best defined as factors that assist or enable the desistance process (de Vries Robbé, Mann, Maruna, & Thornton, 2015; Meinck, Cluver, Boyes, & Mhlongo, 2014) as they help to decrease the likelihood of unwanted behaviours (usually offending) (Dowling et al., 2017). They do this through either a direct reduction of the effects of a risk factor, or indirectly by serving as a buffer; that is, the protective factor serves to mitigate the impact of the risk factor (Hall et al., 2012). Promotive factors, on the other hand, tend to be variables such as character strengths, situations, or conditions (Baglivio et al., 2016) that have a direct effect on desistance (Farrington, Loeber, Jolliffe, & Pardini, 2008), regardless of the risk level. Others argue that protective and promotive factors operate on a continuum and are thus simple opposites. However, it is acknowledged that the presence or absence of factors is unique to each person. For one person, a variable may serve as a protective factor, whereas for others, the variable may be a risk (Stouthamer-Loeber, Loeber, Wei, Farrington, & Wikström, 2002). It is beyond the scope of this chapter to fully explore the differences between the nature, construct, and definition of strengths, protective factors, and promotive factors; however, these differences are important and must be considered. Please see Fortune and Ward (2017) for discussion. The literature and examination of these issues are still in their infancy. It is therefore appropriate that examination of each of these factors and approaches continue so that our understanding of these issues can strengthen (Polaschek, 2017).

Ultimately, assessment tools are designed to help practitioners determine the risk and needs within a client, identify areas of treatment, and help reduce recidivism and future harm. In one review of strengths-based assessments, Wanamaker, Jones, and Brown (2018) examined eight assessment tools used in the assessment of forensic populations. They did not restrict examination to either protective or promotive factors, and as such found some interesting results. Of the eight tools included in the review, when measuring for recidivism, they found empirical evidence of a promotive effect across all eight tools. However, when considering the protective effect of each tool, they found empirical evidence for only two of the tools (the Structured Assessment Protective Factors [SAPROF] and the Youth Assessment and Screening Instrument [YASI] and Service Planning Instrument [SPIn]), with one having mixed results (Short-term Assessment of Risk and Treatability [START]). For the purpose of this chapter, the SAPROF, SPIn, and self-report measures are described, as they report benefits when assessing both promotive and protective factors.

Structured Assessment Protective Factors (SAPROF)

In light of the absence of assessment tools that considered protective factors for forensic psychiatric patients, de Vogel, de Vries Robbé, de Ruiter, and Bouman (2011) developed the SAPROF between 2004 and 2011. They note that its intention was to be used for adult forensic patients with a history of (sexually) violent offending and was designed to be completed alongside structured professional judgement tools such as the Historical Clinical Risk Mangement-20 (HCR-20) (Webster, Douglas, Eaves, & Hart, 1997).

The SAPROF tool is divided into three subscales – internal, motivational, and external items. Internal items include intelligence, secure attachment in childhood, empathy, coping, and self-control. The items in the motivational subscale include work, leisure activities, financial management, motivation for treatment, attitudes towards authority, life goals, and medication. Finally, external items include social network, intimate relationships, professional care, living circumstances, and external control. Apart from the item intelligence and secure attachment in childhood, de Vogel et al. (2011) note that all items are dynamic. A note regarding dynamic factors is included at the end of this chapter. Each item is scored on a three-point scale, where the assessor first establishes if it is present or not and the degree to which it applies to the client: 0 = the item does not apply; 1 = the item probably or partially applies; and 2 = the item definitely applies. The assessor then determines how critical individual items are to aid prevention; these are marked as either key items (currently present) or goal items (to be gained during treatment). Finally, the assessor codes a 'final protection judgement,' classifying a low, moderate, or high level of protection. This final judgement is incorporated into the broader SPJ assessment framework, resulting in an integrated final risk score for future violent behaviour.

The interrater reliability (IRR) of the tool and the predictive validity of the tool has been examined on several occasions. In the examination of 83 sexual offenders, de Vries Robbé, de Vogel, Koster, and Bogaerts (2015) found the SAPROF to have a good IRR for both first scoring (ICC=.85) and the final protection judgement (ICC=.73), and moderate to excellent rates for individual factors. In terms of its predictive power for future offending, de Vries Robbé, de Vogel et al. (2015) retrospectively examined recidivism and both one to three years and up to 15 years of follow up. While the final protection judgement was less accurate in predicting sexual violence when compared to the total SAPROF score, when combined with the HCR-20 it was as equally predictive. The tool demonstrated good predictive strength for sexually violent offences.

From a forensic perspective, whilst results are mixed, they remain encouraging. In Yoon et al.'s (2016) validity study, they examined retrospectively a sample of incarcerated adult male sexual offenders (*n*=450) in Austria. They compared the predictive strength of the SAPROF when compared to the SVR-20. The interrater reliability measures for this study were reasonable, although two of the five internal items and all external items demonstrated variability and poor reliability. However, while the sum of protective factors for general, nonsexual, and sexual violence recidivism in a sexual offending population was found to be reasonably predictive, the predictive power for sexual recidivism alone was not significant. While the SAPROF was a significant predictor of various recidivism categories, it did not add any predictive value beyond SVR-20. This study was a retrospective study and research was completed using the retrieval of archived case files. As

Yoon et al. (2016) note, the limitation of this type of study may be responsible for the low predictive accuracy.

When looking at a broader community sample, Haines et al. (2018) compared the results of SAPROF, HCR-20, and the Hare Psychopathy Check List – Screening Version in a sample of forensic (*n*=55), non-forensic (*n*=100), and community (*n*=106) mental health service clients. They argue any opportunity to support the assessment and treatment process with people with mental health needs, by using strengths-based approaches, ought to be encouraged. They found that the use of the SAPROF enabled greater inclusion with clients through the assessment process. Likewise, it was holistic and motivational, as its inclusive approach relies heavily on service user involvement and is thus likely to achieve greater commitment to treatment plans. In terms of its validity, Haines et al. (2018) found good concurrent validity overall when compared with the other two tools and the predictive validity was good overall.

SPIn

In another assessment tool that uses protective factors, the Service Planning Instrument (SPIn) (Orbis Partners, 2003) is used for male and female adult incarcerated and community populations. The tool requires assessors to evaluate 90 items that include risks, needs, and strengths across 11 domains. The domains include criminal history, response to supervision, aggression/violence, substance abuse, social influences, family, employment, attitudes, social/cognitive skills, stability, and mental health. Following an in-depth interview and review of case records, assessors score items on the SPIn using a six-point Likert-type scale; the totals of scores cumulate to both domain level and overall level scoring for classification. Clients can be classified as low, moderate, or high on both risk and strength scales. For example, a person might be assessed as high risk but have high strengths too.

In a study examining the predictive validity of the pre screen SPIn, Jones, Brown, Robinson, and Frey (2015) found high levels of accuracy in the tool when testing for recidivism over an 18-month period. Importantly, it was the addition of the strengths scores that provided incremental validity of the tool over and above the risk score itself. It was noted that in cases where high strength scores were recorded along with high risk classifications, the recidivism rates were buffered, indicating the importance strengths may play in helping mitigate some of the challenges people face when attempting to reintegrate into the community. Findings from this study demonstrate the importance of including strengths in assessment when considering the possible risk a person presents. Indeed, it is argued that by adding strength components into these tools, prediction of recidivism with greater accuracy and precision occurs (Jones & Robinson, 2018). Thus, the incorporation of strengths during assessment helps practitioners and clinicians direct resources and treatment appropriately. For example, if we were to consider a client with a mixture of positive and antisocial influences in his life, and if a practitioner were to consider an assessment based on risk alone, he might be assessed as a high risk of recidivism based on his antisocial relationships. Yet when combined with a strengths approach, his risk of recidivism is likely to reduce when the positive influences and meaningful relationships are taken into consideration.

In an excellent review of strengths-based assessments, Wanamaker et al. (2018) found studies demonstrating greater predictive accuracy with the quantitative inclusion of strengths. Although individual strength items are yet to be fully understood or tested to date, the strengths included in this tool appear protective.

Self-report measures

There also exists the development of several quantitative self-report measures aimed to assess the risk and needs of people convicted of offending. For example, the Inventory of Offender Risk, Needs, and Strengths (IORNS), which is a 130-item self-report measure, aims to measure both static and dynamic risks, needs, and strengths of factors related to general, violent, and sexual offending behaviour (Miller, 2006). The tool is intended for use in a variety of correctional contexts such as parole hearings, evaluations of offender progress, or assignment to specific risk classification. However, aside from the key purpose of assessing the likelihood of further offending, initial intentions were to address a gap in provision that might help practitioners identify and quantify treatment needs and goals and thus measure progress of treatment and management interventions (Miller, 2018). One of the unique aspects of the tool is its utilisation of needs and strengths. Practitioners can draw from the findings of a completed IORNS and develop plans that can help mitigate risk, as well as help clients develop new strengths or use protective factors to buffer against future situations related to offending. Arguably, by working with the client after they have identified their own strengths through the self-reported measure, the client can not only see the strengths they have but can be supported in exploring ways of capitalising upon these strengths. One issue of self-report is, however, that a client may not be able to self-report or identify strengths, which may be quite demotivating for a client. This is particularly the case for people convicted of sexual offences who often present, post-conviction, with extremely low levels of self-worth and self-esteem. Practitioners must therefore look to support a strategy that can help develop areas of strength, and follow up with a further self-report measure to quantify the change – such a process is likely to be rewarding for both client and practitioner.

Young people

A positive criminological perspective can be helpful for younger people, regardless of the type of crime they have committed. For young people there are added layers of concern when dealing with criminal behaviours, particularly when consequences of labelling are experienced by those convicted of sexual crime. In particular, issues of vulnerability and stages in development make it less appropriate to criminalise young people and more emphasis is needed to care for and support young people following the commission of a crime, particularly a sexual one. A movement known as Children First/Offenders Second (CFOS) helps bring young people back into focus and away from current reductionist approaches that are risk-led, overly punitive, and adult centric (Norris, Griffith, & Norris, 2017). Instead, CFOS promotes the notion that children are themselves not the problem, but are part of a problem, and even as children need to be at the centre of solutions. One of the ways youth offending services across England and Wales assess the needs of young people following the commission of any crime is through a framework known as AssetPlus (Wilson & Hings, 2011). The foundations of the framework are built upon desistance literature and the Good Lives Model (Baker, 2014) in that assessments require identification of both the risks and protective factors the young person presents. By incorporating these approaches, assessors are required to consider the range of interactions in the young person's life, the context and situation of their behaviour, the young person's own perspective, and what needs or goals were being met by the behaviours. As well as identifying risks that may take the person closer to problematic behaviour, assessors must also identify existing and potential strengths in the young person. By contextualising these in the person's life, they can then develop intervention plans that incorporate and develop strengths and protective factors in the young person's life. One of the encouraging features of AssetPlus is that it is designed to be flexible and thus respond to the changing needs of the young person. Assessments are not fixed in one point in time but are fluid and responsive to change. Young people are at the centre of the assessment and planning process, and their input through self-assessment and engagement with assessors is equally valuable to those deemed as 'experts,' making judgements and decisions on the young person's life. This type of strengths-based assessment/approach is conducive to a positive criminological approach. However, for all assessments of this kind, including those discussed in this chapter, caution is needed, as the theoretical basis upon which all these assessments are built are likely to be theoretically limited.

While the notion of engaging in strengths-based approaches or considering protective factors in risk assessment has been well received, there remain issues that need to be addressed. Like those raised by Ward and Beech (2015) regarding the lack of theoretical construction of dynamic risk factors, protective factors face the same problem (Ward, 2017). It appears instinctive that by adding protective factors to existing risk assessment tools they are strengthened; yet without theoretical foundation and empirical testing of protective factors, we cannot yet be confident in their validity (Wanamaker et al., 2018).

Ward (2016a) provides a detailed discussion regarding the conceptual problems of dynamic risk factors, but in summary, he argues that protective factors, like dynamic risk factors, are as yet not clearly defined, they lack clarity regarding their nature (it is unclear if they are causal or predictive), and as a result of these theoretical limitations practitioners cannot be confident when using them in assessments or when applying to treatment. The issue of defining protective factors (and dynamic risk factors) is therefore important. The literature tends to imply (Fortune & Ward, 2017), incorrectly, that these factors are causally related to offending and thus factors, if changed through treatment, will reduce reoffending. However, because risk and protective factors are normative in nature, in that they describe a particular way in which an activity ought to be carried out, usually through socially accepted standards, such factors cannot be causal (Heffernan & Ward, 2019).

Risk and protective factors are multi-variable in nature, made up of composite constructs. They lack theoretical coherency, and are limited in terms of explanatory value. For example, the factor of 'antisocial cognition' includes variables of attitudes, values, rationalisations, and identity. Without any clarity regarding how these variables operate, either together or individually, the notion of the factor of antisocial cognition cannot be causally linked to crime. This is an issue for clinicians when determining appropriate treatment pathways for clients. It is therefore advised that when working with clients, a case formulation approach is adopted in which the full range and presence of risks and strengths are considered. This allows the client's situation to be understood through a biological, psychological, and sociological lens. The multifaceted nature of these factors needs to be considered and not just addressed in the form of a list of dynamic risk and protective factors.

Conclusion

Given that the results of any assessment carried out in a forensic setting is likely to inform life changing decisions regarding the client (being released from or sent to a prison/secure hospital, having restrictions or requirements placed upon them, etc.), carrying out a full and robust assessment is critical from both a public protection perspective as well as a humane and ethical one. While current risk approaches rightly focus on the identification of risk and harm reduction, this is sometimes at the cost of the client, when consideration of the strengths or protective factors in their life may well buffer or mitigate some of the identified risks. There are, as detailed in this chapter, a number of strength- and risk-based tools already in operation across forensic settings, yet they require further examination and testing to ensure practitioners can be confident that their assessments are based on a sound theoretical foundation. Granted, much further work is needed, but early indications suggest assessments that adopted positive criminological principles (considers individual strengths, is integrative, peruses a positive outcome for the client) would enable assessors to focus equally on the risks and strengths of a person, and any decisions regarding subsequent management or treatment plans could be considered comprehensive and meaningful.

References

Baglivio, M. T., Wolff, K. T., Piquero, A. R., Howell, J. C., & Greenwald, M. A. (2016). Risk assessment trajectories of youth during juvenile justice residential placement: Examining risk, promotive, and "buffer" scores. *Criminal Justice and Behavior*, *44*(3), 360–394.

Baker, K. (2014). AssetPlus rationale. *Youth Justice Board*. Retrieved from https://assets.publishing.service.gov.uk/government/uploads/system/uploads/attachment_data/file/367782/AssetPlus_Rationale_revised_October_2014_1_0.pdf de Vogel, V., de Vries Robbé, M., de Ruiter, C., & Bouman, Y. H. (2011). Assessing protective factors in forensic psychiatric practice: Introducing the SAPROF. *International Journal of Forensic Mental Health, 10*(3), 171–177.

de Vries Robbé, M., de Vogel, V., Koster, K., & Bogaerts, S. (2015). Assessing protective factors for sexually violent offending with the SAPROF. *Sexual Abuse: A Journal of Research and Treatment, 27*(1), 51–70.

de Vries Robbé, M., Mann, R. E., Maruna, S., & Thornton, D. (2015). An exploration of protective factors supporting desistance from sexual offending. *Sexual Abuse: A Journal of Research and Treatment, 27*(1), 16–33.

Dowling, N. A., Merkouris, S. S., Greenwood, C. J., Oldenhof, E., Toumbourou, J. W., & Youssef, G. J. (2017). Early risk and protective factors for problem gambling: A systematic review and meta-analysis of longitudinal studies. *Clinical Psychology Review, 51*, 109–124.

Dubreuil, P., Forest, J., & Courcy, F. (2014). From strengths use to work performance: The role of harmonious passion, subjective vitality, and concentration. *The Journal of Positive Psychology, 9*(4), 335–349.

Farrington, D. P., Loeber, R., Jolliffe, D., & Pardini, D. A. (2008). Promotive and risk processes at different life stages. In R. Loeber, D. P. Farrington, M. Stouthamer-Loeber, & H. Raskin White (Eds.), *Violence and serious theft: Development and prediction from childhood to adulthood* (pp. 169–230). New York: Routledge Taylor & Francis Group.

Feeley, M. M., & Simon, J. (1992). The new penology: Notes on the emerging strategy of corrections and its implications. *Criminology, 30*(4), 449–474.

Fortune, C. A., & Ward, T. (2017). Problems in protective factor research and practice. *Aggression and Violent Behavior, 32*, 1–3.

Foucault, M., Simon, J., & Elden, S. (2017). Danger, crime and rights: A conversation between Michel Foucault and Jonathan Simon. *Theory, Culture & Society, 34*(1), 3–27.

Haines, A., Brown, A., Javaid, S. F., Khan, F., Noblett, S., Omodunbi, O., . . . Whittington, R. (2018). Asessing protective factors for violence risk in UK general mental health services using the structured assessment of protective factors. *International Journal of Offender Therapy and Comparative Criminology, 62*(12), 3965–3983.

Hall, J. E., Simon, T. R., Mercy, J. A., Loeber, R., Farrington, D. P., & Lee, R. D. (2012). Centers for disease control and prevention's expert panel on protective factors for youth violence perpetration: Background and overview. *American Journal of Preventive Medicine, 43*(2), S1–S7.

Harrison, K. (2011). *Dangerousness, risk and the governance of serious sexual and violent offenders*. Oxon, UK: Routledge.

Heffernan, R., & Ward, T. (2019). Dynamic risk factors, protective factors, and value-laden practices. *Psychiatry, Psychology & Law, 26*(2), 312–328. Retrieved from www.tandfonline.com/doi/abs/10.1080/13218719.2018.1506721

Jolliffe, D., Farrington, D. P., Loeber, R., & Pardini, D. (2016). Protective factors for violence: Results from the pittsburgh youth study. *Journal of Criminal Justice, 45*, 32–40.

Jones, N. J., Brown, S. L., Robinson, D., & Frey, D. (2015). Incorporating strengths into quantitative assessments of criminal risk for adult offenders: The service planning instrument. *Criminal Justice and Behavior, 42*(3), 321–338.

Jones, N. J., & Robinson, D. (2018). Service Planning Instrument (SPIn). In J. P. Singh, D. G. Kroner, J. S. Wormith, S. L. Desmarais, & Z. Hamilton (Eds.), *Handbook of recidivism risk/needs assessment tools* (pp. 181–198). West Sussex, UK: John Wiley & Sons.

Marshall, W. L., Marshall, L. E., Serran, G. A., & O'Brien, M. D. (2011). *Rehabilitating sexual offenders: A strength-based approach.* Washington, DC: American Psychological Association.

Meinck, F., Cluver, L. D., Boyes, M. E., & Mhlongo, E. L. (2014). Risk and protective factors for physical and sexual abuse of children and adolescents in Africa: A review and implications for practice. *Trauma, Violence, & Abuse*, *16*(1), 81–107.
Miller, H. A. (2006). A dynamic assessment of offender risk, needs, and strengths in a sample of pre-release general offenders. *Behavioral Sciences & the Law*, *24*(6), 767–782.
Miller, H. A. (2018). The inventory of offender risk, needs, and strengths (IORNS). In J. P. Singh, D. G. Kroner, J. S. Wormith, S. L. Desmarais, & Z. Hamilton (Eds.), *Handbook of recidivism risk/needs assessment tools* (pp. 101–116). West Susex: John Wiley & Sons.
Norris, G., Griffith, G., & Norris, H. (2017). Risk assessment in youth justice: A child-centered approach to managing interventions. In W. Petherick & G. Sinnamon (Eds.), *The psychology of criminal and antisocial behavior* (pp. 211–231). Oxford: Academic Press.
Oliver, C., & Charles, G. (2015). Which strengths-based practice? Reconciling strengths-based practice and mandated authority in child protection work. *Social Work*, *60*(2), 135–143.
Orbis Partners. (2003). Service Planning Instrument (SPIn). Ottawa, Canada.
Polaschek, D. L. L. (2017). Protective factors, correctional treatment and desistance. *Aggression and Violent Behavior*, *32*, 64–70.
Quinlan, D. M., Swain, N., Cameron, C., & Vella-Brodrick, D. A. (2015). How 'other people matter'in a classroom-based strengths intervention: Exploring interpersonal strategies and classroom outcomes. *The Journal of Positive Psychology*, *10*(1), 77–89.
Seligman, M. E. P., & Csikszentmihalyi, M. (2000). Positive psychology: An introduction. *American Psychologist*, *55*(1), 5–14.
Stouthamer-Loeber, M., Loeber, R., Wei, E., Farrington, D. P., & Wikström, P.-O. H. (2002). Risk and promotive effects in the explanation of persistent serious delinquency in boys. *Journal of Consulting and Clinical Psychology*, *70*(1), 111–123.
Wanamaker, K. A., Jones, N. J., & Brown, S. L. (2018). Strengths-based assessments for use with forensic populations: A critical review. *International Journal of Forensic Mental Health*, *17*(2), 202–221.
Ward, T. (2016a). Dynamic risk factors: Scientific kinds or predictive constructs. *Psychology, Crime & Law*, *22*(1–2), 2–16.
Ward, T. (2017). Prediction and agency: The role of protective factors in correctional rehabilitation and desistance. *Aggression and Violent Behavior*, *32*, 19–28.
Ward, T., & Beech, A. R. (2015). Dynamic risk factors: A theoretical dead-end? *Psychology, Crime & Law*, *21*(2), 100–113.
Webster, C. D., Douglas, K. S., Eaves, D., & Hart, S. D. (1997). *HCR-20. Assessing the risk of violence. Version 2*. Burnaby, Canada: Simon Fraser University and Forensic Psychiatric Services Commission of British Columbia.
White, M. A., & Waters, L. E. (2015). A case study of 'The good school:'Examples of the use of Peterson's strengths-based approach with students. *The Journal of Positive Psychology*, *10*(1), 69–76.
Wilson, E., & Hings, S. (2011). Assessing the predictive validity of the asset youth risk assessment tool using the Juvenile Cohort Study (JCS). *Ministry of Justice Research Series 10/11*. Retrieved from https://assets.publishing.service.gov.uk/government/uploads/system/uploads/attachment_data/file/217365/assessing-predictive-validity.pdf
Yoon, D., Turner, D., Klein, V., Rettenberger, M., Eher, R., & Briken, P. (2016). Factors predicting desistance from reoffending: A validation study of the SAPROF in sexual offenders. *International Journal of Offender Therapy and Comparative Criminology*, *62*(3), 697–716.

8 Current positive criminology applications in terms of treatment and management

Introduction

As outlined in Chapter 6, positive criminology is an aspirational concept. As such, there are no formal treatment, management, interventions, or programmes labelled as 'positive criminology.' Yet there are several examples whereby practitioners are working in ways that perhaps inadvertently adhere to the principles of positive criminology. The purpose of this chapter therefore is to explore current interventions, programmes, or approaches when working with people convicted of sexual offending, and the extent to which they fit the positive criminology vision. Interventions or approaches detailed in this chapter do not themselves claim to be a positive criminological programmes. Instead, following our cursory review of the literature, it is our own interpretation and application of the principles of positive criminology to these programmes that are discussed.

For interventions or programmes to be included in our analysis and thus defined as meeting the principles of positive criminology, they had to meet all three core themes of positive criminology. Ronel and Segev (2014, p. 1390) detail these as:

> a) an accentuated orientation toward integration at any level (individual, social, and spiritual), b) achievement of this integration by means of forces and effects that target individuals' experience as positive, and c) the belief that these forces and effects might assist individuals or groups in refraining from crime and deviance.

In addition to these three themes, we further employed Ronel and Segev's (2014) six categories or explanations of positive criminology. They state that a positive criminological approach can a) help reduce reoffending, b) foster a holistic approach in which all aspects of the person's life are considered, c) be mutually driven, in that the person takes ownership of both their problems and the solution in collaboration with practitioners, d) be socially inclusive, e) enable a spiritual effect, and f) serve as a role model for change and transformation. In our review, we judged the degree to which any of these six categories were present within the approaches or interventions being considered. Clearly, the greater the number of Ronel and Segev's six categories that could be mapped onto an approach or intervention in this review equated to our assumption that the approach was more akin to a positive criminological philosophy. Our aim here is to simply explore the extent to which existing interventions delivered to people convicted of sexual offending can be applied to a positive criminology approach.

As discussed in Chapter 6, the earliest introduction to the notion of positive criminology was made by Ronel and Elisha (2011). We wanted to allow a reasonable period in which we might expect to see studies reference aspects of positive criminology, and so allowed two years post this introduction. We thus limited our search of the published literature to between 2013 and 2018. We used EBSCO MEDLINE, PsycINFO, and Web of Science electronic databases to search and retrieve articles. We used search terms that included ("sex offender treatment" OR "offender treatment" OR "sex offender management" OR "offender management") AND ("positive criminology" OR "positive psychology" OR "strengths-based"). We also carried out a 'hand search,' using a Google Scholar function to search for articles citing Ronel and/or Elisha. After the removal of duplicate papers, those that were discussion or theoretical papers only, those that did not feature people with sexual convictions, and papers we were unable to access in full or in English, a total of nine studies were obtained. These are each presented in Table 8.1. Study information and findings are tabulated to enable comparison. In addition, Table 8.2 indicates which of Ronel and Segev's (2014) six positive criminological categories the study explicitly meets. It is important to note here that we were not looking for authors to specifically cite or indicate an association with the notion of positive criminology. Instead, we wanted to map, for the purpose of discussion, the categories onto the intervention as a result of our understanding of each category. This allows early exploration of the extent to which positive criminology is already being delivered in practice in the treatment and management of people convicted of sexual offending.

A small sum of nine studies from a five-year period were included in our review for this chapter. While this is a disappointing number, it is perhaps unsurprising given that positive criminology as a concept was in its early years of formation. By way, therefore, of an early and introductory discussion of positive criminology, the following section explores how the six positive criminology categories as outlined by Ronel and Segev (2014) feature in each of the papers included in our review, as abridged in Table 8.2. It is not our aim to include a full discussion about each paper. Instead we attempt to simply provide a flavour of how these papers support Ronel and Segev's (2014) claims.

Reducing recidivism

We begin with Ronel and Segev's (2014) first reason as to why adopting a positive criminological approach is important, which is such an approach helps reduce recidivism, not only in cohorts who have sexually offended but across all offender populations. These claims are supported by extensive strengths-based/positive psychology (Marshall, Marshall, Serran & O'Brien, 2011), desistance (Farmer et al., 2015; Ward & Laws, 2010), and rehabilitation theories

Table 8.1 Summary of selected studies for their adherence to positive criminology classifications

Paper	*Aim of study*	*Location, intervention, and/or programme*	*Method of study*	*Results*
1 Fox (2016)	To explore relationships between people with convictions and community members who support them	US – Circles of Support and Accountability (COSA)	Qualitative interviews with 20 core members individually and 59 groups of COSA team members, nine COSA coordinators and unknown correctional staff	COSA helped to re-build trust between the core member and community, helped monitor behaviour, helped develop new relationships, helped decriminalise identity, and reduced recidivism
2 Bows and Westmarland (2018)	To explore how risk should be managed in an older population	England and Wales – no specific intervention; more a discussion regarding strategies to manage an older population	Qualitative interviews with nine police offender managers working with people with sexual convictions	Reported increased number of older clients. This group has specific challenges, e.g. health, housing, trust
3 Farmer, McAlinden, and Maruna (2015)	To explore desistance process in people with sexual convictions	UK – no specific intervention examined although references to probation programmes and supervision made	Qualitative interviews with 32 men convicted of sexual offending – comparison group of men desisting and those not desisting from crime. Narrative analysis	Found that ‘situation’ was important to those desisting in terms of the nature of their initial offence. The role of employment and relationships with others was important

4	Ricci and Clayton (2016)	To explain the offense drivers model used to justify use of Eye Movement Desensitisation and Reprocessing (EMDR)	Delivery of EMDR therapy to help resolve early life trauma in sex offenders	Description of the process, not study as such – but use of a case as an example	Authors make the case that through EMDR, clients' 'offence drivers,' i.e. those that take the persons closer to offending (affective, cognitive, and behavioural variables), are addressed
5	Yoder, Hansen, Lobanov-Rostovsky, and Ruch (2015)	To examine the impact of a family service involvement on the recidivism and treatment completion of young people convicted of sexual offences	US – family service involvement	Probation file review and recidivism data on 81 young people convicted of sexual offences	Family is a protective factor and those with family service involvement were more likely to complete treatment and less likely to recidivate or re-offend – current study did not support association with family service involvement and recidivism, but those living at home were less likely to reoffend
6	Ryan, McCauley, and Walsh (2019)	To explore the experiences of men on a community-based Good Lives Model (GLM) programme	Irish community-based GLM programmes	Semi-structured interviews of 13 men engaged in GLM community-based treatment programme	Aspects of loyalty and therapeutic alliance were important for the success of the group. Model of therapeutic change, i.e. 'virtuous circle of change,' whereby men engaged in a cyclical process – they experienced psychological growth which in turn helped them engage in treatment; group featured as a microcosm in society
7	Vanhooren, Leijssen, and Dezutter (2015)	To explore the experiences of people with sexual convictions when considering post-traumatic growth and psychological stress	US – prison therapy	Mixed method design interviewing and surveying 30 men engaged in prison treatment and convicted of sexual offending	Post-traumatic growth is negatively related to psychological stress. The process of therapy helped participants explore early trauma and develop emotional support and emotional skills to cope with past experiences. Post prison, participants reported drawing on skills learnt in therapy and while in prison to help cope with life's challenges

(Continued)

Table 8.1 (Continued)

Paper	*Aim of study*	*Location, intervention, and/or programme*	*Method of study*	*Results*
8 Merdian, Kettleborough, McCartan, and Perkins (2017)	To explore the application of strengths-based approaches in the self-reported experiences of men desisting from accessing child sexual exploitation material online	Participants were drawn from a UK community treatment centre. However, this study does not focus on a particular programme; instead it examines the personal experiences of participants	Mixed method using online questionnaire with open questions for qualitative analysis	Findings explored what behaviours participants desisting from sexual offending engaged in to support this process. They reported changes in external factors such as a new job, internal factors such as no longer feeling guilt, and a change in their underlying motivation to offend. These findings were applied to the GLM, demonstrating that through strengths-based approaches desistance can be supported, in particular through positive social relationships and fulfilling work or hobbies
9 Elisha, Idisis, and Ronel (2013)	To identify internal strength and external forces that might help those imprisoned for sexual offending make changes in their life	Israel prison – this study does not focus on a particular programme; instead it examines the personal experiences of participants	Qualitative interviews of 38 men incarcerated for sexual offending	Personal and social changes were a result of the support and acceptance from professionals, family members, and religious role models. Internal shifts in motivations also supported change; for example participants recognised their previous self-centred attitudes towards others

Table 8.2 Matrix of positive criminology categories

Paper	*Aim is to reduce recidivism*	*Works with person as a whole*	*Client takes responsibility for self and actions*	*Socially inclusive*	*Spiritual platform*	*Intervention or staff serves as a role model*	*Total*
1	Yes	Yes	Yes	Yes		Yes	5
2	Yes	Yes		Yes			3
3	Yes	Yes	Yes	Yes		Yes	5
4	Yes						1
5	Yes			Yes			2
6	Yes	Yes	Yes	Yes	Yes	Yes	6
7	Yes	Yes	Yes	Yes	Yes	Yes	6
8	Yes	Yes	Yes	Yes			4
9	Yes		Yes	Yes	Yes	Yes	5

(Ward & Maruna, 2007). Indeed, it is argued that by engaging with clients in ways that help achieve personal goals, enhance individual strengths, and improve their lives, as opposed to only focussing on treating individual risk factors, that general risk is, by default, reduced. Reducing recidivism is of course a shared aim, not only for those engaged in the criminal justice system, but for the majority within society (we set to one side here those who are consciously and actively determined to cause harm). It is thus unsurprising to note that all nine papers included in our review discuss the relationship between recidivism and the intervention or approach in focus.

In her discussion of the role of civic engagement, Fox (2016) highlights that further harm is prevented through the development of social relationships during a Circles of Support and Accountability (COSA) intervention because a 'mutual obligation' emerges. It is participants' commitment not to offend that appears to impact recidivism and not just their own personal change. It is their desire to please and maintain ties with others and to not 'let them down' that leads to the risk of recidivism being likely reduced. Likewise, participants in the Farmer et al. (2015) study reported on the importance of relationships to help them desist from crime. The risk of losing longer-term partners far outweighed any benefits to crime. These were often partners who had endured the lengthy process of participants' prison sentences, and as such, the strong bond between them provided more of a motivation to desist and not commit further crime than other controls.

Bows and Westmarland (2018) found genuine vulnerability in older populations who, without appropriate support and help, may be at risk of reoffending. Of concern was the lack of access, knowledge, and resources available to practitioners to effectively help address many of the inadequate housing, poor physical and mental health, and limited social support challenges faced by this older population. It is noteworthy that while Bows and Westmarland (2018) call to address the vulnerabilities in older populations with sexual convictions, the very nature of their age and perceived vulnerability was found to be a risk in and of itself. According to offender managers interviewed in their study, the often incorrectly perceived trust automatically given to people of an older generation was capitalised upon by some clients. While most risk is reduced as people age, Bows and Westmarland (2018) reported that offender managers found some older clients convicted of sexual offending to be a greater risk, due to them exploiting a perceived trustworthiness, allowing them access to potential victims.

It is worth noting that the Bows and Westmarland (2018) study examined the perspectives of offender managers working in a risk dominant culture. It is therefore expected that while offender managers recognise the need to help and support clients in need, for example, by addressing homelessness or loneliness, it is unsurprising that they reported this through a risk-filtered lens. While it is fair that offender managers perceived clients to exploit the notion of older people as safe and harmless, through an alternative lens, offender managers might begin to examine the underlying motivations for this exploitation. A positive criminological approach considers the notion of risk by working with the whole picture, which means that a person's risks and needs ought to be equally addressed. As outlined in the GLM, by understanding the means by which clients aim to achieve primary life goals and by helping them to achieve these through legitimate and adaptive means, risk is reduced.

Fostering a holistic approach

A positive criminological approach requires interventions or approaches to consider the person as an individual, in contrast to reductive approaches that consider individual risks or deficits in isolation. A positive criminological approach is holistic in that it helps the person consider problems or challenges in a global sense, and as a whole person with history, autonomy, subjectivity, and lived experience. Thus, the person's strengths, characteristics, and talents should also be considered. A holistic approach was present in six of our nine studies in this review. In their examination of a community based GLM programme, Ryan et al. (2019) interviewed 16 men who had undergone offender behaviour treatment. They found that participants particularly valued being considered and treated holistically. They felt that the GLM approach, used by practitioners, meant that there was a genuine sense of empathy and "unconditional positive regard" (p. 15). Adopting a person-centred approach provided a valuable platform in which therapists engaged and developed a strong therapeutic alliance with men in the programme. As a result, clients were more open to consider challenges and develop realistic and meaningful good life plans.

Similar findings were reported by Fox (2016). Her participants valued the sense that the COSA team members cared and believed in them as people, rather than only wanting to focus on tackling isolated deficits. By providing support and direction in a broad and general sense, participants' social, human, and cultural capital were all developed. Working with the client also helped to decriminalise their own sense of self. One participant reported that they could now "truly see there is [*sic*] people out there that do care for me and they care for me for who I am" (p. 86). Fox (2016) concludes her study with an important point regarding the unnatural environment of the criminal justice system. Unlike normative communities, the criminal justice system and those working in it can often unintentionally focus, and even obsess, on single variables or individual treatment goals, without considering the person. Fox (2016) notes how an intervention such as COSA can provide a sense of normalcy, in that the person is part of a broader community who in turn considers the person as an individual rather than a set of deficits to treat.

Finally, as a result of Farmer et al's. (2015) life course approach to examining lived experience, valuable life stories were generated. This approach enabled authors to draw to examine different points in time and varying factors across the person's life, enabling an exploration of variables related to both offending and desisting. Authors argued that understanding the person's behaviours, attitudes, and life experiences both prior to offending and during their periods of desistance helped generate greater understanding of the range of behaviours and factors linked to both crime and desistance. By understanding and examining both processes, rather than the traditional examination of the offending (risk) journey, Farmer et al. (2015) argued that approach goal strategies, rather than only avoidance strategies, can be considered for the client. Strongly featured in this study is the importance of the complexity of the individual client, not only in terms of their lived histories, but also the intricate social relations developed over time. To ignore these contextual and temporal factors arguably fails to support the person as they attempt to reintegrate into the community.

Working holistically with clients, particularly those who are in the criminal justice system, requires some recognition of the harm that the system itself can cause people, as well as the fact that many criminalised populations have themselves experienced trauma in their lives. Vanhooren et al. (2015) found that through prison treatment programmes in which early traumatic experiences are explored, participants are provided the opportunity to grow from these often damaging experiences. By addressing both the deficits and pain within clients, through treatment, participants reported being able to draw emotional support from others and appreciate life more fully when reflecting on their own earlier trauma. Indeed, for many participants, their experience of loss or trauma enabled them to grow and change, and continue post-treatment and post-imprisonment.

Taking responsibility/being accountable

Ensuring that a client takes responsibility for both themselves and their past and future actions is said to help support the change process. Indeed, when any change is needed, not just crime-related, some internal recognition and accountability is required. Taking responsibility for one's own actions often requires autonomy and choice. Autonomy is important when considering how we support people to reintegrate into the community; in most cases where sexual abuse has been committed, people are usually imprisoned, and thus, their autonomy is removed. Much work supports the notion that when a person has the freedom to choose and is committed to making change, there is a greater likelihood of change being realised. Therefore, if a person's sense of autonomy following conviction or imprisonment can be returned, they are more likely to feel in control and commit to change. However, wanting to make change is not something that can be enforced; this must come from within the autonomous agent. There must be self-determination and motivation to make personal change.

Accountability and responsibility featured strongly in six of the nine studies in our review. One interesting example is found in the experiences of Vanhooren et al.'s (2015) participants, where an essential part of the process of therapy was for participants to take responsibility for themselves and their own actions. Examining personal traumatic experiences can be difficult. People can both internalise the responsibility for the trauma and blame themselves, or externalise blame to the person who caused the harm. Both positions of responsibility taking can prevent a person from moving on safely from the experience. It is encouraging to note that by enabling and supporting people with convictions to engage in a process of post-traumatic growth treatment, they are able to develop new self-narratives regarding themselves and their trauma, and take responsibility for their criminal behaviour, even when they too had been victims of abuse.

In the description of their Model of Therapeutic Change, Ryan et al. (2019) demonstrate how the use of a strengths-based intervention enables participants to explore a sense of autonomy and responsibility prior to offending and while in treatment. While participants' sense of autonomy and responsibility developed over a period, the process was not linear or static. Instead, autonomy and responsibility developed within participants as a result of key core conditions applied during this intervention. The authors of the study found that the development of therapeutic alliance, as well as group alliance, should not be underestimated in helping to provide confidence in participants' capacity to take account of their own actions. It is likely that as a result of the care and compassion group members and facilitators had for each other, an environment of challenge was enabled whereby individual members were able to hold each other accountable. In addition, through the installation of hope and confidence in participants' ability to change, they were able to build confidence in themselves and their futures. As a result, clients were able to take greater responsibility for their own futures. Likewise, the GLM approach used in this treatment programme helped reduce prior resistance in participants and encourage greater willingness to consider the perspectives of others.

While the process of taking responsibility to gain acceptance of others was a strong factor in the reported experiences of the Elisha et al. (2013) study, participants also had to experience a process of self-acceptance. For them to do this, accountability was needed, requiring acknowledgement of the nature of their offending and their role in causing harm to others. By engaging in a process of reintegrative shaming, applied to the self, participants were able to acknowledge and take responsibility for their own harmful behaviours.

Adopting a socially inclusive approach

Positive criminology calls for interventions and programmes to ensure they are socially inclusive. Ronel and Segev (2014) summarise the nature of reintegration as essentially a social one, thus failure to include strategies, opportunities, and mechanisms for people to engage with society limits their ability to reintegrate effectively. Of importance here is not only the commitment and attempt by the person with a conviction to re-engage with society, but for society to embrace the person returning to the community. It is likely that both the person with a conviction as well as those living within the community will need support and assistance. A positive criminological approach ensures and recognises the reciprocal process and need for social engagement and integration. Eight of the nine studies included aspects of social inclusivity in their examination of this client group.

In their exploration of the impact of family service involvement for young people with sexual convictions, Yoder et al. (2015) found where young people experienced a greater input from family services, they were almost three times more likely to complete treatment, which in turn is likely to help support the young person in living a life free from future crime. While the authors note some limitations with this study in terms of methodological problems, small sample size, missing data, and possible impact of variables that could not be controlled for, the study still provides an excellent platform to support the notion that in order to support young people convicted of sexual offending, their social and familial environment must be supported too. While most young people who sexually offend do so within the family, collaboration between professionals, educators, health providers, and guardians is essential. Yoder et al. (2015) highlight the importance of a socially inclusive approach, both for the reintegration of the young person but also support for the recovery of extended family members following abuse. While studies are limited, family treatment interventions and therapies appear to offer a promising avenue to support young people engaged in sexual offending behaviours and their family members.

This finding is echoed in the self-reported findings of Farmer et al. (2015), whose participants describe the protective nature of their partnerships and family relationships. Participants expressed concern regarding the harm they caused, either directly or indirectly, to family members through their sexual offending, recognising the need to repair damage and remain offence-free to maintain relations. Similarly, engaging in post-traumatic treatment/therapy, Vanhooren et al's. (2015) participants reported how their success was partly a result of support of group members during and after treatment.

In both the Fox (2016) and Merdian et al. (2017) studies, securing informal or unofficial social support was perhaps the most important factor to support the re-entry and desistance process. However, of equal importance was the meaning of these relationships. For example, Fox (2016) discusses one participant who highlights that the relationships within a COSA programme are mandatory and therefore to some extent meaningless. Given that these relationships are not naturally formed, it is understandable that developing trust may take some time. A positive criminological approach, however, recognises that all relationships require an element of trust, whether these are professional or personal, and as such, all interventions that aim to help develop social integration must be designed to support formal and informal networks. The value of formal and official relationships are understandably perceived as less worthy than those naturally developed outside of the criminal justice context, particularly as participants often reported volunteers as "do gooders" (Fox, 2016, p. 77). Yet for those who have no family or friends, engaging in COSA is perhaps the first step to developing any social capital.

Critical to the reintegration of participants in the study carried out by Elisha et al. (2013) was also the notion of social acceptance. Here the importance of the person and community accepting the individual returning to the community following a conviction of sexual abuse is clearly demonstrated. Participants report how acceptance gained from intimate partners, even after they were found to have lived a double life, was invaluable. The support of partners did not come without condition; however, participants were clear that their responsibility and commitment to change was essential for continued support. This enabled participants to engage in a more productive relationship. Likewise, extended family support was also vital. Participants reported that family were able to draw on other aspects of the person's life and character and see beyond their sexual offending behaviour.

Spiritual horizon

Like the primary good of *spirituality* in the GLM (Ward & Stewart, 2003), positive criminology suggests that interventions ought to provide a spiritual platform upon which people can begin to examine deeper meaning within their lives (we provide greater focus on this issue in Chapter 9). This factor is not about attending a religious place of worship or adhering to a religious ideal (although for some it may be so). The focus instead is on helping the person increase connectedness with the world around them, found in nature, art, relationships with others, or even an inner peace within oneself. Ultimately, a positive criminological approach would support the development of an individual's capacity to move away from a self-centred position. But let's provide some discussion here more generally. Indeed, there are many examples of this within the criminal justice system and the general offending population. However, in the context of this review, only three of the nine papers appear to have explored the notion of a spiritual platform. Ryan et al.'s (2019) participants engaged in a GLM programme. The authors reported shifts in empathy towards others, which is arguably the movement of a self-centred focus to a position where the feelings and experiences of others are considered. However, empathy in this sense appeared to relate more to accountability and a recognition of the harm caused by offending behaviour rather than any deeper meaning. The development of a person's spirituality or inner peace as defined in the GLM is related more to the importance of connecting with something bigger than ourselves; this is often achieved through activities such as yoga, meditation, and time spent out in nature. The participants in the Vanhooren et al. (2015) study were able to reflect upon their personal experiences of trauma and draw meaning from personal growth. For example, participants were able to begin to understand themselves within a global context or perspective. By drawing deeper meaning of their purpose in life, participants were able to recognise the self-centred nature of their motivations to cause sexual harm to others and put strategies in place to move away from this type of behaviour.

Being accepted by spiritual leaders provided a vital source of support for Elisha et al's. (2013) participants. The nature of their relationships with a faith allowed them to repent and seek forgiveness. In addition, engaging in religious practice and values provided them with the opportunity to present a particular self to others that might help demonstrate to others their committed change. Engaging in and being accepted by a religious community also helped provide some boundaries, both external and internal, which participants felt helped them in their rehabilitation process.

Role models for change and transformation

The final factor used to define a positive criminological approach includes the idea that the intervention, or staff members delivering the programme, serve as a role model for change and transformation. Ronel and Segev (2014) highlight that for a positive criminological approach to be effective, practitioners must operate from a perspective of tolerance, respect, and dignity. This has the potential to conflict with traditional forms of criminal justice, such as the application of punishment. While certain interventions cause unintentional harm, many forms of punishment (such as the death penalty) are intended to harm the person convicted of a crime. For example, an official executioner can behave in a respectful manner towards the person on death row; their action of administering a lethal injection conflicts with the notion of a respectful role model. Likewise, criminal justice officials can attempt to treat inmates with dignity and respect, but this fails in cases where innocent people are imprisoned and the guilty go free, yet the order of the court is still required of the criminal justice official. This presents the world in a particularly unjust and inconsistent light. Thus, adopting a position whereby practitioners and programmes serve as mechanisms of change and models of human virtue arguably provides an opportunity to practice what it promotes. Evidence of this approach was found in five of the nine studies we identified.

Fox (2016) found that participants (both core members and volunteers) embraced the COSA relationship as one of both mentor and friend. Participants described the relationships in a way that endorses this factor. They labelled the relationships as a "kind of parent, mentor, teacher, friend, or peer advocate . . . we are a group of wise aunts and uncles" (p. 80). Farmer et al. (2015) also notes how appreciative participants were about their probation officers. They felt that even under formal correctional conditions, the personal characteristics of their probation officer were positive in that they demonstrated personal interest in them but were also firm when appropriate. Finally, Ryan et al. (2019) report that to support a model of change, a therapeutic alliance between the treatment facilitator and client is essential. Participants reported how respect and unconditional positive regard between facilitator and client were essential to the transformation process. They observed that facilitators were able to model effective conflict resolution, which in turn provided opportunities for clients to develop their own coping strategies and improve communication during treatment. Working with female therapists also provided further role modelling in relation to positive healthy interactions and relationships with women. For many of the participants in this study, their offences targeted women, and as such, this type of modelling served as an excellent platform to help them grow as individuals.

Conclusion

Within this chapter, we reported on a small number of approaches and interventions working to support and treat people convicted of sexual offending, using the principles of positive criminology. It is important to note that these interventions exist and operate in a punitive climate and a regime of risk management. Thus, it is unreasonable to expect interventions and approaches to be able to fully embrace and operate within a pure positive criminological paradigm. Despite this, our review found reports of clients, practitioners, volunteers, and family members sharing the responsibility of addressing harmful behaviour. Where a shared strategy took place, bonds were strengthened and stigma reduced. Indeed, through this type of social integration, the complexity of sexual offending and the lives of those causing harm was recognised. Thus, solutions to crime were not risk focussed, but instead centred on the needs of the client, and in some cases their post-traumatic growth. Paradoxically, the sharing of solutions and commitment from communities to support the person created greater responsibility taking and autonomy in those convicted of sexual offending.

References

Bows, H., & Westmarland, N. (2018). Older sex offenders – Managing risk in the community from a policing perspective. *Policing and Society*, *28*(1), 62–74.

Elisha, E., Idisis, Y., & Ronel, N. (2013). Positive criminology and imprisoned sex offenders: Demonstration of a way out from a criminal spin through acceptance relationships. *Journal of Sexual Aggression*, *19*(1), 66–80.

Farmer, M., McAlinden, A.-M., & Maruna, S. (2015). Understanding desistance from sexual offending a thematic review of research findings. *Probation Journal*, *62*(4), 320–335.

Fox, K. J. (2016). Civic commitment: Promoting desistance through community integration. *Punishment & Society*, *18*(1), 68–94.

Marshall, W. L., Marshall, L. E., Serran, G. A., & O'Brien, M. D. (2011). *Rehabilitating sexual offenders: A strength-based approach*. Washington, DC: American Psychological Association.

Merdian, H., Kettleborough, D., McCartan, K., & Perkins, D. E. (2017). Strength-based approaches to online child sexual abuse: Using self-management strategies to enhance desistance behaviour in users of child sexual exploitation material. *Journal of Criminal Psychology*, *7*(3), 182–191.

Ricci, R. J., & Clayton, C. A. (2016). EMDR with sex offenders: Using offense drivers to guide conceptualization and treatment. *Journal of EMDR Practice and Research*, *10*(2), 104–118.

Ronel, N., & Elisha, E. (2011). A different perspective: Introducing positive criminology. *International Journal of Offender Therapy and Comparative Criminology*, *55*(2), 305–325.

Ronel, N., & Segev, D. (2014). Positive criminology in practice. *International Journal of Offender Therapy and Comparative Criminology*, *58*(11), 1389–1407.

Ryan, M., McCauley, M., & Walsh, D. (2019). The virtuous circle: A grounded theory exploration of the good lives model. *Sexual Abuse*, *31*(8), 908–929.

Vanhooren, S., Leijssen, M., & Dezutter, J. (2015). Posttraumatic growth during incarceration: A case study from an experiential – Existential perspective. *Journal of Humanistic Psychology*, *58*(2), 144–167.

Ward, T., & Laws, D. R. (2010). Desistance from sex offending: Motivating change, enriching practice. *International Journal of Forensic Mental Health*, *9*(1), 11–23.

Ward, T., & Maruna, S. (2007). *Rehabilitation: Beyond the risk paradigm*. London: Routledge.

Ward, T., & Stewart, C. A. (2003). The treatment of sex offenders: Risk management and good lives. *Professional Psychology: Research and Practice*, *34*(4), 353–360.

Yoder, J. R., Hansen, J., Lobanov-Rostovsky, C., & Ruch, D. (2015). The impact of family service involvement on treatment completion and general recidivism among male youthful sexual offenders. *Journal of offender Rehabilitation*, *54*(4), 256–277.

9 Religion, spirituality, and positive criminology

Religion, religiosity, and spirituality

The terms religion, religiosity, and spirituality are often used interchangeably, although "from the point of view of research, there are no true and false definitions of religion, but only more and less fruitful ones" (Glock & Stark, 1965, p. 29). Clarity of both the definition and differences between religion, religiosity, and spirituality is lacking within the literature (Bjarnason, 2007), although it is not our aim to debate and discuss these issues here. Instead, we intend to apply religion in its purest sense, in that it "refers to a set of habits, practices and disciplines associated with a particular faith tradition" (Beedon, 2019, p. 16). Here the individual prays, attends places of worship, and adheres to rituals/sacrifices in accordance to the standards, values, and guidance of their chosen religion. Religiosity, however, is a "characteristic of individuals and collectives that display various features of beliefs" (Sherkat, 2015, p. 377). Furthermore, it is complex, multidimensional, and involves cognitive, emotional, motivational, and behavioural elements (Hackney & Sanders, 2003) associated with an existing religion (Stolz, 2009). The term spirituality brings with it some vagueness, as well as a degree of neutrality (Beedon, 2019). On one hand it can stand apart from the notion of religion and religiosity, as it is less affiliated with our conventional understanding of religion, yet on the other hand, it can also sit comfortably within it. Spirituality is often referred to in the context of a person's spiritual needs (religious or not), relating more to our conscious connection with existential existence. Thus, the drive to enhance our spiritual richness need not be attained through religious affiliation, but could equally be achieved through engagement with, for example, nature.

Over the last century, a growth in criminal justice religious and spiritual (non-faith) interventions has emerged. Many studies report that through religious practice, affiliation, and spiritual belief, positive psychological effects can be experienced. For example, regular and positive attendance at religious gatherings opens social networks and improves feelings of life satisfaction (Lim & Putnam, 2010) and a sense of growth and purpose can be experienced (Greenfield, Vaillant, & Marks, 2009). Furthermore, personal prayer can help emotional management, problem solving, and self-reflection (Sharp, 2010) and therefore religious practice can reduce anxiety and depression (Mela et al., 2008). Finally, for those engaged in religious meditation, improved coping strategies and hope can be experienced (Hasson-Ohayon, Braun, Galinsky, & Baider, 2009). As previously stated, offending populations such as juveniles (Cox & Matthews, 2007; Hirschi & Stark, 1969; Lanza-Kaduce & Lane, 2007) and substance users (Chu, 2007; Scott, Crow, & Thompson, 2010) have received much research interest, but until very recently, few studies have examined the effects of faith or the impact religious affiliation might have on persons who sexual offend (for examples of most recent studies, please see Kewley, Larkin, Harkins, & Beech, 2016, 2018; Winder et al., 2019; Winder, Blagden, & Lievesley, 2018). This lack of academic interest is of concern, as evidence from desistance-based literature indicates religious or spiritual contexts might foster environments that promote desistance from sexual abuse (Kewley, 2019).

Positive criminology and the notion of spirituality

When making their case as to why a positive criminology ideology ought to be considered, Ronel and Segev (2014) contextualise the current regime first. Noting that those with criminal convictions live (in or out of prison) under harsh punitive conditions, they point out that these people are often socially isolated and rejected by family, thus making it hard to emerge from a sentence without experiencing trauma, harm, or rejection. We would argue, for those with sexual convictions, this reality is perhaps understated. Thus, Ronel and Segev (2014) present six reasons as to why a positive criminology ideology ought to be considered. One reason, they note, is that positive criminology "offers a spiritual horizon that can increase offending individuals' ability to step away from a self-centredness and inspire them to find a meaning greater than that of their everyday struggle in a materialistic world of criminality and social responses" (p. 1394). The idea is that through engagement, affiliation, or association with a religious or spiritual community or activity, a person might move away from a life of crime, but also grow, reaching new possibilities, including a new social acceptance from others (Elisha, Idisis, & Ronel, 2013). In light of this, we will now consider the current religious and/or spiritual offers for those with convictions for sexual offending within the current criminal justice context.

Religious and spiritual interventions within the criminal justice system

The connection between religious or faith communities and criminal justice systems is an already powerful bond. Faith communities have worked together in partnership with criminal justice agencies for centuries; probation and prison services are rooted in the history of missionaries who often worked in the courts, to 'advise, assist, and befriend' in an attempt to divert people away from custody (Dominey, 2012). Thus, an embedded and active stakeholder in the work of corrections, the religious and faith community, has always played a key role in supporting and enriching the lives of people with criminal convictions, ostensibly including those with sexual convictions.

It is worth noting that at this point a slight distinction between the types of religious and faith-based organisations within the criminal justice system. For some organisations, the aim is to primarily intervene to reduce reoffending, and the faith element of their work is to some degree secondary. An example of one such organisation is Circles of Support and Accountability (COSA). As discussed in Chapter 5, this intervention was originally founded by a Canadian Mennonite minister, who gathered support within his local faith community to work with high-risk sexual offenders who were without statutory restraints and had no support on release from custody (Hanvey, Wilson, & Philpot, 2011). COSA in the UK was implemented by the Religious Society of Friends (Quakers), and like its Canadian counterpart, originally drew volunteers from their faith community, but now recruits support from the wider community, where religious denomination is unrelated (Harper, Wilson, Hocken, Awan, & Lievesley, 2019). The person at the core of the Circle is not required to adopt or practice a Christian faith (Wilson, Picheca, Prinzo, & Canada, 2005).

Similarly, The Mothers Union, a Christian organisation, helps families when a member of the community/church is incarcerated. Some examples of the supports they offer are to help with prison visits, provide support for children and parents, run groups for women, and provide safe areas for children to play during prison visits. There is no commitment required by beneficiaries to follow the Christian faith (The Mothers Union, 2007).

Conversely, there are faith-based organisations where the practice of faith is the predominant activity; rehabilitation is a positive outcome of engaging with offenders but perhaps secondary to the commitment of religious faith and practice. For example, the Islamic Guidance Programme (IGP) (Awan, 2019) is designed to cater to the needs of Muslims with convictions for extremism, or who are at risk of radicalisation. The programme has ten outcomes including the development of an understanding of "the concept of a meaningful/purposeful life in Islam" (p. 456). Leaders of the programme challenge the often distorted and antisocial thinking of learners, using a critical-theoretical approach. Harper et al. (2019) argue that methods and teaching used in this programme are likely to be as effective for those convicted of sexual offences. This is because people with sexual convictions might draw on outdated religious texts or misinterpretations of text to support patriarchal attitudes towards women and children, which support sexual offending.

At the InnerChange Freedom Initiative, offenders engage in a structured 16- to 24-month prison programme and a 6- to 12-month community programme, including the development of life skills, education, housing, employment referrals, mentoring and developing relationships, and regular support groups focussing on topics such as substance abuse and victim awareness. These activities are, however, embedded within regular Christian spiritual and religious teachings, religious services, self-exploration, and moral guidance (Johnson & Larson, 2003). Likewise, the Kainos Community's Challenge-to-Change programme in English prisons combines structured cognitive behavioural therapy programmes with life in a therapeutic community (Ellis, Shalev, & Findings, 2008). Here, offenders learn skills and have opportunities to practice them within the community receiving feedback from mentors and staff; they are exposed to prosocial interactions and are required to take responsibility for their community. The fundamental religious preaching of the Kainos Community is Christian, and although offenders are not required to be of Christian faith, the religious practice and teachings within the Kainos prison are overtly Christian (Adler, Burnside, Loucks, & Viki, 2008). Additionally, the Muslim Youth Helpline offers support to young Muslims over the period of Ramadan. The charity aims to ensure that young Muslims in custody are contacted during the festival to prevent feelings of isolation from their wider Muslim community. Gifts, messages of support, and copies of the Quran are sent to young offenders (Aitken, 2009). Lastly, the Prison Chaplaincy provides a presence of ministry in custody. Although they appear to spend a large percentage of their time completing administrative tasks and coordinating volunteers within the prison regime rather than missionary time (Sundt & Cullen, 2008), they offer support and care for inmates whilst balancing security needs of the prison. Chaplains work with the needs of people on a humanistic and spiritual level (Thomas & Lankau, 2009).

Finally, there are also interventions that adopt a religious perspective as part of the delivery of certain activities within a criminal justice context. One of the most prominent, in prison establishments, is that of Buddhism, and its practice of techniques such as mindfulness and yoga (Harper et al., 2019). In a study of spirituality and gangs, Deuchar (2018) draws attention to the benefits of Sudarshan Kriya Yoga (SKY) as a mechanism for cognitive change, emotional release, and desistance. SKY is an advanced form of cyclic breathing, with slow, medium, and fast cycles. Deuchar (2018) researched ex-gang members and his findings corroborate clinical research that suggests that SKY is an antidepressant therapy, supporting emotional processing, the management of stress, and increased feelings of eudemonic well-being. This intervention, while developed for gang members, shares the principles of positive criminology and could easily transfer to any offending population, particularly one in which emotional management and unhelpful patriarchal attitudes are risk factors.

The presence of religious and spiritual organisations within our criminal justice system is therefore encouraging, as the opportunity to facilitate a positive criminological ideology for those convicted of sexual offending is, at the very least, accessible. We will now consider the way in which a religious or spiritual connection for those with sexual convictions might support their process of reintegration and ultimately desisting from crime.

Desistance

Desistance theory explains how individuals move away and cease offending. It suggests that building on individuals' strengths, developing positive prosocial self-narratives, fostering strong social bonds and social capital, along with encouraging and supporting motivation for change (Giordano, Cernkovich, & Rudolph, 2002; Göbbels, Ward, & Willis, 2012; Maruna, 2001; McNeill & Farrall, 2013; Paternoster & Bushway, 2009) will not only assist people to rehabilitate and 'go straight,' but will do so while maintaining peoples' dignity (Laws & Ward, 2011). Environments such as those provided by religious and spiritual communities might offer opportunities whereby the factors that promote desistance can be accessed (Kewley et al., 2018). Given that the process of desistance, although an individual one, always occurs within a social context (McNeill, 2012), religious or spiritual communities are likely to be conducive contexts. While much work is needed to empirically test this concept, we can draw on an already robust pool of literature (referred to earlier) that informs our understanding of desistance. It is of note that there is no evidence to suggest that those with criminal histories, sexual in nature, desist differently from those with non-sexual offences. While it is likely that the desistance experience is a greater challenge due to additional barriers, the psychosocial process is the same as a general offending population (Harris, 2014). We present the case here that affiliation with a religious and spiritual organisation will provide the opportunity for those with sexual criminal offences to step away from their self-centredness and develop new meaning in their lives (Ronel & Segev, 2014) through at least two mechanisms, forgiveness and identity transformation.

Forgiveness

Forgiveness is a human adaption that has evolved as a response to wrongdoing. Forgiveness is critical to many ancient religious and spiritual philosophies, most centrally Christianity (Rye et al., 2000), and is a complex, multi-faceted phenomenon. It involves aspects of behaviour, cognition, emotion, and affect; the process usually involves the 'wrong-doer' and at least one person who has been transgressed (possible observers/witnesses of the transgression). In spite of this, the concept of forgiveness has only received scholarly interest in the last five decades (Worthington, 2007).

While the notion of forgiveness is central to many religious and spiritual philosophies, it can also be found within the Western ideals of criminal justice and punishment. Drawn from 'moral' philosophers such as Immanuel Kant, forgiveness is rejected and deemed unnecessary in a fair criminal justice system. Meyer (2010) states that Kant's moral (and legal) philosophy centres on the understanding of autonomy. He notes that if a 'reasonable' man transgresses and commits a criminal act, he does so with free will. Thus, there is no place for mercy or forgiveness, as according to Kant, the judicial system is fair and flawless, and it is the transgressor who failed to conform to the demands of universal *reason* as institutionalised in law. This, therefore, is a wilful and punishable rejection of a gift from God (Kant, 1998). Given that Kant claims citizens are autonomous beings, capable of determining their own moral status through choice, the concept of forgiveness sits uncomfortably in his moral thought (Satne, 2016). One of the key issues with this position is that it runs counter to more deterministic philosophies that argue that not all humans are equal, and as such, do not have the ability or freedom to make rational or logical choices. Whilst many current criminal justice responses to crime still have the essence of early classical philosophy, there are some shifts that demonstrate more inclusive approaches. These include policies and approaches that encourage greater humanity, compassion, and respect. We do not have the scope to discuss these here; please refer to a discussion paper by Kewley (2017) for details, as for now, our focus is on the concept of forgiveness.

In spite of there being some shift towards strengths-based opportunities for those in the criminal justice system (Kewley, 2017), there remain significant barriers and challenges for people to be accepted beyond the criminal justice system itself. It is extremely challenging for people with criminal convictions to seek and experience redemption and forgiveness for their crimes, particularly those with sexual convictions. Instead, once a criminal conviction is issued, the person is often stigmatised and shamed, and this usually extends to their family members. One of the reasons this is experienced, as proposed by Maruna (2001), is the lack of opportunity or provision to publicly display and demonstrate change and redemption. On the one hand, criminal trials, convictions, and sentencings are publicly staged; yet once a person has successfully completed their sentence, there is no equal public show of change. This is regrettable, as rituals that support reintegration would help de-label and reinstate a person's identity to a time prior to their transgression, and thus help them live a life free from crime (Maruna, 2001); forgiveness might support this process. There is a great deal of literature detailing and evidencing the process of forgiveness, its health and well-being benefits, and the effects of forgiving others (please refer to Exline, Worthington, Hill, & McCullough, 2003; McCullough & Witvliet, 2002). Yet much less is known of the components required and of the experiences of those seeking, receiving, and feeling forgiven (Ashby, 2003; Krause & Ellison, 2003), while for those convicted of sexual offending a 'true' process of forgiveness might be inappropriate and unethical, and therefore understanding the process for the receiver in the absence of those transgressed is equally important.

Ashby (2003) suggests that the four-stage process of those seeking forgiveness is like those looking to forgive others. The first stage requires the seeker to acknowledge that their actions caused harm to another person(s); they must, therefore, take and accept full responsibility for their behaviour, meaning they should no longer blame the victim or minimise their role in the offence. The second stage requires the seeker of forgiveness to make the decision to seek forgiveness; here they commit to the restorative nature of reparation. Third, they make an apology to the injured person; they must take full responsibility for their actions. Finally, regardless of the form or content of the forgiveness, the seeker must receive and accept the forgiveness given. Even in cases where forgiveness cannot be directly sought or given (as with many people convicted of sexual offending, who for legal and public protection reasons are not permitted to make contact with their victim(s)), then a process of forgiveness can occur internally. Following the third stage, the seeker should turn inward or to a higher being to request forgiveness. It is at this stage, that a religious or spiritual affiliation is likely to be of benefit.

Whilst many recognise the value practising religion offers to those with criminal convictions (Giordano, Longmore, Schroeder, & Seffrin, 2008; Hallett & McCoy, 2015; Schroeder & Frana, 2009), others have identified the opportunity religious engagement offers in providing a moral compass that enables people the opportunity to express remorse for acts of harm (Clear & Sumter, 2002; Kewley et al., 2016; Maruna, 2001, 2011; Robinson-Edwards & Kewley, 2018; Ronel & Segev, 2015). By engaging in religious activity, a new language and framework for seeking forgiveness is provided (O'Connor & Duncan, 2011), which according to Deuchar (2018) is integral for achieving alternative, non-offending identities. Yet there is minimal evidence of the power of forgiveness in populations convicted of sexual offences. Some preliminary examination by Kewley and colleagues (2016, 2018) found both benefits and challenges for this population when seeking and receiving forgiveness through religious or spiritual means. While on the one hand love and support was experienced by participants from their religious network, true forgiveness was arguably unattainable for all. While efforts were made to facilitate self-forgiveness or indirect forgiveness, this was not to the satisfaction of all participants, who felt forgiveness from actual victims would be the only point to which they would be able to forgive themselves.

There are, of course, victim-offender mediation initiatives, such as restorative justice (see Chapter 6 for a more detailed discussion). These are themselves not faith-led, but work with the principles of forgiveness. These interventions facilitate a dialogue between the victim and transgressor with the aim of providing both parties the opportunity to tell and hear each others' perspectives of the offence, with the view of mutually repairing harm. Restorative approaches offer people a platform to make amends and seek forgiveness; of equal importance is victim empowerment – the process helps with post-traumatic growth, and where appropriate, offers forgiveness (Ronel & Toren, 2012; Wager, 2015). As discussed in Chapter 6, debate regarding the appropriateness of this type of intervention for sexual crimes persists. While there are clearly some sexual assault cases in which a restorative approach would be inappropriate, there are some for which this platform might be of benefit, not only for the perpetrator, but also the victim. Thus, when considering opportunities to enable a process of forgiveness, a restorative solution might provide this.

Identity transformation

Aside from the often harmful effects of entering criminal justice systems (Liebling & Maruna, 2005), being categorised as belonging to a highly stigmatised group can have negative psychological consequences (Tajfel & Turner, 1979). Being labelled 'criminal' and losing one's identity often damages well-being and mental health (Jetten, O'Brien, & Trindall, 2002). This is perhaps unsurprising as identity is important – it provides meaning and purpose in life; it determines and explains who we are (Stryker, 1968). Indeed, social identity theory informs our sense of self, which is derived from the "membership of a social group (or groups) together with the value and emotional significance attached to that membership"

(Tajfel & Turner, 1979, p. 2). Identity is therefore defined not only by the groups we belong to, but by the groups we do not belong to.

Belonging to groups with shared characteristics and values helps us to make sense of who we are, where we have come from, as well as defining ourselves to others. For those with sexual convictions, particularly those who receive a prison sentence, original identities become lost; people are no longer attached to non-offending social groups, but instead are forced to identify with a stigmatised and condemned group of 'sex offenders.' Maruna, Wilson, and Curran (2006) report this loss of identity as central to the stigmatising process. Once criminally convicted, a new negative label pervades, and the consequences of such labels are great. The stigma imposed by others causes many external challenges; for example, when having to disclose prior offending history, it might impact on the ability to access new accommodations, start a new relationship, or gain employment. However, when the stigma is internalised and the person adopts the negative label, their identity is compromised and the ability to desist from crime becomes more challenging (Maruna, 2014). Maruna, Lebel, Mitchell, and Naples (2004) outline the notion of Lemert's (1951) primary and secondary deviation process. They note how primary deviation processes involve a mere testing out of the deviant behaviours, whereas at the secondary deviation stage, the person accepts the deviant behaviour as central to themselves, the label becoming the core of their identity.

In order to restore a non-offending identity, people need to (re-)align themselves with more socially acceptable groups (Tajfel & Turner, 1979). However, the stigma and label of being affiliated with a group such as those convicted of sex crimes makes the ability to join new groups extremely difficult. One solution is to turn to religious and spiritual groups for support. Indeed, many people convert to a religion (either rejuvenating old beliefs or adopting new ones) whilst in prison (Maruna et al., 2006). Religion and spirituality can assist people in processing the experiences of trauma, loss, and suffering often associated with an offence and/or subsequent prison sentence, and help people develop new identities, taking into consideration their changed circumstances (Sedikides & Gebauer, 2014). Yet, little is known of the effects religion and spirituality have on identity (Ysseldyk, Matheson, & Anisman, 2010) and even less is known about how religious or spiritual affiliation is experienced by those convicted of sexual offences (Kewley, Beech, & Harkins, 2015).

As discussed, desistance is widely accepted to be the cessation of deviant or criminal behaviour (Maruna, 2011). One aspect of desistance, known as 'knifing off,' requires people to detach from their immediate antisocial network and environment and attach to new prosocial peers, institutional structures, and routines (Laub & Sampson, 2001). It has been proposed that a religious or spiritual context might facilitate this desistance process as it gives support to the process of identity transformation and secondary desistance (Giordano et al., 2008; Maruna, 2011). Control theory helps explain this in that by affiliating with a religious or spiritual community, the person is provided an opportunity to bond with others and conform to the new group norms (Giordano et al., 2008; Schroeder & Frana, 2009;

Hallett & McCoy, 2015; Deuchar, 2018) and thus begin to endorse and adopt a new identity. Indeed, life-course research indicates identity transformation occurs as a result of people developing new religious social bonds, being exposed to an increase in social capital, experiencing a spiritual awakening, and having the opportunity to take part in religious practice and church fellowship (Hallett & McCoy, 2015; Giordano et al., 2008). Research has also identified how religion and spiritual affiliation can act as a protective shield for those who engage in risky or unhealthy sexual behaviours (Schiff, 2006; Hardy, Steelman, Coyne, & Ridge, 2013) and substance abuse (Kim-Spoon, Farley, Holmes, & Longo, 2014).

The stigma for those with sexual convictions is considerable and in part has developed in response to the criminal justice strategies to manage this group. Indeed, the management of people with sexual convictions often includes control strategies, as much for their own protection as the protection of others (e.g. specialised segregated wings in prison). Yet one of the unintended consequences of these management strategies is the amplification of the belief that this group is highly 'dangerous' and should be separated from all of society, even other 'criminals' (West, 1985). The result of this segregation (and restrictions placed on individuals) inevitably limits the opportunity for those with sexual convictions to engage in broader social activities. This is of concern. As Ronel and Segev (2015) highlight, the last few decades have experienced a growth of 'spiritual-but-not-religious' approaches for the rehabilitation of those with criminal convictions, providing valuable 'hooks for change' (Giordano et al., 2002). Yet from the limited research available, it appears that where the opportunity has been provided for those with sexual convictions to engage with such groups, identity transformation occurs, even in those with a history of sexual offending (Kewley et al., 2016, 2018; Winder et al., 2018, 2019).

Caution is, however, needed. As with any community, a religious or spiritual one can provide those intent on harming others with the opportunity to engage in sexually harmful behaviour (Smallbone, Marshall, & Wortley, 2013). Indeed, there are people who are either unable to make changes in their life, who are influenced by situational factors, who misuse religious texts or doctrines to support or distort attitudes and beliefs (Micklethwaite, Blagden, & Winder, 2019), or who are simply motivated and determined to cause harm and abuse to others. We are not endorsing free access to religious and spiritual communities to everyone with a sexual conviction; instead, we aim to highlight how identity transformation can be achieved through engagement in a religious or spiritual community for those who are motivated and committed to make changes in their lives and live a life free from crime (notwithstanding continued assessment of risk).

Conclusion

This chapter has presented the case that religious or spiritual communities or programmes can support a process of desistance in those convicted of sexual offending. While not appropriate for all, for those who it is deemed safe to engage in a religious or spiritual community, it can help foster opportunities in which people can seek and receive forgiveness, exist in a place with little stigma, and thus develop new prosocial identities. Religious and spiritual communities are already embedded within our criminal justice systems; therefore, the opportunity for those with sexual convictions to engage with these groups exist. However, religious or spiritual approaches cannot function in isolation, and for a positive criminology ideology to exist, a multidisciplinary, integrated approach is essential. Criminal justice practitioners, academics, community stakeholders, people with convictions, and victims need to work collaboratively so that risk and needs-led solutions enable an effective desistance process.

References

Adler, J. R., Burnside, J., Loucks, N., & Viki, G. T. (2008). Measuring religion in prisons: Offenders' beliefs and attitudes. *Journal of Forensic Psychology Practice*, *8*(2), 130–149.

Aitken, J. (2009). *Breakthrough Britain: Locked up potential a strategy for reforming prisons and rehabilitating prisoners*. Retrieved from www.centreforsocialjustice.org.uk/library/locked-potential-strategy-reforming-prisons-rehabilitating-prisoners

Ashby, H. U., Jr. (2003). Being forgiven: Toward a thicker description of forgiveness. *Journal of Pastoral Care & Counseling*, *57*(2), 143–152.

Awan, T. M. (2019). Engaging with the narrative of radical extremism: A spiritually based diagnostic and intervention model. *Journal of Ecumenical Studies*, *54*(3), 455–465.

Beedon, D. K. (2019). Religion and the Criminal Justice System (CJS): A socio-historical overview. In B. Winder, N. Blagden, K. Hocken, H. Elliott, R. Lievesley, & P. Banyard (Eds.), *Sexual crime, religion and spirituality* (pp. 1–24). Switzerland: Palgrave Macmillan.

Bjarnason, D. (2007). Concept analysis of religiosity. *Home Health Care Management & Practice*, *19*(5), 350.

Clear, T. R., & Sumter, M. T. (2002). Prisoners, prison, and religion: Religion and adjustment to prison. *Journal of Offender Rehabilitation*, *35*(3–4), 125–156.

Cox, M., & Matthews, B. (2007). Faith-based approaches for controlling the delinquency of juvenile offenders. *Fed. Probation*, *71*, 31.

Chu, D. C. (2007). Religiosity and desistance from drug use. *Criminal Justice and Behavior*, *34*(5), 661–679.

Deuchar, R. (2018). *Gangs and spirituality: Global perspectives*. London: Palgrave Macmillan.

Dominey, J. (2012). A mixed market for probation services: Can lessons from the recent past help shape the near future? *Probation Journal*, *59*(4), 339–354.

Elisha, E., Idisis, Y., & Ronel, N. (2013). Positive criminology and imprisoned sex offenders: Demonstration of a way out from a criminal spin through acceptance relationships. *Journal of Sexual Aggression*, *19*(1), 66–80.

Ellis, T., Shalev, K., & Findings, K. (2008). *An evaluation of the effectiveness of the Kainos community 'Challenge-to-Change' programme in English prisons*. University of Portsmouth: Institute of Criminal Justice Studies. Retrieved from https://researchportal.port.ac.uk/portal/en/publications/an-evaluation-of-the-effectiveness-of-the-kainos-community-challengetochange-programme-in-english-prisons(ad1cc643–13d8–408b-b296-ea99ff0593ab).html

Exline, J. J., Worthington, J. E. L., Hill, P., & McCullough, M. E. (2003). Forgiveness and justice: A research agenda for social and personality psychology. *Personality & Social Psychology Review*, *7*(4), 337–348.

Giordano, P. C., Cernkovich, S. A., & Rudolph, J. L. (2002). Gender, crime, and desistance: Toward a theory of cognitive transformation. *American Journal of Sociology*, *107*(4), 990–1064.

Giordano, P. C., Longmore, M. A., Schroeder, R. D., & Seffrin, P. M. (2008). A life-course perspective on spirituality and desistance from crime. *Criminology*, *46*(1), 99–132.

Glock, C., & Stark, R. (1965). *Religion and society in tension*. Chicago: Rand McNally.

Göbbels, S., Ward, T., & Willis, G. M. (2012). An integrative theory of desistance from sex offending. *Aggression and Violent Behavior*, *17*(5), 453–462.

Greenfield, E., Vaillant, G., & Marks, N. (2009). Do formal religious participation and spiritual perceptions have independent linkages with diverse dimensions of psychological well-being? *Journal of Health and Social Behavior*, *50*(2), 196.

Hackney, C. H., & Sanders, G. S. (2003). Religiosity and mental health: A meta-analysis of recent studies. *Journal for the Scientific Study of Religion*, *42*(1), 43–56.

Hallett, M., & McCoy, J. S. (2015). Religiously motivated desistance: An exploratory study. *International Journal of Offender Therapy and Comparative Criminology*, *59*(8), 855–872.

Hanvey, S., Wilson, C., & Philpot, T. (2011). *A community-based approach to the reduction of sexual reoffending: Circles of support and accountability*. London, England: Jessica Kingsley Publishers.

Hardy, A., Steelman, M., Coyne, S., & Ridge, R. (2013). Adolescent religiousness as a protective factor against pornography use. *Journal of Applied Developmental Psychology*, *34*(3), 131–139.

Harper, C. A., Wilson, C., Hocken, K., Awan, T. M., & Lievesley, R. A. (2019). Religiously responsive treatment for prople convited of sexual offences. In B. Winder, N. Blagden, K. Hocken, H. Elliott, R. Lievesley, & P. Banyard (Eds.), *Sexual crime, religion and spirituality* (pp. 115–138). Switzerland: Palgrave Macmillan.

Harris, D. A. (2014). Desistance from sexual offending: Findings from 21 life history narratives. *Journal of Interpersonal Violence*, *29*(9), 1554–1578.

Hasson-Ohayon, I., Braun, M., Galinsky, D., & Baider, L. (2009). Religiosity and hope: A path for women coping with a diagnosis of breast cancer. *Psychosomatics*, *50*(5), 525.

Hirschi, T., & Stark, R. (1969). Hellfire and delinquency. *Social Problems*, *17*(2), 202–213.

Jetten, J., O'Brien, A., & Trindall, N. (2002). Changing identity: Predicting adjustment to organizational restructure as a function of subgroup and superordinate identification. *British Journal of Social Psychology*, *41*(2), 281–297.

Johnson, B. R., & Larson, D. B. (2003). *The innerchange freedom initiative: A preliminary evaluation of a faith-based prison program*. University of Pennsylvania. Retrieved from www.baylor.edu/content/services/document.php/25903.pdf

Kant, I. (1998). *Groundwork of metaphysics and moral*. Cambridge: Cambridge University Press.

Kewley, S. (2017). Strength based approaches and protective factors from a criminological perspective. *Aggression and Violent Behavior*, *32*, 11–18.

Kewley, S. (2019). How might faith communities promote desistance from sexual crime? An exploration of theory. In B. Winder, N. Blagden, K. Hocken, H. Elliott, R. Lievesley, & P. Banyard (Eds.), *Sexual crime, religion and spirituality* (pp. 53–70). Switzerland: Palgrave Macmillan.

Kewley, S., Beech, A. R., & Harkins, L. (2015). Examining the role of faith community groups with sexual offenders: A systematic review. *Aggression and Violent Behavior*, *25*, 142–149.

Kewley, S., Larkin, M., Harkins, L., & Beech, A. R. (2016). Restoring identity: The use of religion as a mechanism to transition between an identity of sexual offending to a non-offending identity. *Criminology and Criminal Justice*, *17*(1), 79–96.

Kewley, S., Larkin, M., Harkins, L., & Beech, A. R. (2018). Incarcerated child sexual offenders and the reinvention of self through religious and spiritual affiliation. In K. R. Kerley (Ed.), *Finding freedom in confinement: The role of religion in prison life* (pp. 366–394). Santa Barbara, CA: Praeger.

Kim-Spoon, J., Farley, J., Holmes, C., & Longo, G. (2014). Does adolescents' religiousness moderate links between harsh parenting and adolescent substance use? *Journal of Family Psychology*, *28*(6), 739–748.

Krause, N., & Ellison, C. G. (2003). Forgiveness by god, forgiveness of others, and psychological well – Being in late life. *Journal for the Scientific Study of Religion*, *42*(1), 77–93.

Lanza-Kaduce, L., & Lane, J. (2007). Initiating faith-based juvenile corrections: Exercising without establishing religion. *Youth Violence and Delinquency: Monsters and Myths*, *2*, 131–148.

Laub, J. H., & Sampson, R. J. (2001). Understanding desistance from crime. *Crime and Justice*, *28*, 1–69.

Laws, D. R., & Ward, T. (2011). *Desistance from sex offending: Alternatives to throwing away the keys*. New York: Guilford Press.

Lemert, E. (1951). Primary and secondary deviation. In P. Bean (Ed.), *Crime. Critical concepts in sociology* (Vol. 3, pp. 603–607). London: Routledge.

Liebling, A., & Maruna, S. (2005). *The effects of imprisonment*. London: Routledge.

Lim, C., & Putnam, R. D. (2010). Religion, social networks, and life satisfaction. [Electronic version]. *American Sociological Review*, *75*(6), 914–933.

Maruna, S. (2001). *Making good: How ex-offenders reform and reclaim their lives*. Washington, DC: American Psychological Association.

Maruna, S. (2011). Reentry as a rite of passage. *Punishment & Society*, *13*(1), 3–28.

Maruna, S. (2014). Reintegration as a right and the rites of reintegration: A comparative review of de-stigmatization practices. In J. A. Humphrey & P. Cordella (Eds.), *Effective interventions in the lives of criminal offenders* (pp. 121–138): New York: Springer.

Maruna, S., Lebel, T., Mitchell, N., & Naples, M. (2004). Pygmalion in the reintegration process: Desistance from crime through the looking glass. *Psychology, Crime & Law*, *10*(3), 271–281.

Maruna, S., Wilson, L., & Curran, K. (2006). Why god is often found behind bars: Prison conversions and the crisis of self-narrative. *Research in Human Development*, *3*(2–3), 161–184.

McCullough, M. E., & Witvliet, C. V. (2002). The psychology of forgiveness. In C. R. Snyder & S. J. Lopez (Eds.), *Handbook of positive psychology* (pp. 446–458). New York, NY: Oxford University Press.

McNeill, F. (2012). Four forms of 'offender'rehabilitation: Towards an interdisciplinary perspective. *Legal and Criminological Psychology*, *17*(1), 18–36.

McNeill, F., & Farrall, S. (2013). A moral in the story? Virtues, values and desistance from crime. In M. Cowburn, M. Duggan, A. Robinson, & P. Senior (Eds.), *Values in criminology and community justice* (pp. 147–164). Bristol, UK: Policy Press.

Meyer, L. (2010). *The justice of mercy*. Michigan: Michigan University Press.

Mela, M., Marcoux, E., Baetz, M., Griffin, R., Angelski, C., & Deqiang, G. (2008). The effect of religiosity and spirituality on psychological well-being among forensic psychiatric patients in Canada. *Mental Health, Religion & Culture*, *11*(5), 517–532.

Micklethwaite, D., Blagden, N., & Winder, B. (2019). Understanding the expereinces of religious perpetrators of sexual abuse. In B. Winder, N. Blagden, K. Hocken, H. Elliott, R. Lievesley, P. Banyard (Eds.), *Sexual crime, religion and spirituality* (pp. 71–114). Switzerland: Palgrave Macmillan.

The Mothers Union. (2007). Retrieved from www.themothersunion.org

O'Connor, T., & Duncan, J. (2011). The sociology of humanist, spiritual, and religious practice in prison: Supporting responsivity and desistance from crime. *Religions*, *2*(4), 590–610.

Paternoster, R., & Bushway, S. (2009). Desistance and the "feared self": Toward an identity theory of criminal desistance. *The Journal of Criminal Law and Criminology*, *99*(4), 1103–1156.

Robinson-Edwards, S., & Kewley, S. (2018). Faith-based intervention: Prison, prayer, and perseverance. *Religions*, *9*(4), 130.

Ronel, N., & Segev, D. (2014). Positive criminology in practice. *International Journal of Offender Therapy and Comparative Criminology*, *58*(11), 1389–1407.

Ronel, N., & Segev, D. (2015). *Positive criminology*. London: Routledge.

Ronel, N., & Toren, Y. (2012). Positive victimology – An innovation or "more of the same"? *Temida*, *15*(2), 171–180.

Rye, M. S., Pargament, K. I., Ali, M. A., Beck, G. L., Dorff, E. N., Hallisey, C., . . . Williams, J. G. (2000). Religious perspectives on forgiveness. In M. E. Mcculloch, K. I. Pargament, & C. E. Thoresen (Eds.), *Forgiveness: Theory, research and practice* (pp. 17–40). New York: Guilford Press.

Satne, P. (2016). Forgiveness and moral development. *Philosophia*, *44*(4), 1029–1055.

Schiff, M. (2006). Living in the shadow of terrorism: Psychological distress and alcohol use among religious and non-religious adolescents in Jerusalem. *Social Science and Medicine*, *62*(9), 2301–2312.

Schroeder, R., & Frana, J. (2009). Spirituality and religion, emotional coping, and criminal desistance: A qualitative study of men undergoing change. *Sociological Spectrum*, *29*(6), 718–741.

Scott, D., Crow, M., & Thompson, C. (2010). Tempest in a therapeutic community: Implementation and evaluation issues for faith-based programming. *Journal of Offender Rehabilitation*, *49*(1), 39–51.

Sedikides, C., & Gebauer, J. E. (2014). Religion and the self. In V. Saroglou (Ed.), *Religion, personality, and social behavior* (pp. 46–70). New York: Psychology Press.

Sharp, S. (2010). How does prayer help manage emotions? *Social Psychology Quarterly*, *73*(4), 417–437.

Sherkat, D. E. (2015). Religiosity. In J. D. Wright (Ed.), *International encyclopedia of the social & behavioral sciences* (2nd ed., pp. 377–380). Oxford: Elsevier.

Smallbone, S., Marshall, W. L., & Wortley, R. (2013). *Preventing child sexual abuse: Evidence, policy and practice*. Devon, UK: Routledge.

Stolz, J. (2009). Explaining religiosity: Towards a unified theoretical model. *The British Journal of Sociology*, *60*(2), 345–376.

Stryker, S. (1968). Identity salience and role performance: The relevance of symbolic interaction theory for family research. *Journal of Marriage and Family*, *30*(4), 558–564. doi:10.2307/349494

Sundt, J., & Cullen, F. (2008). Doing god's work behind bars: Chaplains' reactions to employment in prison. *Journal of Offender Rehabilitation*, *45*(3), 131–157.

Tajfel, H., & Turner, J. C. (1979). An integrative theory of intergroup conflict. In W. G. Austin & S. Worchel (Eds.), *The social psychology of intergroup relations* (pp. 33–47). Monterey, CA: Brooks-Cole.

Thomas, C., & Lankau, M. (2009). Preventing burnout: The effects of LMX and mentoring on socialization, role stress, and burnout. *Human Resource Management*, *48*(3), 417–432.

Wager, N. (2015). Restorative justice and domestic violence: A view from a positive victimological perspective. In N. Ronel & D. Segev (Eds.), *Positive criminology*. London: Routledge.

West, D. J. (1985). Helping imprisoned sex offenders: Discussion paper. *Journal of the Royal Society of Medicine*, *78*(11), 928–932.

Wilson, R., Picheca, J., Prinzo, M., & Canada, C. S. (2005). *Circles of support and accountability: An evaluation of the pilot project in south-central Ontario*. Ottawa: Citeseer.

Winder, B., Blagden, N., Hocken, K., Elliott, H., Lievesley, R., & Banyard, P. (Eds.). (2019). *Sexual crime, religion and spirituality*. Switzerland: Palgrave Macmillan.

Winder, B., Blagden, N., & Lievesley, R. (2018). "Because you've got faith it doesn't mean that you've got wings on your back": A qualitative analysis of the accounts of Christian prisoners serving time for a sexual offence. *Journal of Sexual Aggression*, *24*(2), 240–256.

Worthington, E. L., Jr (Ed.). (2007). *Handbook of forgiveness*. New York: Routledge.

Ysseldyk, R., Matheson, K., & Anisman, H. (2010). Religiosity as identity: Toward an understanding of religion from a social identity perspective. *Personality and Social Psychology Review*, *14*(1), 60–71.

Conclusion

The term positive criminology is relatively new in the field of criminology, yet positive criminological approaches, theories, and models are not. Indeed, many great contemporary scholars have paved the way in their exploration of crime and criminal justice systems from a positive criminological perspective. Several scholars have sought to explore how positive experiences might be encountered by people affected by crime, and how even during challenging and testing times, people are able to grow and flourish (including work by, but not limited to, Pepinsky, 2013; Gal & Wexler, 2015; Wager, 2015; Ronel & Segev, 2014; Braithwaite, 1989; Bazemore, 1998; Bogdan & Taylor, 1987). Furthermore, scholars have sought to examine the transformational processes that support people's ability to change their harmful belief systems, thoughts, emotions, and behaviours so that criminal behaviour can be prevented (including work by Maruna, 2001; Marshall et al., 2005; Elisha, Idisis, & Ronel, 2013; Giordano, Cernkovich, & Rudolph, 2002; Birgden, 2004). Finally, scholars have developed and examined theories that support integration on a social/interpersonal, intrapersonal, and spiritual level so that true reintegration and rehabilitation following criminal behaviour can be supported (including the work of Ronel & Elisha, 2011; Weaver & McNeil, 2015; LeBel, Burnett, Maruna, & Bushway, 2008; Best, 2012; O'Connor & Bogue, 2010; Farrall & Calverley, 2005). While mainstream criminological research and criminal justice policy and practice continues to be dominated by a 'risk paradigm' (Maruna & Mann, 2019), it is encouraging that these and other positive criminological approaches have entered and started to embed into (albeit to varying degrees) our criminal justice systems.

This text has made a preliminary attempt to examine the scope and scale of existing positive criminological approaches that might help prevent sexual abuse and harm while working with those with convictions for sexual offending. It examines an approach that runs somewhat contrary to the more orthodox criminological approaches used in contemporary criminal justice systems, whereby a punitive 'justice' orientated approach to sexual violence is more favourable. We have argued that these approaches tend to exclude and pathologise people convicted of sexual abuse through a process of labelling and 'othering.' While it is with good intention that these strategies aim to protect the public and reintegrate people into the community, for those with histories of sexual offending, such strategies are often counterproductive and result in the failed reintegration of people and at times an increased risk of harm. We have presented the notion that positive criminology offers an approach worthy of much greater examination, and one that serves to complement the current regime.

We have presented several key benefits to a positive criminological approach. It will reduce recidivism, eradicate harm, prevent reoffending, and help to truly reintegrate those with histories of sexual abuse into the community. First, we have argued that by adopting a positive criminological approach, the responsibility for sexual abuse becomes a shared one. As discussed in Chapter 5, prevention strategies tend to target potential victims, resulting in an implicit notion that the prevention of sexual abuse becomes the victim's responsibility. Yet when the responsibility for preventing sexual abuse becomes a shared responsibility, solutions to the problem also become shared. Instead of imposing responsibility on victims, families, and perpetrators, the wider society also becomes part of the solution. When responsibility is shared, a positive criminological approach means the benefits are also shared. By taking a global perspective to addressing the problem of sexual abuse, the benefits of these solutions go beyond immediate stakeholders and reach wider elements of society.

A positive criminological approach allows ethical and humanistic ways of dealing with a subject matter that is highly sensitive. Working with the notion of deviance allows society to move towards a place of social acceptance. For decades the examination of deviant behaviours and the exclusion of 'deviant' people has been the focus of traditional criminological approaches, yet understanding how communities can accept difference and deviance is a less explored area (Bogdan & Taylor, 1987). Understanding how deviance can be accepted within society must reach beyond intimate relationships and the nuclear family. Instead, it must look and consider institutional and societal structures.

The current regime appears partially effective. Recidivism rates for those with sexual convictions are low when compared to the general offending population. Indeed, the longer a person lives in the community offence-free, the faster risk declines (Hanson, Harris, Helmus, & Thornton, 2014). Yet this is only part of the solution. Current strategies tend to focus solely on the risk/needs of those convicted of crime (Van Ness & Strong, 2006), often at the exclusion of their victims. As has been outlined in this text, for those with sexual convictions, current strategies to rehabilitate and reintegrate tend to adopt a 'community protection' model. The characteristics of such solutions tend to be those that punish and control. Thus, true rehabilitation can never be achieved in a climate whereby citizens and their families who have served their sentence continue to live with inequality, stigma, and a lifetime of controls.

A further benefit likely to be experienced from the application of positive criminological approaches is the empowerment of criminal justice practitioners supporting those working towards desistance and true rehabilitation. While practitioners are currently tasked with supporting a rehabilitation process, they do this within a regime that involves the control, registration, and management of clients. Indeed, beyond the criminal justice system practitioners operate within a climate of fear and risk aversion. As a result, clients are stigmatised and excluded from fully re-entering society. Thus, any attempts to support meaningful employment, secure safe housing, or help develop social capital are undermined by the limitations and restrictions, both internal and external, to the criminal justice system. Positive criminological approaches would mean practitioners could engage with clients in ways that assist personal growth and social integration. They would be accepted more readily by communities and thus access the capital needed to support the desistance process and fully reintegrate into the community.

Within this text several existing positive criminological initiatives and approaches that aim to prevent future sexual violence have been explored and show real promise. However, key challenges must be overcome before a positive criminological movement can fully support the prevention of sexual violence, protect past and possible future victims, and help to truly rehabilitate people perpetrating violence. Thanks to the work of Natti Ronel and colleagues, the unification of positive criminological approaches has begun. Yet the process is in its infancy. A unified force is needed to help with this momentum so that the development of a shared language amongst researchers, practitioners, and policy makers is achieved. In spite of apparent incompatible methods and practice, all of which are much debated, including recent attempts to reconcile perceived opposing paradigms (see Maruna and Mann's (2019) astute discussion around the reconciliation of the 'desistance' and 'what works' literature), a clear and shared research methods for a positive criminological movement is essential. Understanding human behaviour is a complex matter. Thus, understanding our response to deviant behaviours and solutions to harmful responses is a huge challenge. A unified approach to this problem can be achieved through the consideration of positive criminological approaches.

A further challenge faced by a positive criminological movement that aims to address sexual violence is the need for criminal justice structures and systems to adopt public health approaches. Until the response to sexual violence moves away from the individual and towards a whole systems approach, potential solutions and responses to sexual violence will continue to be directed to individuals within society. Thus, the role of social structures and organisational conditions will continue to stigmatise and exclude those involved in sexual violence (victims, their families, and perpetrators). Instead, more positive criminological methods that adopt public health approaches might help begin to shift society's perspective and response to sexual violence in a way that is inclusive, integrative, and a problem shared by all. One of the major obstacles to helping provide this shift is the public perception of sexual violence. Positive criminological approaches will help evidence alternative strategies to prevent sexual abuse, as well as successful reintegration of those convicted of sexual violence. Education and awareness strategies with the use of the media, communities, and policies are very much needed.

In the words of Ward, Polaschek, and Beech (2006, p. 340), "thought and action are both essential elements of effective practice," and we hope that this text has provided new ways of thinking to be put to action by policymakers, practitioners, and academics who might begin to engage with the notion of preventing sexual harm and abuse, not only through current 'community protection' measures, but also through positive and strengths-based approaches.

References

Bazemore, G. (1998). Restorative justice and earned redemption: Communities, victims, and offender reintegration. *American Behavioral Scientist, 41*(6), 768–813.

Best, D. (2012). *Addiction recovery: A movement for social change and personal growth in the UK*. Brighton: Pavilion Publishing.

Braithwaite, J. (1989). *Crime, shame and reintegration*. Cambridge: Cambridge University Press.

Birgden, A. (2004). Therapeutic jurisprudence and responsivity: Finding the will and the way in offender rehabilitation. *Psychology, Crime & Law, 10*(3), 283–295.

Bogdan, R., & Taylor, S. (1987). Toward a sociology of acceptance: The other side of the study of deviance. *Social Policy, 18*(2), 34–39.

Elisha, E., Idisis, Y., & Ronel, N. (2013). Positive criminology and imprisoned sex offenders: Demonstration of a way out from a criminal spin through acceptance relationships. *Journal of Sexual Aggression, 19*(1), 66–80.

Farrall, S., & Calverley, A. (2005). *Understanding desistance from crime*. Berkshire: McGraw-Hill Education.

Gal, T., & Wexler, D. B. (2015). Synergizing therapeutic jurisprudence and positive criminology. In *Positive criminology* (pp. 109–121). Oxon: Routledge.

Giordano, P. C., Cernkovich, S. A., & Rudolph, J. L. (2002). Gender, crime, and desistance: Toward a theory of cognitive transformation. *American Journal of Sociology, 107*(4), 990–1064.

Hanson, R. K., Harris, A. J. R., Helmus, L., & Thornton, D. (2014). High-risk sex offenders may not be high risk forever. *Journal of Interpersonal Violence, 29*(15), 2792–2813.

LeBel, T. P., Burnett, R., Maruna, S., & Bushway, S. (2008). The 'chicken and egg' of subjective and social factors in desistance from crime. *European Journal of Criminology, 5*(2), 131–159.

Maruna, S. (2001). *Making good*. Washington, DC: American Psychological Association.

Maruna, S., & Mann, R. (2019). Reconciling "Desistance" and "What Works." *HM Inspectorate of Probation Academic Insights 2019/1*. Retrieved from www.justiceinspectorates.gov.uk/hmiprobation/wp-content/uploads/sites/5/2019/02/Academic-Insights-Maruna-and-Mann-Feb-19-final.pdf

Marshall, W. L., Ward, T., Mann, R. E., Moulden, H., Fernandez, Y. M., Serran, G., & Marshall, L. E. (2005). Working positively with sexual offenders: Maximizing the effectiveness of treatment. *Journal of Interpersonal Violence, 20*(9), 1096–1114.

O'Connor, T. P., & Bogue, B. (2010). Collaborating with the community, trained volunteers and faith traditions: Building social capacity and making meaning to support desistance. *Offender Supervision: New Directions in Theory, Research and Practice*, 301–319.

Pepinsky, H. (2013). Peacemaking criminology. *Critical Criminology, 21*(3), 319–339.

Ronel, N., & Elisha, E. (2011). A different perspective: Introducing positive criminology. *International Journal of Offender Therapy and Comparative Criminology, 55*(2), 305–325.

Ronel, N., & Segev, D. (2014). Positive criminology in practice. *International Journal of Offender Therapy and Comparative Criminology, 58*(11), 1389–1407.

Wager, N. (2015). Restorative justice and domestic violence: A view from a positive victimological perspective. In *Positive Criminology* (pp. 261–275). Routledge.

Ward, T., Polaschek, D. L. L., & Beech, A. R. (2006). Ward and Siegert's pathways model. *Theories of Sexual Offending*, 61–77.

Weaver, B., & McNeill, F. (2015). Lifelines: Desistance, social relations, and reciprocity. *Criminal Justice and Behavior*, *42*(1), 95–107.

Van Ness, D. W., & Strong, K. H. (2006). *Restoring justice: An introduction to restorative justice* (3rd ed.). Cincinnati, OH: Anderson Publishing.

Index

accountability 121–122, 125
Adam Walsh Act, The (2006) 90
arts-based therapy 92–94

case formulation 3, 45–49, 111
character strengths 105–106
Circles of Support and Accountability (COSA) 76, 80–82, 116–121, 124–125, 130
community protection model 143
community rehabilitation companies 35
community sentences 28–31
crime survey 18, 26
Criminal Justice Act, The (2003) 26, 28, 31
Criminal Justice and Immigration Act, The (2008) 29
Crown Prosecution Service (CPS) 20

dangerousness 104
desistance 2, 15, 59–61, 81, 86–87, 89, 106, 110, 115–118, 121, 123, 129, 131–137, 143–144
Domestic Abuse Bill, The (2019) 5
dynamic risk factors 39, 45, 10

ecological 10, 15, 70–73, 81
ecological model of violence 71
electronic or satellite tracking/monitoring systems/tagging 30
employment 31, 35, 39, 46–48, 87–90, 98, 104–105, 108, 116, 130, 134, 144
European Convention of Human Rights 29
Eye Movement Desensitisation and Reprocessing (EMDR) 117

faith communities/faith-based organisations 129–131
feminist perspective 73
forgiveness 125, 132–134

Her Majesty's Prison and Probation Service (HMPPS) 41, 60
holistic approach 79, 114, 120–121
Horizon programme 60–61

identity transformation 134–136
Indeterminate Public Protection (IPP) 29
InnerChange Freedom Initiative 130–131
Islamic Guidance Programme (IGP) 130

juveniles or young people 20, 26, 71, 79, 87, 89, 109–111, 117, 123, 129

Kainos Community's Challenge-to-Change 130
Kaizen programme 60–61

labelling/labels 6–7, 27, 98, 109, 135, 142

Management of Sexual or Violent Offenders (MOSOVO) 36
media 1, 6–7, 71, 75, 144
meditation 92, 124, 129
Megan's Law 30
Mental Health Act, The (1983) 31
mindfulness 12, 92, 131
Mothers Union, The 130
motivational interviewing (MI) 60, 94
Multi-Agency Public Protection Arrangements (MAPPA) 2, 31–36, 104
Muslim Youth Helpline 131

National Probation Service (NPS) 35, 76
News of the World 6–7

Offender Rehabilitation Act, The (2014) 34

peer support and self-help groups 89–91
person-centred approach 120

phallometry 45, 50–51, 58
polygraph testing 29–30, 32, 45, 51–52, 62, 77
positive criminology: definition 2; principles or core themes 114–126
positive psychology 14, 115
positive sexuality 87, 97–98
post-traumatic growth 2, 117, 122, 126, 134
Prevention Project Dunkelfeld (PPD) 75
primary prevention 69–73, 81
principles of sentencing 26–27
Prison Chaplaincy 131
prisoner education 87–89
promotive factors 105–106
Protection of Children Act (1978) 5
protective factors 32, 39, 48, 52, 105–111
psychological stress 117
psychometrics 49–50
public health approaches 59, 144

registered sex offenders (RSOs) 31–36
registration 29, 76–77, 88, 143
rehabilitation 26, 29, 34–36, 58–59, 64, 79, 87, 92, 115, 125, 130, 136, 142–143
relapse prevention approaches/model 58, 64, 76
religion, religiosity, and spirituality 129–137
responsible authorities 32–33
restorative justice (RJ) 80, 87, 94–97, 133
risk and need 13, 27, 32–33, 41, 46, 60, 104, 106, 106, 137
risk assessment approaches 40–53
risk assessment tool development 39–40
risk assessment tools: Active Risk Management System (ARMS) 32, 36, 41, 48; ACUTE 2007 46; Historical Clinical Risk Management-20 (HCR-20) 47–48, 107–108; Juvenile Sex Offender Assessment Protocol (J-SOAP) 44; Minnesota Sex Offender Screening Tool-Revised (MnSOST-R) 44; Offender Assessment System (OASys) 32–33, 42; Rapid Risk Assessment for Sex Offence Recidivism (RRASOR) 43; Risk for Sexual Violence Protocol (RSVP) 41, 47; Risk Matrix 2000 (RM2000) 32, 41; self-report measures 106, 109; The Service Planning Instrument (SPIn) 106, 108–109; Sexual Offender Risk Appraisal Guide (SORAG) 42; The Sexual Violence Risk-20 (SVR-20) 46; STABLE 2007 46; Static-99 43; Static-2002 43; Structured Anchored Clinical Judgement Scale (SACJ) 42; The Structured Assessment of Protective Factors for Violent Risk (SAPROF) 48, 106–108; Structured Assessment of Risk and Need (SARN) 41, 45; Structured Risk Assessment (SRA) 48
risk management/risk management plan (RMP) 30, 32–36, 126
risk prediction 39–40, 52
Rockwood Psychological Services 93–94
Rotherham Metropolitan Borough Council 6

secondary prevention 73–76
self-regulation model 59
sentence planning 33–34
sentencing 26–36
sentencing guidelines 31
sexual abuse: causes (*see* theoretical explanations of sexual offending); classification/type 16–17; consequences 8–16; definition 5–7; prevalence/incidence and prosecution rates 17–22
Sexual Harm Prevention Orders (SHPO) 33
Sexual Offences Act, The (2003) 5–6
Sexual Offences Prevention Order (SOPO) 33
social acceptance 2, 124, 129, 143
social construction 6
social, human, and cultural capital 13, 60–61, 88, 120, 124, 131, 136, 144
social learning theory 15, 58
socially inclusive (approach) 87, 115, 119, 123–124
spiritual criminology x–xii
static factors 40–41
stigma/stigmatisation 7, 80, 88, 90, 93, 97–98, 126, 133–137, 142–144
Stop it Now! 75, 81
strengths-based 3, 14, 52, 88, 92–94, 103–110, 118, 122, 133, 145
Sudarshan Kriya Yoga (SKY) 131
supervision 29–32, 35, 46, 51, 72, 108, 116

tertiary prevention 59, 76–81
theoretical explanations of sexual offending: attachment-based theory 9; cognitive distortions of child sexual

abusers 11–12; the confluence mediational model of sexual aggression 9; desistance from sexual offending 15; the four preconditions model 9; the Good Lives Model (GLM) 14, 59, 76, 79, 110; incentive theory of sexual motivation 10; integrated model of change for the treatment of sexual offending 13; the integrated theory of sexual offending – revised 10; intimacy deficits/attachment problems in sexual offenders 11; models of modus operandi in sexual offending 13; multimodal self-regulation theory of sexual offending 10; Risk-Need-Responsivity (RNR) 15, 59–60; situational theories 12; strengths-based theories and sexual offending 14; a theoretical integration of aetiological and typological models of rape 10; theories of deviant sexual fantasy 11; theories of emotion regulation 21; theories of empathy deficits 12; theories of the offence and relapse process 13
therapeutic community xi, 131
therapeutic jurisprudence (TJ) 91–92
therapeutic style 94
transformation 87, 114, 125–126, 143; identity 132, 134–136
trauma 1–3, 16–17, 47, 61, 75, 87, 89, 96, 117, 121–126, 129, 134–135
treatment: aversion therapy 57, 63; behavioural therapy 58, 75–76; cognitive behavioural treatment/approaches 58, 75–76, 92, 131; electric shock treatment 57, 64; Medical Management of Sexual Arousal (MMSA) 62–64; Model of Therapeutic Change 117, 122; penile plethysmography (PPG) 50–51, 57; pharmacology 62–64, 76–78; relapse prevention approaches 58, 64, 76; sexual offender treatment programmes (SOTPs) 59–62, 94; therapists' style 94; victim empathy 58, 61, 76

United Nations 16–17, 88–89

vipassana course xi, 92

what works 58–59, 61, 64, 78, 144
World Health Organisation 5, 16

For Product Safety Concerns and Information please contact our EU representative GPSR@taylorandfrancis.com
Taylor & Francis Verlag GmbH, Kaufingerstraße 24, 80331 München, Germany

www.ingramcontent.com/pod-product-compliance
Ingram Content Group UK Ltd.
Pitfield, Milton Keynes, MK11 3LW, UK
UKHW011018180926
475701UK00004B/814
9780367624095